TEACHER'S GUIDE

CONNECTED 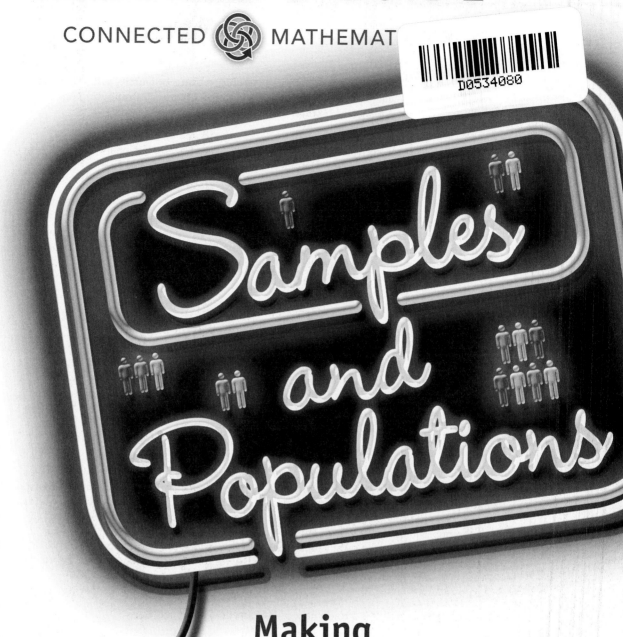 MATHEMAT

Samples and Populations

Making Comparisons and Predictions

Glenda Lappan, Elizabeth Difanis Phillips,
James T. Fey, Susan N. Friel

PEARSON

Boston, Massachusetts • Chandler, Arizona • Glenview, Illinois • Hoboken, New Jersey

Connected Mathematics™ was developed at Michigan State University with financial support from the Michigan State University Office of the Provost, Computing and Technology, and the College of Natural Science.

 This material is based upon work supported by the National Science Foundation under Grant No. MDR 9150217 and Grant No. ESI 9986372. Opinions expressed are those of the authors and not necessarily those of the Foundation.

As with prior editions of this work, the authors and administration of Michigan State University preserve a tradition of devoting royalties from this publication to support activities sponsored by the MSU Mathematics Education Enrichment Fund.

Acknowledgments appear on page 240, which constitutes an extension of this copyright page.

13-digit ISBN 978-0-13-327661-9
10-digit ISBN 0-13-327661-9
4   16

PEARSON

A Team of Experts

Glenda Lappan is a University Distinguished Professor in the Program in Mathematics Education (PRIME) and the Department of Mathematics at Michigan State University. Her research and development interests are in the connected areas of students' learning of mathematics and mathematics teachers' professional growth and change related to the development and enactment of K–12 curriculum materials.

Elizabeth Difanis Phillips is a Senior Academic Specialist in the Program in Mathematics Education (PRIME) and the Department of Mathematics at Michigan State University. She is interested in teaching and learning mathematics for both teachers and students. These interests have led to curriculum and professional development projects at the middle school and high school levels, as well as projects related to the teaching and learning of algebra across the grades.

James T. Fey is a Professor Emeritus at the University of Maryland. His consistent professional interest has been development and research focused on curriculum materials that engage middle and high school students in problem-based collaborative investigations of mathematical ideas and their applications.

Susan N. Friel is a Professor of Mathematics Education in the School of Education at the University of North Carolina at Chapel Hill. Her research interests focus on statistics education for middle-grade students and, more broadly, on teachers' professional development and growth in teaching mathematics K–8.

With... Yvonne Grant and Jacqueline Stewart

Yvonne Grant teaches mathematics at Portland Middle School in Portland, Michigan. Jacqueline Stewart is a recently retired high school teacher of mathematics at Okemos High School in Okemos, Michigan. Both Yvonne and Jacqueline have worked on all aspects of the development, implementation, and professional development of the CMP curriculum from its beginnings in 1991.

Development Team

CMP3 Authors

Glenda Lappan, University Distinguished Professor, Michigan State University

Elizabeth Difanis Phillips, Senior Academic Specialist, Michigan State University

James T. Fey, Professor Emeritus, University of Maryland

Susan N. Friel, Professor, University of North Carolina – Chapel Hill

With...

Yvonne Grant, Portland Middle School, Michigan

Jacqueline Stewart, Mathematics Consultant, Mason, Michigan

In Memory of... **William M. Fitzgerald,** Professor (Deceased), Michigan State University, who made substantial contributions to conceptualizing and creating CMP1.

Administrative Assistant

Michigan State University
Judith Martus Miller

Support Staff

Michigan State University
Undergraduate Assistants:
Bradley Robert Corlett, Carly Fleming,
Erin Lucian, Scooter Nowak

Development Assistants

Michigan State University
Graduate Research Assistants:
Richard "Abe" Edwards, Nic Gilbertson,
Funda Gonulates, Aladar Horvath,
Eun Mi Kim, Kevin Lawrence, Jennifer Nimtz,
Joanne Philhower, Sasha Wang

Assessment Team

Maine
Falmouth Public Schools
Falmouth Middle School: Shawn Towle

Michigan
Ann Arbor Public Schools
Tappan Middle School:
Anne Marie Nicoll-Turner

Portland Public Schools
Portland Middle School:
Holly DeRosia, Yvonne Grant

Traverse City Area Public Schools
Traverse City East Middle School:
Jane Porath, Mary Beth Schmitt

Traverse City West Middle School:
Jennifer Rundio, Karrie Tufts

Ohio
Clark-Shawnee Local Schools
Rockway Middle School: Jim Mamer

Content Consultants

Michigan State University
Peter Lappan, Professor Emeritus,
Department of Mathematics

Normandale Community College
Christopher Danielson, Instructor,
Department of Mathematics & Statistics

University of North Carolina – Wilmington
Dargan Frierson, Jr., Professor,
Department of Mathematics & Statistics

Student Activities
Michigan State University
Brin Keller, Associate Professor,
Department of Mathematics

Consultants

Indiana
Purdue University
Mary Bouck, Mathematics Consultant

Michigan
Oakland Schools
Valerie Mills, Mathematics Education Supervisor

Mathematics Education Consultants:
Geraldine Devine, Dana Gosen

Ellen Bacon, Independent Mathematics Consultant

New York
University of Rochester
Jeffrey Choppin, Associate Professor

Ohio
University of Toledo
Debra Johanning, Associate Professor

Pennsylvania
University of Pittsburgh
Margaret Smith, Professor

Texas
University of Texas at Austin
Emma Trevino, Supervisor of
Mathematics Programs, The Dana Center

Mathematics for All Consulting
Carmen Whitman, Mathematics Consultant

Reviewers

Michigan
Ionia Public Schools
Kathy Dole, Director of Curriculum
and Instruction

Grand Valley State University
Lisa Kasmer, Assistant Professor

Portland Public Schools
Teri Keusch, Classroom Teacher

Minnesota
Hopkins School District 270
Michele Luke, Mathematics Coordinator

Field Test Sites for CMP3

Michigan
Ann Arbor Public Schools
Tappan Middle School: Anne Marie Nicoll-Turner*

Portland Public Schools
Portland Middle School: Mark Braun,
Angela Buckland, Holly DeRosia, Holly Feldpausch,
Angela Foote, Yvonne Grant*, Kristin Roberts,
Angie Stump, Tammi Wardwell

Traverse City Area Public Schools
Traverse City East Middle School:
Ivanka Baic Berkshire, Brenda Dunscombe,
Tracie Herzberg, Deb Larimer, Jan Palkowski,
Rebecca Perreault, Jane Porath*, Robert Sagan,
Mary Beth Schmitt*

Traverse City West Middle School:
Pamela Alfieri, Jennifer Rundio,
Maria Taplin, Karrie Tufts*

Maine
Falmouth Public Schools
Falmouth Middle School: Sally Bennett,
Chris Driscoll, Sara Jones, Shawn Towle*

Minnesota
Minneapolis Public Schools
Jefferson Community School:
Leif Carlson*,
Katrina Hayek Munsisoumang*

Ohio
Clark-Shawnee Local Schools
Reid School: Joanne Gilley
Rockway Middle School: Jim Mamer*
Possum School: Tami Thomas

*Indicates a Field Test Site Coordinator

Contents

Samples and Populations
Making Comparisons and Predictions

Unit Planning

▼ Unit Overview

Unit Description

You can use concepts from probability as tools for understanding sampling procedures in statistics. You can use statistics as tools for representing and analyzing data. The Problems in *Samples and Populations* help students make connections between probability concepts and statistics concepts. These Problems help students learn how to draw conclusions about samples and populations.

Samples and Populations applies statistics concepts introduced in the Grade 6 Unit, *Data About Us*. Students use what they learned in Grade 6 about data analysis to more deeply investigate distributions in Grade 7. The focus in Grade 7 is on the use of measures of center and spread to describe and compare samples and populations.

Investigation 1 reviews concepts introduced in *Data About Us*, but with an additional focus of comparing distributions. In Investigations 2 and 3, students extend this by exploring samples and populations. They define *samples*, describe how samples are related to populations, determine what sampling procedures are best to use, select random samples, and compare samples. Students will also discuss representative samples.

In this Unit, students generally work with samples rather than populations of data. This may not be explicitly stated in many cases. As you go through the Unit, be sure that students understand when they are working with samples and when they are working with populations. Students should also understand and properly use the terms *samples* and *populations*.

In many of the Problems in this Unit, data are provided. Many students in Grade 7 have had prior experience collecting data as part of statistical investigations. If they have not, you may want to have your class collect their own data for some of the Problems. The Problems can be applied either to the data provided or to data collected by students. If you choose to collect data, please be sensitive about which statistics to collect. Some Problems address "unexpected" or "unusual" values; it is important to make sure that students don't feel as though some personal attributes of theirs are "unexpected" or "unusual."

► UNIT
OVERVIEW

GOALS AND
STANDARDS

MATHEMATICS
BACKGROUND

UNIT
INTRODUCTION

Summary of Investigations

Investigation 1: Making Sense of Samples

Investigation 1 focuses on comparing two or more sets of data (each set of data having the same number or different numbers of data values) using a variety of strategies first introduced in *Data About Us*. It also guides students toward using data from samples to make predictions about populations.

Three of the Problems (1.1, 1.2, and 1.4) involve numerical data; Problem 1.3 uses categorical data. The Problems focus attention on the use of measures of center and variability (or spread). Measures of center (mode with respect to categorical data, mean, and median) describe what is typical of the center of a distribution of data. Measures of variability (range, mean absolute deviation, and interquartile range) describe how data are spread about the center of a distribution. Students rely on measures of variability, in conjunction with measures of center, to make comparisons.

The intent is to build a deeper foundation—connecting measures of center and spread to compare data sets. In subsequent Investigations, students will use their knowledge to compare samples with samples and samples with populations.

Investigation 2: Choosing a Sample From a Population

In Investigation 2, students consider the statistical distinctions between samples and populations. They also use results of data analyses from samples to draw conclusions about characteristics or behaviors of a population. First, students consider the implications of making estimates about the entire U.S. population based on an Internet survey involving a few thousand people. The survey raises the issue of projecting the results collected from a sample to an entire population.

Next, students consider the differences among different types of samples: convenience, voluntary-response, systematic, and random. They explore techniques for choosing samples randomly from a population—such as using spinners, number cubes, and random-number generators on calculators—and think about why random samples are often preferable to other types of sampling methods. Then, they investigate the relationship between sample size and accuracy of population estimates. Students study sampling distributions of means and medians, noticing that the means or medians from larger samples (e.g., 30 values) taken from the same population are less variable than those from smaller samples (e.g., 5 or 10 values). This helps students realize that measures of center from larger samples are more similar; it is possible to use the mean from a large sample to draw reliable conclusions about the given population.

Investigation 3: Using Samples to Draw Conclusions

Students apply what they have learned about samples and populations to engaging real-world problems in Investigation 3.

First, they analyze measurements of Native American arrowheads found at six different archeological sites. Scientists know the approximate time periods during which four of the sites were settled. The time periods for two newer sites are unknown. Students explore how data from the known sites may be used to draw conclusions about the newer sites.

In Problem 3.2, students determine whether the differences found between two samples of basketball player heights (one sample from a male professional basketball player population and the other from a female professional basketball player population) are most likely due to naturally occurring variability or meaningful differences between the distributions of heights in the two populations. They base this analysis on the relationship of the samples' means and MADs.

Next, students use a sampling procedure to investigate how many chocolate chips must be added to a batch of cookie dough to ensure that each cookie in the batch will contain at least five chips. They use concepts that they have learned about sampling techniques and probability to solve this real-world quality control problem.

Last, in Problem 3.4, students simulate the **capture–tag–recapture** method that scientists and policymakers often use to sample and draw conclusions about the sizes of wildlife populations. In this Problem, students use containers of beans to represent deer populations.

Unit Vocabulary

- capture–tag–recapture
- census
- convenience sampling
- population
- random sampling

- relative frequency
- representative sample
- sample
- sampling distribution
- sampling plan

- simulate
- systematic sampling
- voluntary-response (or self-selected) sampling

The following vocabulary terms are included in the Glossary as review but are not defined within the exposition of the Student Edition.

- bar graph
- box-and-whisker plot (box plot)
- categorical data
- distribution
- five-number summary
- frequency

- histogram
- interquartile range (IQR)
- line plot
- mean
- mean absolute deviation (MAD)
- median

- mode
- numerical data
- outlier
- quartile
- range

Planning Charts

Investigations & Assessments	Pacing	Materials	Resources
Unit Readiness	Optional		• Unit Readiness*
1 Making Sense of Samples	4 days	**Labsheet 1.2** Fundraising Money Collected **Labsheet 1.3** Roller Coaster Survey Responses **Labsheet 1.4A** Sample of 30 Steel-Frame Roller Coasters **Labsheet 1.4B** Sample of 30 Wood-Frame Roller Coasters **Labsheet 1.4C:** Dot Plots of Top-Speed Data (accessibility) **Labsheet 1ACE:** Exercises 3–7 (accessibility)	**Teaching Aid 1.2** Line Plots of Fundraiser Data **Teaching Aid 1.3** Bar Graphs for Roller Coaster Survey Responses • Data and Graphs
Mathematical Reflections	½ day		
Assessment: Check Up	½ day		• Check Up • Spanish Check Up

continued on next page

Planning Charts *continued*

Investigations & Assessments	Pacing	Materials	Resources
2 Choosing a Sample From a Population	5 days	**Labsheet 2.3A** Responses to Grade 7 Movie and Sleep Survey **Labsheet 2.3B** Blank Number Lines for Movies Watched Line Plots **Labsheet 2.3C** Blank Number Lines for Hours Slept Box Plots **Labsheet 2.4A** Blank Number Lines for Movies Watched Last Week (Means) **Labsheet 2.4B** Blank Number Lines for Movies Watched Last Week (Medians) **Labsheet 2.4C** Blank Number Lines for Hours of Sleep Last Night (Means) **Labsheet 2.4D** Blank Number Lines for Hours of Sleep Last Night (Medians) **Labsheet 2.4E** Group Organizer for Sample-Size Statistics **Labsheet 2.4F** Class Organizer for Sample-Size Statistics **Labsheet 2ACE:** Exercises 20–22 (accessibility) • 10-Section Spinners 10-sided solids paper clips or bobby pins	**Teaching Aid 2.1** Honesty Survey **Teaching Aid 2.3** Graphs for Grade 7 Survey (Whole Population) • Probability • Data and Graphs • Expression Calculator
Mathematical Reflections	½ day		
Assessment: Partner Quiz	1 day		• Partner Quiz • Spanish Partner Quiz

continued on next page

Planning Charts *continued*

Investigations & Assessments	Pacing	Materials	Resources
3 Using Samples to Draw Conclusions	5½ days	**Labsheet 3.1A** Arrowhead Data **Labsheet 3.1B** Blank Tables for Arrowhead Summary Statistics **Labsheet 3.1C** Arrowhead Summary Statistics **Labsheet 3.1D** Box Plots for Arrowhead Data **Labsheet 3.2** Heights of Basketball Players **Labsheet 3.3** Cookie Simulation Tables **Labsheet 3.4** Capture–Tag–Recapture Table **Labsheet 3ACE:** Exercises 3–6 (accessibility) **Labsheet 3ACE:** Exercise 7 (accessibility) **Labsheet 3ACE** Exercises 8 and 9 **Labsheet 3ACE:** Exercise 11 (accessibility) • Graph Paper • 12-Section Spinners spinners, number cubes, coins, containers of beans (one container per group; at least 200 beans per container)	• Data and Graphs • Probability • Coordinate Grapher
Mathematical Reflections	½ day		
Looking Back	½ day	• Labsheet: Looking Back	
Assessment: Self-Assessment	Take Home		• Self-Assessment • Notebook Checklist • Spanish Self-Assessment • Spanish Notebook Checklist

continued on next page

Planning Charts *continued*

Investigations & Assessments	Pacing	Materials	Resources
Assessment: Unit Test	1 day		• Unit Test • Spanish Unit Test
Total	19 days	**Materials for All Investigations:** calculators, student notebooks, colored pens, pencils, or markers	

* Also available as an assignment in MathXL.

Block Pacing (Scheduling for 90-minute class periods)

Investigation	Block Pacing
1 Making Sense of Samples	2½ days
Problem 1.1	½ day
Problem 1.2	½ day
Problem 1.3	½ day
Problem 1.4	½ day
Mathematical Reflections	½ day
2 Choosing a Sample From a Population	3 days
Problem 2.1	½ day
Problem 2.2	½ day
Problem 2.3	½ day
Problem 2.4	1 day
Mathematical Reflections	½ day

Investigation	Block Pacing
3 Using Samples to Draw Conclusions	4 days
Problem 3.1	1 day
Problem 3.2	½ day
Problem 3.3	1 day
Problem 3.4	1 day
Mathematical Reflections	½ day

Parent Letter

• Parent Letter (English)
• Parent Letter (Spanish)

UNIT
OVERVIEW
► GOALS AND
STANDARDS
MATHEMATICS
BACKGROUND
UNIT
INTRODUCTION

Goals and Standards

Goals
....

The Process of Statistical Investigation Deepen the understanding of the process of statistical investigation and apply this understanding to samples

- Pose questions, collect data, analyze data, and interpret data to answer questions

Analysis of Samples Understand that data values in a sample vary and that summary statistics of samples, even same-sized samples, taken from the same population also vary

- Choose appropriate measures of center (mean, median, or mode) and spread (range, IQR, or MAD) to summarize a sample

- Choose appropriate representations to display distributions of samples

- Compare summary statistics of multiple samples drawn from either the same population or from two different populations and explain how the samples vary

Design and Use of Simulations Understand that simulations can model real-world situations

- Design a model that relies on probability concepts to obtain a desired result

- Use the randomly generated frequencies for events to draw conclusions

Predictions and Conclusions About Populations Understand that summary statistics of a representative sample can be used to gain information about a population

- Describe the benefits and drawbacks to various sampling plans

- Use random-sampling techniques to select representative samples

- Apply concepts from probability to select random samples from populations

- Explain how sample size influences the reliability of sample statistics and resulting conclusions and predictions

- Explain how different sampling plans influence the reliability of sample statistics and resulting conclusions and predictions

- Use statistics from representative samples to draw conclusions about populations

- Use measures of center, measures of spread, and data displays from more than one random sample to compare and draw conclusions about more than one population

- Use mean and MAD, or median and IQR, from random samples to assess whether the differences in the samples are due to natural variability or due to meaningful differences in the underlying populations

Standards

Common Core Content Standards

7.RP.A.2 Recognize and represent proportional relationships between quantities. *Investigation 3*

7.NS.A.1 Apply and extend previous understandings of addition and subtraction to add and subtract rational numbers; represent addition and subtraction on a horizontal on vertical number line diagram. *Investigations 1 and 3*

7.NS.A.1b Understand $p + q$ as the number located a distance $|q|$ from p, in the positive or negative direction depending on whether q is positive or negative. . .Interpret sums of rational numbers by describing real-world contexts. *Investigations 1 and 3*

7.SP.A.1 Understand that statistics can be used to gain information about a population by examining a sample of the population; generalizations about a population from a sample are valid only if the sample is representative of that population. Understand that random sampling tends to produce representative samples and support valid inferences. *Investigations 2 and 3*

7.SP.A.2 Use data from a random sample to draw inferences about a population with an unknown characteristic of interest. Generate multiple samples (or simulated samples) of the same size to gauge the variation in estimates or predictions. *Investigations 2 and 3*

7.SP.B.3 Informally assess the degree of visual overlap of two numerical data distributions with similar variabilities, measuring the difference between the centers by expressing it as a multiple of a measure of variability. *Investigations 1 and 3*

7.SP.B.4 Use measures of center and measures of variability for numerical data from random samples to draw informal comparative inferences about two populations. *Investigations 1 and 3*

7.SP.C.5 Understand that the probability of a chance event is a number between 0 and 1 that expresses the likelihood of the event occurring. Larger numbers indicate greater likelihood. A probability near 0 indicates an unlikely event, a probability around 1/2 indicates an event that is neither unlikely nor likely, and a probability near 1 indicates a likely event. *Investigation 3*

7.SP.C.7 Develop a probability model and use it to find probabilities of events. Compare probabilities from a model to observed frequencies; if the agreement is not good, explain possible sources of the discrepancy. *Investigations 2 and 3*

7.SP.C.7a Develop a uniform probability model by assigning equal probability to all outcomes, and use the model to determine probabilities of events. *Investigations 2 and 3*

UNIT
OVERVIEW

▶ GOALS AND
STANDARDS

MATHEMATICS
BACKGROUND

UNIT
INTRODUCTION

Facilitating the Mathematical Practices

Students in *Connected Mathematics* classrooms display evidence of multiple Standards for Mathematical Practice every day. Here are just a few examples of when you might observe students demonstrating the Standards for Mathematical Practice during this Unit.

Practice 1: Make sense of problems and persevere in solving them.

Students are engaged every day in solving problems and, over time, learn to persevere in solving them. To be effective, the problems embody critical concepts and skills and have the potential to engage students in making sense of mathematics. Students build understanding by reflecting, connecting, and communicating. These student-centered problem situations engage students in articulating the "knowns" in a problem situation and determining a logical solution pathway. The student-student and student-teacher dialogues help students not only to make sense of the problems, but also to persevere in finding appropriate strategies to solve them. The suggested questions in the Teacher Guides provide the metacognitive scaffolding to help students monitor and refine their problem-solving strategies.

Practice 2: Reason abstractly and quantitatively.

Throughout Investigation 3, students rely on statistics and data displays to draw conclusions about samples and populations.

Practice 3: Construct viable arguments and critique the reasoning of others.

In Investigation 1, students critique reports of two fictitious characters. Students compare the two reports and identify whether there are flaws in the arguments. Students improve the arguments and justify their understanding.

Practice 4: Model with mathematics.

In Investigation 3, students use simulations to solve problems. These simulations are models of real-world situations, which can help students to understand what might happen if they encountered that scenario in real life.

Practice 5: Use appropriate tools strategically.

Throughout the entire Unit, students use calculators. Rather than spending too much time calculating statistics, students use calculators or other tools to find summary statistics more efficiently. Additionally, when students need to generate numbers at random in Investigations 2 and 3, they use appropriate probability tools (such as spinners, number cubes, and coins) to generate these numbers.

Practice 6: Attend to precision.

In Investigations 1 and 3, students look at values within one and two MADs of the mean of a distribution. Students use these observations to decide whether certain data values are expected or unexpected. A misstep in precision could potentially lead to incorrect conclusions.

Practice 7: **Look for and make use of structure.**

Throughout Investigation 2, students explore how samples are chosen from a population. Students randomly select samples of size 5, 10, and 30. Then all samples are collected in the classroom to analyze the data. The smaller and individual samples are used as building blocks for the larger and collective samples. Thus, students are better able to make predictions about the whole population.

Practice 8: **Look for and express regularity in repeated reasoning.**

In Investigation 3, students complete simulations that mimic real-world situations. During these simulations, students repeat trials multiple times and modify their conclusions after each repetition.

Students identify and record their personal experiences with the Standards for Mathematical Practice during the Mathematical Reflections at the end of each Investigation.

UNIT
OVERVIEW

GOALS AND
STANDARDS

▶ MATHEMATICS
BACKGROUND

UNIT
INTRODUCTION

▼ Mathematics Background

The Process of Statistical Investigation
....

In *Samples and Populations*, students use their background knowledge of statistical investigations and probability to draw conclusions about samples and populations. Statistical investigations involve four parts:

- Posing questions

- Collecting data

- Analyzing data distributions

- Interpreting the data and the analysis to answer the questions

At the end of a statistical investigation, students need to communicate the results.

Students learned about data and statistical measures in Grade 6 during *Data About Us*. There are opportunities in Investigation 1 to review the Grade 6 content. The focus of *Samples and Populations*, however, is not on reviewing the material introduced in Grade 6. The focus is to extend the concepts developed in Grade 6. You should gauge whether or not your students would benefit from an additional quick refresher of concepts.

....

In *Samples and Populations*, students will use both data that are provided for them in the Student Edition and data that they generate. In both cases, students need to consider the process of statistical investigation.

When students collect their own data, they naturally tend to follow through with the process of statistical investigation. When students analyze a data set they have not collected, however, they need to understand the data first in order to complete any analysis. Have students think about why and how the data might have been collected.

Questions students should ask themselves
- What question might have been asked in order to collect the data?
- How do you think the data were collected?
- Why are these data represented with this kind of display?
- How can you describe the data distribution?
- How can you use the results of the analysis to answer the original question?

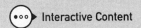
Reviewing Types of Data and Attributes

Attributes

In *Samples and Populations* students use the word *attributes*, rather than *variables*, to describe qualities that certain data have. This is so that students do not confuse statistics concepts with algebra concepts. An *attribute* names a particular characteristic of a person, place, or thing about which data are being collected. For example, height is an attribute of male professional basketball players.

Categorical and Numerical Data Values

Statistical questions result in answers that are either categorical or numerical data values.

Numerical data arise from questions for which the answers are numbers, counts, or measurements. For example, "How tall are these basketball players?" will result in answers such as 81 inches.

Categorical data arise from questions for which the answers are nonnumerical. For example, "Does each cookie in this batch of cookies have five chips?" will result in either the answer "yes" or the answer "no."

Knowing whether an attribute is described with categorical or numerical values helps students to determine which measures of center to report and which displays to use. Students use both categorical and numerical data in *Samples and Populations*.

Reviewing Measures of Center and Measures of Spread

When students work with data, they are often interested in individual cases, particularly if the data are about themselves. Statisticians like to look at the overall distribution of a data set, however, rather than at individual cases. When statisticians analyze distributions rather than individual cases, they can consider properties of the distribution, such as measures of center, measures of spread, or shape. They also use graphs to help clarify the distribution.

Measures of Central Tendency

Three measures of central tendency were addressed in *Data About Us*. In *Samples and Populations*, students deepen their understanding of and explore relationships between two measures of center, mean and median.

UNIT
OVERVIEW

GOALS AND
STANDARDS

▶ MATHEMATICS
BACKGROUND

UNIT
INTRODUCTION

- The *median* is the numerical location that divides an ordered distribution into two equal parts. It is a good measure to use when working with skewed distributions because it is not influenced by extreme data values.

Examples

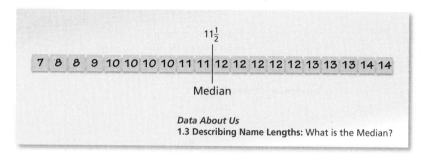

$11\frac{1}{2}$

| 7 | 8 | 8 | 9 | 10 | 10 | 10 | 10 | 11 | 11 | 12 | 12 | 12 | 12 | 12 | 13 | 13 | 13 | 14 | 14 |

Median

Data About Us
1.3 Describing Name Lengths: What is the Median?

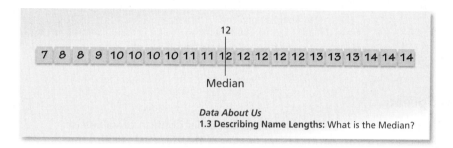

12

| 7 | 8 | 8 | 9 | 10 | 10 | 10 | 10 | 11 | 11 | 12 | 12 | 12 | 12 | 12 | 13 | 13 | 13 | 14 | 14 | 14 |

Median

Data About Us
1.3 Describing Name Lengths: What is the Median?

- The *mean* is the numerical value that marks the balance point of a distribution, or the value of each individual case if the values were evenly shared. The mean is influenced by all values of the distribution, including extreme values. It is a good measure to use when working with distributions that are generally symmetric.

Example

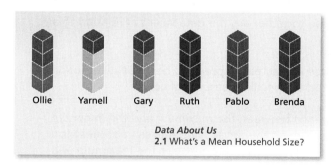

Ollie   Yarnell   Gary   Ruth   Pablo   Brenda

Data About Us
2.1 What's a Mean Household Size?

continued on next page

- The *mode* is the most frequent value in a data set. In *Samples and Populations*, students will work with the mode on occasion, because it is the only measure of center that can be found for categorical data.

Example

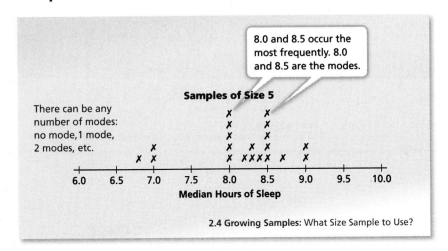

2.4 Growing Samples: What Size Sample to Use?

Measures of Spread

Variability measures how close together or spread out a distribution of values is. Measures of spread describe the degree of variability of the data values and the data values' deviations from, or differences from, the measures of center.

When students analyze the variability of a distribution, they consider the following.

- How alike or different are the data values from each other?

- Which data values occur more frequently or less frequently?

- How spread out or close together are the data values in relation to each other?

- How spread out or close together are the data values in relation to a measure of center?

Students in Grade 7 use three measures of spread to describe distributions of data, two of which are related to specific measures of center.

- The *range* is the difference between the maximum and the minimum data values. When considering the range, students can also describe where gaps exist or how the data cluster between the maximum and the minimum.

UNIT
OVERVIEW

GOALS AND
STANDARDS

▶ MATHEMATICS
BACKGROUND

UNIT
INTRODUCTION

Example

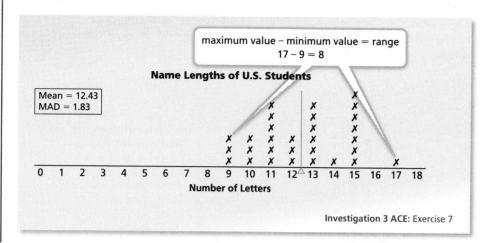

maximum value − minimum value = range
17 − 9 = 8

Name Lengths of U.S. Students

Mean = 12.43
MAD = 1.83

Number of Letters

Investigation 3 ACE: Exercise 7

- The *interquartile range (IQR)* is used in connection with the median. It is the range of the middle 50% of the ordered data values. It provides a numerical measure of how close or widely spread out the data values in the 2nd and 3rd quartiles of a distribution are from the median. The IQR is visually represented by the box of a box-and-whisker plot. The IQR also helps to identify *outliers*, data values that are unexpected compared to the other data values in a distribution.

Example

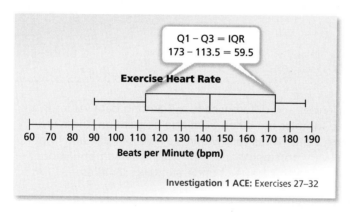

Q1 − Q3 = IQR
173 − 113.5 = 59.5

Exercise Heart Rate

Beats per Minute (bpm)

Investigation 1 ACE: Exercises 27–32

continued on next page

- The *mean absolute deviation (MAD)* is used in connection with the mean. In some sets of data, data values are concentrated close to the mean. In other sets of data, the data values are more widely spread out. The MAD calculates the average distance between each data value and the mean in a distribution.

Example

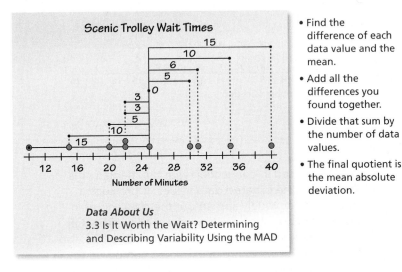

Scenic Trolley Wait Times

Number of Minutes

- Find the difference of each data value and the mean.
- Add all the differences you found together.
- Divide that sum by the number of data values.
- The final quotient is the mean absolute deviation.

Data About Us
3.3 Is It Worth the Wait? Determining and Describing Variability Using the MAD

For all three measures of spread, the smaller the measure, the less variation of the data values; the larger the measure, the greater the variation of the data values. Smaller measures of spread indicate consistency, while larger measures of spread indicate inconsistency.

Exploring Variation

Variation refers to the similarities and differences found among data values in a distribution. When multiple samples are taken from one population, there is a natural variation that occurs. Data values vary within a single sample, and one sample of a population will vary from another sample of the same population. Understanding this variability is at the heart of understanding samples.

In *Samples and Populations*, students encounter the natural variation that occurs when studying different samples taken from the same population. Students will use statistics and data analysis to describe areas of stability (or consistency) in the natural variation of a distribution.

You can use questions such as the ones below to help students think about variation and stability.

> *You analyze the distribution of a sample of 10 students' sleep durations per night in order to draw conclusions about the sleep durations of a population of 40 students.*

UNIT
OVERVIEW

GOALS AND
STANDARDS

▶ MATHEMATICS
BACKGROUND

UNIT
INTRODUCTION

- Suppose you collected a set of data from a different sample of
  10 students from this population. Would you expect the distribution
  of data in the new sample to be the same as or different from the
  distribution of data for the original sample of 10 students?

Sleep Durations of 40 Students

Student Number	Average Hours Slept Per Night	Student Number	Average Hours Slept Per Night	Student Number	Average Hours Slept Per Night
01	7.75	15	8.75	28	9.0
02	8.0	16	7.0	29	6.5
03	8.5	17	7.75	30	8.25
04	8.0	18	7.0	31	8.0
05	7.5	19	8.0	32	7.25
06	7.5	20	9.5	33	7.5
07	9.0	21	8.25	34	7.75
08	9.25	22	7.75	35	8.75
09	7.25	23	6.5	36	6.75
10	8.25	24	8.0	37	7.5
11	8.5	25	8.25	38	8.0
12	6.75	26	7.25	39	7.0
13	8.75	27	7.0	40	7.5
14	7.5				

Sleep Durations of 40 Students

Student Number	Average Hours Slept Per Night	Student Number	Average Hours Slept Per Night	Student Number	Average Hours Slept Per Night
01	7.75	15	8.75	28	9.0
02	8.0	16	7.0	29	6.5
03	8.5	17	7.75	30	8.25
04	8.0	18	7.0	31	8.0
05	7.5	19	8.0	32	7.25
06	7.5	20	9.5	33	7.5
07	9.0	21	8.25	34	7.75
08	9.25	22	7.75	35	8.75
09	7.25	23	6.5	36	6.75
10	8.25	24	8.0	37	7.5
11	8.5	25	8.25	38	8.0
12	6.75	26	7.25	39	7.0
13	8.75	27	7.0	40	7.5
14	7.5				

continued on next page

Sleep Durations of 40 Students

Student Number	Average Hours Slept Per Night	Student Number	Average Hours Slept Per Night	Student Number	Average Hours Slept Per Night
01	7.75	15	8.75	28	9.0
02	8.0	16	7.0	29	6.5
03	8.5	17	7.75	30	8.25
04	8.0	18	7.0	31	8.0
05	7.5	19	8.0	32	7.25
06	7.5	20	9.5	33	7.5
07	9.0	21	8.25	34	7.75
08	9.25	22	7.75	35	8.75
09	7.25	23	6.5	36	6.75
10	8.25	24	8.0	37	7.5
11	8.5	25	8.25	38	8.0
12	6.75	26	7.25	39	7.0
13	8.75	27	7.0	40	7.5
14	7.5				

- If you expect the distributions to be different, in what ways would the data be different (e.g., would there be differences among data values, locations of data values, measures of center or spread, or descriptions of shapes of distributions)?

Sleep Durations

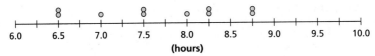

Sleep Durations

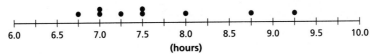

Several questions may be used to highlight interesting aspects of variation.

- *What does a distribution look like?*
- *How much do the data points vary from one another or from a measure of center?*

In addition to these basic questions, students in Grade 7 begin to ask questions such as:

- *Are there reasons why there is variation in these data?*
- *Are there reasons why two samples might vary from each other?*
- *Can you conclude anything about two samples, or about the population (or populations) from which they were drawn, by analyzing the difference between the two samples?*

UNIT
OVERVIEW

GOALS AND
STANDARDS

▶ MATHEMATICS
BACKGROUND

UNIT
INTRODUCTION

Representing Data With Graphical Displays

Statisticians use data displays and statistics during the analysis part of the process of statistical investigation.

Students will construct and analyze graphs in *Samples and Populations* that they have already used a number of times during Grades K–6.

Types of Graphical Displays

Dot plots (or line plots) In a dot plot, each case is represented by a dot (or an "X") positioned over a labeled number line. The dot plot below shows the distribution of heights for a sample of 32 male professional basketball players.

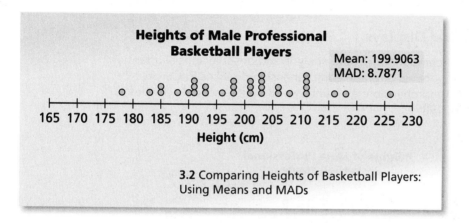

Heights of Male Professional Basketball Players

Mean: 199.9063
MAD: 8.7871

Height (cm)

3.2 Comparing Heights of Basketball Players: Using Means and MADs

Histograms A histogram groups data values into intervals of the same size. The size of the bar over that interval shows the frequency of data values within that interval. Frequencies may be displayed as counts or as percentages. The histogram below shows the distribution of several simulations completed to find the total number of chocolate chips needed to add to a batch of 12 cookies to have at least 5 chips per cookie.

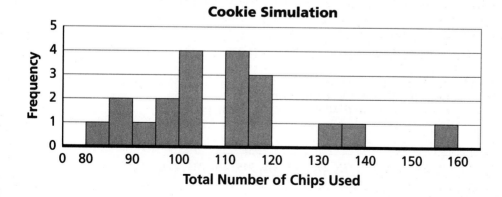

Cookie Simulation

Frequency

Total Number of Chips Used

continued on next page

Box-and-whisker plots Box plots are divided into quartiles and display properties of distributions, such as symmetry or skewness. The graphs below show the distributions of different size dog breeds; outliers and medians are marked.

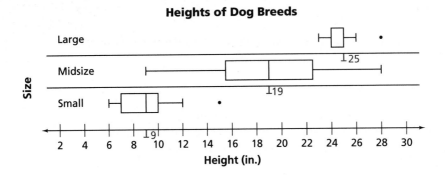

Heights of Dog Breeds

Reading Graphical Displays

Graphs are a central component of data analysis and deserve special attention. There are three components of graph comprehension (Frances R. Curcio, Developing graph comprehension: elementary and middle school activities [Reston, VA: NCTM, 1989]).

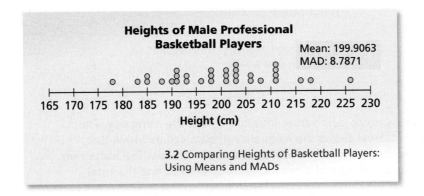

Heights of Male Professional Basketball Players

Mean: 199.9063
MAD: 8.7871

3.2 Comparing Heights of Basketball Players: Using Means and MADs

- *Reading the data* involves taking specific information from a graph to answer explicit questions. For example, how many male professional basketball players are 185 centimeters tall?

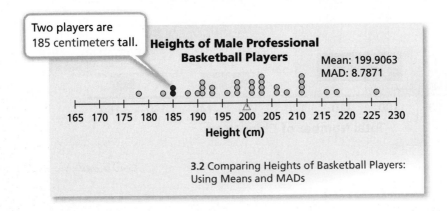

Two players are 185 centimeters tall.

Heights of Male Professional Basketball Players

Mean: 199.9063
MAD: 8.7871

3.2 Comparing Heights of Basketball Players: Using Means and MADs

UNIT
OVERVIEW

GOALS AND
STANDARDS

▶ MATHEMATICS
BACKGROUND

UNIT
INTRODUCTION

- *Reading between the data* includes interpreting and integrating information presented in a graph. For example, what percent of heights for male professional basketball players are greater than the mean of 199.906 centimeters?

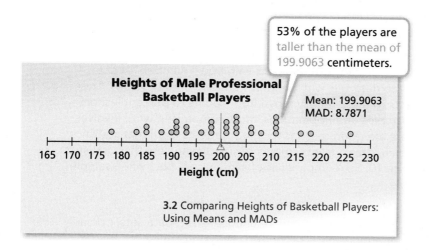

53% of the players are taller than the mean of 199.9063 centimeters.

Heights of Male Professional Basketball Players

Mean: 199.9063
MAD: 8.7871

Height (cm)

3.2 Comparing Heights of Basketball Players: Using Means and MADs

- *Reading beyond the data* involves extending, predicting, or inferring from data to answer implicit questions. For example, what is the typical height for male professional basketball players?

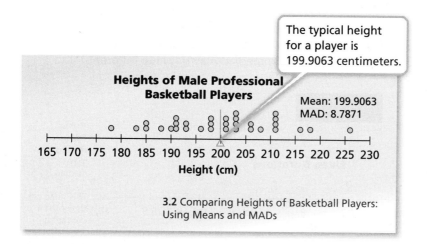

The typical height for a player is 199.9063 centimeters.

Heights of Male Professional Basketball Players

Mean: 199.9063
MAD: 8.7871

Height (cm)

3.2 Comparing Heights of Basketball Players: Using Means and MADs

Once students construct graphs, they use the graphs in the interpretation phase of the data-investigation process. This is when they need to ask questions about the graphs. The first two categories of questions—reading the data and reading between the data—are basic to understanding graphs. However, when students read beyond the data, they are exhibiting higher-order thinking skills, such as inference and justification.

Comparing Distributions

Students can compare two or more data sets with statistics. Students must sort out whether they are comparing data sets with equal numbers of data values (when counts can be used as frequencies) or data sets with unequal numbers of data values (when relative frequencies or percentiles need to be used).

Students often find it easier to start with data sets with equal numbers of data values and then move on to data sets with unequal numbers of data values. This progression helps students to more readily move from counts to percentiles, or relative frequencies. In *Samples and Populations*, most comparison work involves same-sized samples. There are good reasons for this. Students learn that statistics, such as the mean or median, drawn from samples of size 30 vary less than statistics drawn from samples of size 10. So, comparisons of samples are best when sample size is not another variable.

There are a few cases in which students compare unequal-sized data sets, primarily using box plots, a representation already organized using percentiles.

When comparing two or more data sets, the focus is on three features.

Center: Graphically, the center of a distribution is the point at which about half of the observations are on either side (median) or around which the distribution is balanced (mean). The two primary measures are the median and the mean for numerical data. These will have similar values for symmetric distributions, but the mean and median may be quite different for skewed distributions.

Example

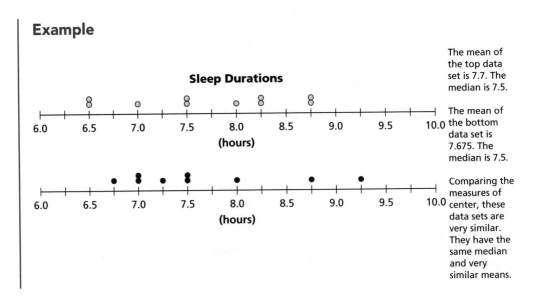

The mean of the top data set is 7.7. The median is 7.5.

The mean of the bottom data set is 7.675. The median is 7.5.

Comparing the measures of center, these data sets are very similar. They have the same median and very similar means.

UNIT
OVERVIEW

GOALS AND
STANDARDS

▶ MATHEMATICS
BACKGROUND

UNIT
INTRODUCTION

Spread: The spread of a distribution refers to the variability of the data. If the observations cover a wide range, the spread is larger. If the observations are clustered around a single value, the spread is smaller. Three primary measures are the range, IQR (median), and MAD (mean).

Example

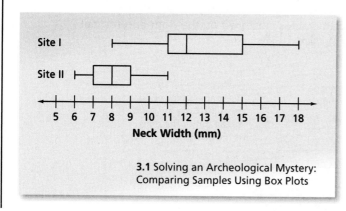

Site 1's arrowhead neck widths are much more variable than Site II's.

The Site I data has a range of 10 (18 – 8), while Site II only has a range of 5 (11 – 6).

Also, Site I's IQR is 4 (15 – 11) while Site II's IQR is only 2 (9 – 7).

3.1 Solving an Archeological Mystery: Comparing Samples Using Box Plots

Shape: The shape of a distribution can be described as symmetrical or skewed. Shape also can be described by noticing number, size, and placement of gaps and clusters.

Example

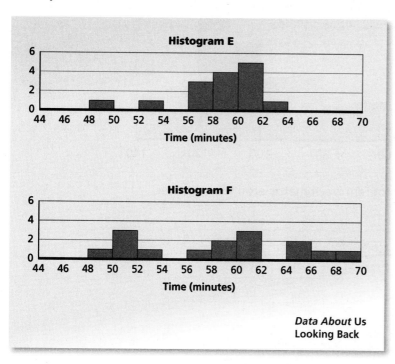

Histogram E is skewed to the left and has a cluster from 56 minutes to 64 minutes.

Histogram F is fairly symmetric but has no large clusters or gaps.

Data About Us
Looking Back

continued on next page

Symmetry is an attribute used to describe the shape of a data distribution. When it is graphed, a **symmetric** distribution can be divided at the center so that each half is a mirror image of the other. A **nonsymmetric** distribution cannot.

When they are displayed graphically, some distributions of data have many more observations on one side of the graph than on the other. Distributions with data values clustered on the left and the tail extending to the right are said to be **skewed right**. Distributions with data values clustered on the right and the tail extending to the left are said to be **skewed left**.

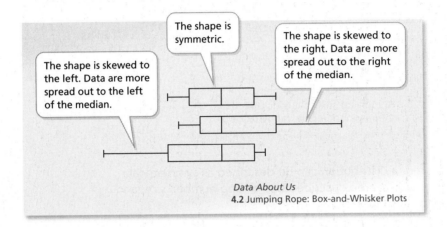

The shape is symmetric.

The shape is skewed to the right. Data are more spread out to the right of the median.

The shape is skewed to the left. Data are more spread out to the left of the median.

Data About Us
4.2 Jumping Rope: Box-and-Whisker Plots

This histogram is skewed to the left.

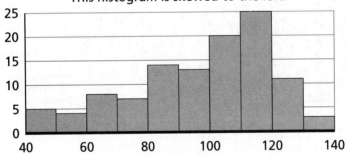

This histogram is symmetric around the center.

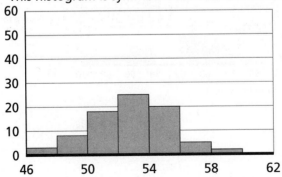

UNIT
OVERVIEW

GOALS AND
STANDARDS

▶ MATHEMATICS
BACKGROUND

UNIT
INTRODUCTION

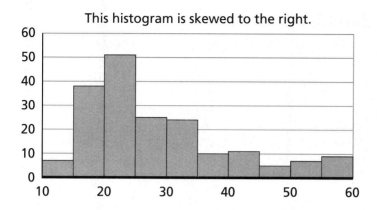

This histogram is skewed to the right.

Unexpected Features: Unexpected features may refer to gaps in the data (areas of the distribution where there are no observations) or the presence of outliers. An outlier is a value that one would not expect when examining the other values in a distribution. An extreme value is considered an outlier if it is at least 1.5 times the IQR less than the first quartile (Q1), or at least 1.5 times IQR greater than the third quartile (Q3). The box plot below shows two outliers. In addition, in some data situations, a data value being greater than 3 MADs less than or greater than the mean would be defined as an outlier.

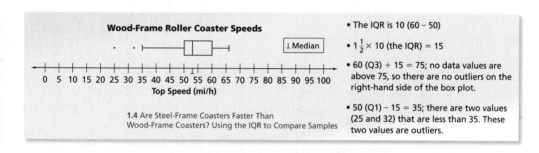

Wood-Frame Roller Coaster Speeds

⊥ Median

Top Speed (mi/h)

1.4 Are Steel-Frame Coasters Faster Than
Wood-Frame Coasters? Using the IQR to Compare Samples

- The IQR is 10 (60 − 50)

- $1\frac{1}{2} \times 10$ (the IQR) = 15

- 60 (Q3) + 15 = 75; no data values are above 75, so there are no outliers on the right-hand side of the box plot.

- 50 (Q1) − 15 = 35; there are two values (25 and 32) that are less than 35. These two values are outliers.

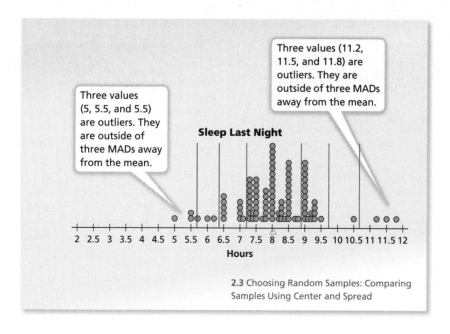

Three values (5, 5.5, and 5.5) are outliers. They are outside of three MADs away from the mean.

Three values (11.2, 11.5, and 11.8) are outliers. They are outside of three MADs away from the mean.

Sleep Last Night

Hours

2.3 Choosing Random Samples: Comparing
Samples Using Center and Spread

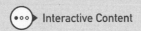
Variability Across Samples: Expected From Natural Variability or Due to Meaningful Differences Between Samples?

Variability is found in any set of data. Not all math test scores are the same, not all students watch the same number of hours of TV, and not all basketball players are the same heights. When students compare two sets of data, they should expect the distributions to be different. They need a way, however, to decide whether the differences are expected due to natural variability or to meaningful differences between samples.

For instance, in Problem 3.1, students compare box plots of six samples of arrowhead data. Looking at the two box plots below, you can see that the differences between the sample data from the Big Goose Creek site and Wortham Shelter site are fairly similar. They have a common attribute: they come from the same time period. Any differences in the samples of these two sites may simply be due to natural variability.

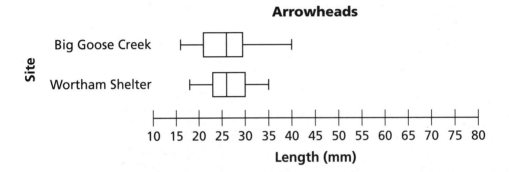

On the other hand, consider the two dot plots below of male professional basketball player heights and female professional basketball player heights.

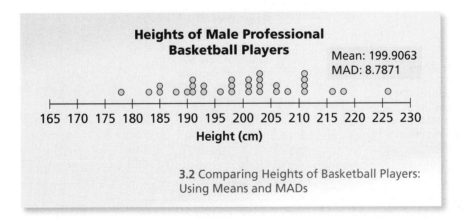

3.2 Comparing Heights of Basketball Players: Using Means and MADs

UNIT
OVERVIEW

GOALS AND
STANDARDS

▶ MATHEMATICS
BACKGROUND

UNIT
INTRODUCTION

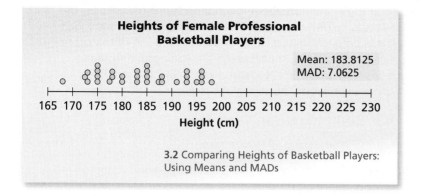

Heights of Female Professional Basketball Players

Mean: 183.8125
MAD: 7.0625

Height (cm)

3.2 Comparing Heights of Basketball Players: Using Means and MADs

Do these two samples provide evidence to support the idea that the difference between the heights of male professional basketball players and the heights of female professional basketball players is meaningful? Or could this difference be due simply to natural variability?

Steps to Decide Whether Samples Come From Different Populations or From the Same Population:

1. Find the MAD of each distribution.

2. Mark the location of two MADs greater than the mean and two MADs less than the mean on each distribution.

3. Mark the mean height of each distribution on the display of the other distribution.

4. If the mean of one distribution is more than two MADs from the mean of the other distribution, we can consider these two distributions to be more variable than what would naturally occur across samples of the same population. Visit Teacher Place at mathdashboard.com/cmp3 to see the video on using the MAD to analyze variability.

Using MAD to Analyze Variability

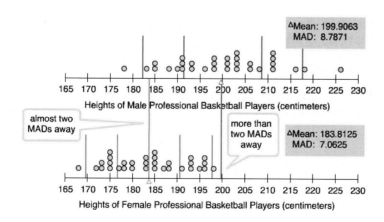

△Mean: 199.9063
MAD: 8.7871

Heights of Male Professional Basketball Players (centimeters)

almost two MADs away

more than two MADs away

△Mean: 183.8125
MAD: 7.0625

Heights of Female Professional Basketball Players (centimeters)

continued on next page

While the two distributions in the animation above overlap in terms of spreads, the difference between the means is 16.047 cm. Additionally, as seen above, the mean height of each set of players is an unexpected value in the distribution of the other set of players. You can conclude, therefore, that there is a meaningful difference between the two distributions that is not due to natural variability. It is not likely that these two populations have similar distributions of heights.

Sampling Plans

A census takes information from the entire population. Generally, conducting a census is not possible or reasonable because of factors such as cost and the size of the population. Instead, sampling is used to gain information about a whole population by analyzing only a part of it.

Representativeness

A central issue in sampling is the need for representative samples. This includes identifying a sampling plan that would result in as representative a sample as possible without concern for the effects of variability or size.

Students often have intuitive notions about representativeness. They can discuss ways in which certain samples may or may not be "fair," or in more technical terms, may or may not represent characteristics of all the members of a population. The terms *representative* and *bias* will help students focus on whether they think data taken from a sample may be used to give a "fair" reflection of what is true about a population.

To ensure that samples are representative, or fair, statisticians try to use **random sampling plans**. Each person or object in the population needs to have an equally likely chance to be included as part of a sample.

The concept of randomness is not an easy one for many students to grasp. One context that may help students think about what it means to choose randomly is the draw-names-from-a-hat strategy. The random sampling plans encountered in this Unit may all be compared to the idea of writing each data value on an identical slip of paper, putting each piece of paper in a hat and mixing thoroughly, and then drawing out one or more slips of paper.

Random samples are not always representative of a population. All types of samples vary. Random samples, however, have two important characteristics:

- Random samples are free from bias.
- Random samples of a large enough size generally give good predictions about the populations from which they are drawn.

UNIT
OVERVIEW

GOALS AND
STANDARDS

▶ MATHEMATICS
BACKGROUND

UNIT
INTRODUCTION

Random Sampling Plans

A number of strategies for selecting samples at random are mentioned in this Unit, such as using spinners, tossing number cubes, and generating lists of values using a calculator. These strategies rely on prior knowledge about probability that students bring to the Unit. There is an equally likely chance for any number to be generated by any spin, toss, or calculator key press. This number may be used to select a member of a population as part of a sample, which means there is an equally likely chance for any member of a population to be included in the sample. Visit Teacher Place at mathdashboard.com/cmp3 to see the video on Random Sampling.

Generating a Random Sample

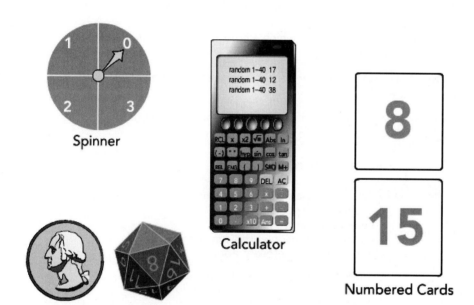

Spinner

Calculator

Numbered Cards

Coin and Numbered Icosahedron

Generating Samples From a Calculator

If you use a calculator to generate random numbers, you will need to think about how random digits are generated on the calculators students are using. Most graphing calculators and many nongraphing calculators have a function for generating decimal numbers. The number of digits in each decimal may be specified (for example, .42 is a two-digit decimal). Students can treat the decimal numbers .00 to .99 as whole numbers for selecting students from the database, with .00 representing student 100, .01 representing student 1, .02 representing student 2, and so on. Some calculators have a random-integer generator. For these calculators, one or more numbers are entered as part of the command. The command consists of the maximum and minimum numbers with which you are working.

continued on next page

It is also important to check whether students' calculators generate the same ordered set of random numbers each time the calculator is turned on. If so, the calculator uses a "seed value" that causes it to begin generating random numbers in a specific way. Consult the manual for each calculator to learn how to change the seed value so that each student can generate a different list of random numbers.

Other Sampling Plans

In addition to random sampling, students consider other types of sampling: **convenience sampling**, **voluntary-response sampling**, and **systematic sampling**. Samples selected using one of these three methods have a greater potential to be biased, or not representative, of the population from which they are drawn.

- **convenience sampling:** a sampling plan in which all of the participants are chosen because they are convenient

- **systematic sampling:** a sampling plan that chooses participants in a methodical or rule-based way

- **voluntary-response sampling:** a sampling plan in which the participants select themselves to be part of the sample

Sampling Plans

Type of Sampling Plan	Examples
Convenience Sampling	• surveying the people in your neighborhood • surveying the people who come through a register at the grocery store
Random Sampling	• choosing Social Security Numbers at random by using a computer's random number generator • assigning each person at a school a student ID number and using a spinner to choose student ID numbers at random
Systematic Sampling	• surveying every third household on your block • surveying every fourth person who comes into a bank.
Voluntary-Response Sampling	• gathering information from callers who agree to answer survey questions at the end of a call • having a voluntary survey booth at a blood drive

UNIT
OVERVIEW

GOALS AND
STANDARDS

▶ MATHEMATICS
BACKGROUND

UNIT
INTRODUCTION

Sample Sizes

Students should develop a sound, general sense about what makes a good sample size. As a rule of thumb, students should use samples with 30 data values. Even with good sampling strategies, summary statistics, such as means and medians, of the samples will vary.

The accuracy of a sample statistic as a predictor of the population statistic improves with the size of the sample. In *Samples and Populations*, Investigation 2, students demonstrate that samples of 30 generally have mean or median distributions that cluster fairly closely around the population mean or median. Sample sizes of 25 to 30 are appropriate for most of the contexts that students at this level encounter.

Sampling Distributions

A sampling distribution is a distribution of data values, each of which is a statistic drawn from a sample. For instance, suppose you collect a sample of size 10. You can find the mean of this sample. This mean is one data value in a sampling distribution.

Repeat the process. Find multiple samples of size 10, and find the mean of each. This distribution of means is called a sampling distribution of means. You can then investigate how much these means vary from each other. The same process can be done with medians.

Interesting concepts arise from studying sampling distributions. For example, the sampling distribution of means from samples of size 30 still shows variation, but it shows much less variation than the sampling distribution of means of samples of size 20, 10, and so on. Moreover, the greater the size of the sample, the more the sampling distribution of means clusters around the true mean of the population. A random sample of size 30 usually gives an accurate prediction of the mean of the population.

▼ Unit Introduction

Using the Unit Opener

In *Samples and Populations*, students explore ways to compare data sets and to use sample data as a way to draw conclusions about a population.

To introduce your students to the Unit, you can begin by posing the following problem.

You are asked to write a survey that collects data on readers' reactions to the cartoon section of the local newspaper. The newspaper is considering removing some cartoons and adding others.

Ask your students the following questions.

- How would you go about planning your survey?

- What types of questions would you ask? What would your survey look like?

- What information would you gather about the personal attributes of the people you are surveying?

- How would you distribute the survey so that you get a variety of useable responses? What are the advantages and disadvantages of any surveying technique that you might use?

- How would you analyze the data? Which graphs would you display? Which statistics would you report?

Discuss this problem in relation to the process of statistical investigation. Suppose that a newspaper surveys the cartoon preferences of their readership by publishing a survey and asking readers to respond. Talk with your class about the issues that arise from this sort of sampling technique. Talk with your class about how the wording of survey questions might influence the answers to those questions, and how imprecise wording may therefore lead to erroneous conclusions.

Refer students to the three questions posed in the Looking Ahead of the Student Edition. You may want to have a class discussion about these questions. At this time, however, do not focus on finding the "correct" answers. Each question is posed again in the Unit at the time when your students have learned the mathematical concepts required to answer it. Ask your students to keep these questions in mind as they work through the Investigations. They should think about how they might use the ideas they are learning to help them figure out the answers to these questions.

UNIT
OVERVIEW

GOALS AND
STANDARDS

MATHEMATICS
BACKGROUND

▶ UNIT
INTRODUCTION

Using the Mathematical Highlights

The Mathematical Highlights page in the Student Edition provides information to students, parents, and other family members. It gives students a preview of the mathematics and some of the overarching questions that they should ask themselves while studying *Samples and Populations*.

As they work through the Unit, students can refer back to the Mathematical Highlights page to review what they have learned and to preview what is still to come. This page also tells students' families what mathematical ideas and activities will be covered as the class works through *Samples and Populations*.

Looking Ahead

How can you determine whether steel-frame roller coasters or wood-frame roller coasters are faster?

A national magazine posts a survey on its Web site for its readers. **What** population do the survey results describe? Is sampling with this kind of plan a good way to draw conclusions about an entire population?

We need student volunteers for our survey.

How can you estimate the albatross population of an island?

Notes _____

_____

_____

The United States Census attempts to gather information from every household in the United States. Gathering, organizing, and analyzing data from such a large population is expensive and time-consuming. In most studies of large populations, data are gathered from a *sample* of the population.

Sampling is an important tool in statistics and data analysis. You can draw conclusions about a single population or compare samples from different populations. For example, scientists may study a sample of penguins to learn more about the entire population of penguins.

Recall that you can analyze a set of data by finding summary statistics. You can use measures of center and measures of variability to describe a distribution.

In this Unit, you will learn how to choose a sample of data from a large population and use data distributions and statistics to draw conclusions about that population. You will use these ideas to answer questions such as those on the previous page.

Looking Ahead   3

Notes

Mathematical Highlights

Making Comparisons and Predictions

In *Samples and Populations*, you will learn about different ways to collect and analyze data in order to make comparisons and draw conclusions.

You will learn how to:

- Use the process of statistical investigation to answer questions

- Apply concepts from probability to select random samples from populations

- Gather information about a population by examining a sample of the population

- Use information from samples to draw conclusions about populations

- Identify how sample sizes and sampling plans influence the measures of center and variability that describe a sample distribution

- Compare samples using measures of center (mean, median), measures of variability (range, IQR, MAD), and displays that group data (histograms, box-and-whisker plots)

When you encounter a new problem, it is a good idea to ask yourself questions. In this Unit, you might ask questions such as:

What is the population?

What is the sample?

Is the sample a representative sample?

How can I describe the data I collected?

How can I use my results to draw conclusions about the population?

How can I use samples to compare two or more populations?

Notes _____

_____

_____

Common Core State Standards
Mathematical Practices and Habits of Mind

In the *Connected Mathematics* curriculum you will develop an understanding of important mathematical ideas by solving problems and reflecting on the mathematics involved. Every day, you will use "habits of mind" to make sense of problems and apply what you learn to new situations. Some of these habits are described by the *Common Core State Standards for Mathematical Practices* (MP).

MP1 Make sense of problems and persevere in solving them.

When using mathematics to solve a problem, it helps to think carefully about

- data and other facts you are given and what additional information you need to solve the problem;
- strategies you have used to solve similar problems and whether you could solve a related simpler problem first;
- how you could express the problem with equations, diagrams, or graphs;
- whether your answer makes sense.

MP2 Reason abstractly and quantitatively.

When you are asked to solve a problem, it often helps to

- focus first on the key mathematical ideas;
- check that your answer makes sense in the problem setting;
- use what you know about the problem setting to guide your mathematical reasoning.

MP3 Construct viable arguments and critique the reasoning of others.

When you are asked to explain why a conjecture is correct, you can

- show some examples that fit the claim and explain why they fit;
- show how a new result follows logically from known facts and principles.

When you believe a mathematical claim is incorrect, you can

- show one or more counterexamples—cases that don't fit the claim;
- find steps in the argument that do not follow logically from prior claims.

Common Core State Standards   5

Notes _____

_____

_____

MP4 Model with mathematics.

When you are asked to solve problems, it often helps to

- think carefully about the numbers or geometric shapes that are the most important factors in the problem, then ask yourself how those factors are related to each other;
- express data and relationships in the problem with tables, graphs, diagrams, or equations, and check your result to see if it makes sense.

MP5 Use appropriate tools strategically.

When working on mathematical questions, you should always

- decide which tools are most helpful for solving the problem and why;
- try a different tool when you get stuck.

MP6 Attend to precision.

In every mathematical exploration or problem-solving task, it is important to

- think carefully about the required accuracy of results; is a number estimate or geometric sketch good enough, or is a precise value or drawing needed?
- report your discoveries with clear and correct mathematical language that can be understood by those to whom you are speaking or writing.

MP7 Look for and make use of structure.

In mathematical explorations and problem solving, it is often helpful to

- look for patterns that show how data points, numbers, or geometric shapes are related to each other;
- use patterns to make predictions.

MP8 Look for and express regularity in repeated reasoning.

When results of a repeated calculation show a pattern, it helps to

- express that pattern as a general rule that can be used in similar cases;
- look for shortcuts that will make the calculation simpler in other cases.

You will use all of the Mathematical Practices in this Unit. Sometimes, when you look at a Problem, it is obvious which practice is most helpful. At other times, you will decide on a practice to use during class explorations and discussions. After completing each Problem, ask yourself:

- What mathematics have I learned by solving this Problem?
- What Mathematical Practices were helpful in learning this mathematics?

Notes _____

_____

_____

Investigation

1

PLANNING

INVESTIGATION
OVERVIEW

GOALS AND
STANDARDS

Making Sense of Samples

▼ Investigation Overview

Investigation Description

Investigation 1 focuses on comparing two or more sets of data (having the same number or different numbers of data values) using a variety of strategies first introduced in *Data About Us*. It also guides students toward using data from samples to make predictions about populations.

Three of the Problems (1.1, 1.2, and 1.4) involve numerical data; Problem 1.3 uses categorical data. The Problems focus attention on the use of measures of center and variability (or spread). Measures of center (mode with respect to categorical data, mean, and median) describe what is typical of the center of a distribution of data. Measures of variability (range, mean absolute deviation, and interquartile range) describe how data are spread about the center of a distribution. Students rely on measures of variability, in conjunction with measures of center, to make comparisons.

The intent is to build a deeper foundation—connecting measures of center and spread to compare data sets. In subsequent Investigations, students will use their knowledge to compare samples with samples and samples with populations.

Investigation Vocabulary

- census
- population
- relative frequency

The following vocabulary terms are included in the Glossary as review but are not defined within the exposition of the Student Edition.

- bar graph
- box-and-whisker plot (box plot)
- categorical data
- distribution
- frequency

- interquartile range (IQR)
- line plot
- mean
- mean absolute deviation (MAD)

- median
- mode
- numerical data
- outlier
- quartile
- range

Mathematics Background

- The Process of Statistical Investigation
- Reviewing Types of Data and Attributes
- Reviewing Measures of Center and Measures of Spread
- Exploring Variation
- Representing Data With Graphical Displays
- Comparing Distributions

Planning Chart

Content	ACE	Pacing	Materials	Resources
Problem 1.1	1–2, 17–18	1 day		
Problem 1.2	3–7, 19–20	1 day	**Labsheet 1.2** Fundraising Money Collected **Labsheet 1ACE:** Exercises 3–7 (accessibility)	**Teaching Aid 1.2** Line Plots of Fundraiser Data • Data and Graphs
Problem 1.3	8, 21, 27–33	1 day	**Labsheet 1.3** Roller Coaster Survey Responses	**Teaching Aid 1.3** Bar Graphs for Roller Coaster Survey Responses
Problem 1.4	9–16, 22–26	1 day	**Labsheet 1.4A** Sample of 30 Steel-Frame Roller Coasters **Labsheet 1.4B** Sample of 30 Wood-Frame Roller Coasters **Labsheet 1.4C:** Dot Plots of Top-Speed Data (accessibility)	• Data and Graphs
Mathematical Reflections		½ day		
Assessment: Check Up		½ day		• Check Up

Goals and Standards

Goals

The Process of Statistical Investigation Deepen the understanding of the
process of statistical investigation and apply this understanding to samples

- Pose questions, collect data, analyze data, and interpret data to answer
  questions

Analysis of Samples Understand that data values in a sample vary and that
summary statistics of samples, even same-size samples, taken from the same
population also vary

- Choose appropriate measures of center (mean, median, or mode) and
  spread (range, IQR, or MAD) to summarize a sample

- Choose appropriate representations to display distributions of samples

- Compare summary statistics of multiple samples drawn from either the
  same population or from two different populations and explain how the
  samples vary

Predictions and Conclusions About Populations Understand that summary
statistics of a representative sample can be used to gain information about
a population

- Describe the benefits and drawbacks of various sampling plans

- Use random-sampling techniques to select representative samples

- Apply concepts from probability to select random samples from
  populations

- Explain how sample size influences the reliability of sample statistics and
  resulting conclusions and predictions

- Explain how different sampling plans influence the reliability of sample
  statistics and resulting conclusions and predictions

- Use statistics from representative samples to draw conclusions about
  populations

- Use measures of center, measures of spread, and data displays from more
  than one random sample to compare and draw conclusions about more
  than one population

- Use mean and MAD, or median and IQR, from random samples to assess
  whether the differences in the samples are due to natural variability or
  due to meaningful differences in the underlying populations

Mathematical Reflections

Look for evidence of student understanding of the goals for this Investigation in their responses to the questions in *Mathematical Reflections*. The goals addressed by each question are indicated below.

1. **a.** A new term is used in this Investigation: *sample*. What do you think *sample means*?

   b. Suppose you have data from a 7th-grade class. The data are answers to the questions:

   • What is your favorite movie?

   • How many movies do you watch per week?

   i. Which statistics can you use to summarize the results of the data?

   ii. How could you use the data to predict the number of students in the entire 7th grade who would say they watch two movies per week?

   Goals

   • Pose questions, collect data, analyze data, and interpret data to answer questions

   • Choose appropriate measures of center (mean, median, or mode) and spread (range, IQR, or MAD) to summarize a sample

2. **a.** How do graphs of distributions help you compare data sets?

   b. How do measures of center help you compare data sets?

   c. How do measures of spread help you compare data sets?

   Goal

   • Choose appropriate representations to display distributions of samples

3. When does it make sense to compare groups using counts, or frequencies? When does it make sense to compare groups using percents, or relative frequencies? Explain.

   Goal

   • Explain how sample size influences the reliability of sample statistics and resulting conclusions and predictions

Standards

Common Core Content Standards

Essential for 7.SP.A.1 Understand that statistics can be used to gain information about a population by examining a sample of the population; generalizations about a population from a sample are valid only if the sample is representative of that population. Understand that random sampling tends to produce representative samples and support valid inferences. *Problems 1, 3, and 4*

Essential for 7.SP.A.2 Use data from a random sample to draw inferences about a population with an unknown characteristic of interest. Generate multiple samples (or simulated samples) of the same size to gauge the variation in estimates or predictions. *Problems 3 and 4*

Essential for 7.SP.B.3 Informally assess the degree of visual overlap of two numerical data distributions with similar variabilities, measuring the difference between the centers by expressing it as a multiple of a measure of variability. *Problems 2 and 3*

7.SP.B.4 Use measures of center and measures of variability for numerical data from random samples to draw informal comparative inferences about two populations. *Problems 1, 2, 3, and 4*

7.NS.A.1 Apply and extend previous understandings of addition and subtraction to add and subtract rational numbers; represent addition and subtraction on a horizontal or vertical number line diagram. *Problem 2*

7.NS.A.1b Understand $p + q$ as the number located a distance $|q|$ from p, in the positive or negative direction depending on whether q is positive or negative. . . Interpret sums of rational numbers by describing real-world contexts. *Problem 2*

Facilitating the Mathematical Practices

Students in *Connected Mathematics* classrooms display evidence of multiple Common Core Standards for Mathematical Practice every day. Here are just a few examples of when you might observe students demonstrating the Standards for Mathematical Practice during this Investigation.

Practice 1: **Make sense of problems and persevere in solving them.**

Students are engaged every day in solving problems and, over time, learn to persevere in solving them. To be effective, the problems embody critical concepts and skills and have the potential to engage students in making sense of mathematics. Students build understanding by reflecting, connecting, and communicating. These student-centered problem situations engage students in articulating the "knowns" in a problem situation and determining a logical solution pathway. The student-student and student-teacher dialogues help students not only to make sense of the problems, but also to persevere in finding appropriate strategies to solve them. The suggested questions in the Teacher Guides provide the metacognitive scaffolding to help students monitor and refine their problem-solving strategies.

Practice 3: **Construct viable arguments and critique the reasoning of others.**

In Problem 1.4, students critique reports of two fictitious students, Charlie and Rosa. Students compare the two reports and identify whether there is a flaw in the arguments. Students improve the arguments and justify their understanding.

Practice 4: **Model with mathematics.**

In Problem 1.3, students conduct their own classroom survey to mirror the data provided in a table. Using multiple sets of data, students then use percents to find relative frequencies. Students are able to compare samples of different sizes. They identify quantities in a practical situation, mapping and analyzing the relationships to draw conclusions.

Practice 6: **Attend to precision.**

In Problem 1.2, Question D, students are asked to identify data values that are within one MAD of the mean, within two MADs of the mean, or further than two MADs from the mean. They repeat this exercise with six dot plots to determine any patterns. Students must calculate accurately and express answers with a degree of precision.

Students identify and record their personal experiences with the Standards for Mathematical Practice during the *Mathematical Reflections* at the end of the Investigation.

PROBLEM 1.1

Comparing Performances
Using Center and Spread

▼ Problem Overview

> *Focus Question*   Given a set of results, how might you use measures of center and variability (spread) to judge overall performance?

Problem Description

Problem 1.1 provides opportunities for students to review concepts they learned in *Data About Us*. Students analyze math test scores from sample data belonging to two students. They use measures of center and variability to compare performances, calculating the means, medians, ranges, and MADs. Students examine how adding data values changes the summary statistics. They also judge performance based on consistency and see how different measures might result in different conclusions.

Problem Implementation

Have students work in pairs on this Problem.

Materials

There are no additional materials for this Problem.

Vocabulary

The following vocabulary terms are included in the Glossary as review but are not defined within the exposition of the Student Edition.

- mean
- mean absolute deviation (MAD)
- median
- range

Mathematics Background

- The Process of Statistical Investigation
- Reviewing Measures of Center and Measures of Spread
- Exploring Variation
- Representing Data With Graphical Displays
- Comparing Distributions

At a Glance and Lesson Plan

- At a Glance: Problem 1.1 Samples and Populations
- Lesson Plan: Problem 1.1 Samples and Populations

▼ Launch

Launch Video

In this Launch animation, students are introduced to the idea that means of data sets can be identical even when the distributions are very different. Students will see two divers with the same mean score. One diver will be very consistent; however, the other diver will be erratic. You can show this animation to your students before Connecting to Prior Knowledge to have them begin to consider the Focus Question. Visit Teacher Place at mathdashboard.com/cmp3 to see the complete video.

Connecting to Prior Knowledge

Problem 1.1 specifically addresses measures of center and variability (or spread). Students should be familiar with the terms from *Data About Us*. You may need to evaluate how much time should be spent on review; however, Problem 1.1 addresses the review concepts.

As a refresher, measures of center are used to characterize what is typical for a distribution of data. Highlighted are the mean (evened-out value) and the median (midpoint in an ordered set). Students will encounter mode (most frequent value) in Problem 1.3 as it relates to categorical data.

Measures of variability (range and mean absolute deviation (MAD)) are used to describe how the data are spread about the center of a distribution. Range calculates the difference between the maximum and minimum values; it is a measure of spread for the whole distribution. The MAD highlights how the data values, on average, are spread around the mean of a distribution. With MAD as a measure of variability, a small number indicates that the data are grouped closely together around the mean, while a larger quantity shows that the data are more spread out. These measures can be used to compare two distributions.

Problem 1.1 builds a deeper foundation for students as they connect measures of center and spread to compare distributions. Students find that they need to use measures of spread, in conjunction with measures of center, in order to judge performance. In addition, students need to decide on the usefulness of particular measures of spread.

To remind students about what they already know about making comparisons, you might ask:

Suggested Questions

- What might you consider when comparing these sample test scores? (Students might suggest measures of center or variability. Review them if necessary.)

- How do you find a mean? A median? The MAD? What do these statistics tell you? (The mean is found by adding all the data values and dividing the sum by the number of data values. The median is found by locating the midpoint in an ordered set (if there is an odd number of data values, the value of the median is the middle value; however, if there is an even number of data values, then the median value is the average of the two middle values). The mean and median tell you about the center of the distribution by describing what is "typical."

   The MAD is found by taking the distance each data value is from the mean of the data set, totaling all the distances, and dividing by the number of data values. The MAD is a measure of spread indicating how variable the data are.)

Note: Material reviewing MAD is offered as part of the Summarize. You may wish to use it as part of the Launch.

Presenting the Challenge

Use the Investigation introduction to set up Problem 1.1. Discuss what is involved in conducting a statistical investigation: posing a question, collecting data, analyzing the data, and interpreting the results. In thinking about the analysis phase, have students discuss why deciding what is typical for a data set or describing how a set of data varies can help them compare distributions.

▼ Explore

Providing for Individual Needs

Students should have the background to understand and determine measures of center or spread discussed in this Problem having completed *Data About Us*. Be attentive to what questions students have.

If some students are confused by Question A, other teams can help them recall the two measures of center: mean and median. Encourage students to compare these measures for Jun and Mia: they are identical.

Suggested Questions

- How is it possible that Jun and Mia have the same mean and median math scores when their test scores are different? (The median marks the middle of the data; 80 points is the midpoint. Mean answers the question: What would the score be if all the tests had the same score? For both students, the answer is 80 points for both mean and median.)

Students explored making different distributions of data having the same means in *Data About Us*.

For Question B, two measures of variability—range and mean absolute deviation (MAD)—are highlighted. Students may be comfortable finding the range (for Jun, it is 40 points; for Mia, it is 10 points).

Students might not remember what MAD is or how to compute it. You may decide to conduct a whole class session around finding the MAD. Remind students that the MAD is determined using the mean of a distribution. It is used to describe how much, on average, the math test scores (in this example) differ from the mean score.

Questions C and D ask whether having more information (a larger sample) provides better evidence for making a decision, and which measure of spread best reflects the samples.

- Does having more data change any of the measures you found in Questions A and B? (The median scores remained the same (80 points). Mia's mean score goes up slightly (from 80 to 83.33 points).)

- Does having more data change the decision you made in Question C? (The addition of three scores did not change the measures significantly, but the larger sample did illuminate that Jun's earlier inconsistency is a result of one poor score. The MAD is not as influenced by this unusual score as the range, and adding more scores lessens the influence of the poor score on the MAD calculation.)

Planning for the Summary

What evidence will you use in the summary to clarify and deepen understanding of the Focus Question?
What will you do if you do not have evidence?

Summarize

Orchestrating the Discussion

Have students summarize what they found for Question A. It may surprise them that the test scores have the same means and the same medians. *In Data About Us*, however, students completed several activities that should help them to now explain how different sets of data can result in equal measures of center. In this situation, a lower measure of spread indicates a more consistent test performance.

Have students discuss how they found the range and what it means for one range to be 40 points and the other to be 10 points in terms of evaluating performance.

Note: You may need to review the mean absolute deviation (MAD) as a statistic. The MAD is determined using the mean of a distribution. It is used to describe how much, on average, the math test scores (in this example) differ from the mean score.

For Jun's test scores, the mean is 80 points. To calculate the MAD, find the positive difference between the mean and each test score. The results are $80 - 60 = 20$, $80 - 80 = 0$, and $100 - 80 = 20$. Add the differences $(20 + 0 + 20)$ for a sum of 40 points. Find the average difference: $40 \div 3 = 13.33$ points. So, the MAD is 13.33 points. Jun's test scores differ on average by about 13.33 points from the mean test score of 80 points.

For Mia's test scores, the mean is 80 points. To calculate the MAD, find the positive difference between the mean and each test score. The results are $80 - 75 = 5$, $80 - 80 = 0$, and $85 - 80 = 5$. Add the differences $(5 + 0 + 5)$ for a sum of 10 points. Find the average difference: $10 \div 3 = 3.33$ points. So, the MAD is 3.33 points. Mia's test scores differ on average by about 3.33 points from the mean test score of 80 points.

Based on the measures of variability (range and MAD), Mia's results are much less variable than Jun's results. It may be interesting for students to consider that it is not the greater score, but how consistently each student performs overall, that may be used to evaluate success. Other measures being equal, students may determine Mia's performance as being more successful than Jun's performance.

Have students talk about their responses to Question C. Highlight the use of the word *sample* in the Problem.

Suggested Questions

- What do you think the word *sample* means? (A sample is a subset of all the test scores each student earns.)

- Does the sample include all of Jun's or Mia's math test scores? (It is unlikely but not known in this case.)

  If students consider "all" to mean the math test scores for a complete math class, then the selection of three math scores each is probably not "all."

- Does it make sense to make general statements about the two students' performances? (Possibly, but there is probably not enough data. It appears both students are achieving the same average score (80 points), but their consistency in achieving the average indicates variable performance. You would probably need to look at more long-term data if you wanted to generalize about performance.)

In Question D, more data values are included. The table now reflects six tests each. Students look at measures of center and spread to explore how the additional data change their assessment of Jun's and Mia's test performances. The intent is for students to see that the choice of a particular measure can influence conclusions.

For Jun's test scores, the mean (80 points), median (80 points), and range (40 points) remain the same. However, with the additional data values, the MAD has decreased from 13.33 points to 6.67 points. To calculate the MAD, students will need to find the positive difference between the mean and each test score. The results are: $80 - 80 = 0$, $80 - 60 = 20$, $100 - 80 = 20$, $80 - 80 = 0$, $80 - 80 = 0$, and $80 - 80 = 0$. The sum of these differences is 40 ($0 + 20 + 20 + 0 + 0 + 0 = 40$). To find the average difference, the sum is divided by 6 ($40 \div 6 = 6.67$). So, the MAD is 6.67 points. With the addition of more data values, Jun's test performance is less variable (MAD of 6.67 points) than previously thought (MAD of 13.33 points).

For Mia's test scores, the mean increases slightly (83.3 points), the median remains the same (80 points), and the range increases (25 points). To calculate the MAD, finding the positive difference between the mean and each test score results in: $83.3 - 75 = 8.3$, $83.3 - 80 = 3.3$, $85 - 83.3 = 1.7$, $83.3 - 80 = 3.3$, $83.3 - 80 = 3.3$, and $100 - 83.3 = 16.7$. The sum of these differences is 36.6 ($8.3 + 3.3 + 1.7 + 3.3 + 3.3 + 16.7 = 36.6$). To find the average difference, the sum is divided by 6 ($36.6 \div 6 = 6.1$). So, the MAD is 6.1 points, which is more than the original MAD of 3.33 points. So, with the addition of more test scores, Mia's performance is more variable than previously thought (due, in part, to her perfect score of 100%).

The students' performances are almost indistinguishable (the difference being attributed to Jun's one poor test result). Students may still conclude that Mia performs more consistently, since she does not have low values, nor as big a range in scores, as Jun does. You may want to ask students who they would rather be—Jun or Mia—on test day.

Finally, you can return to the Focus Question and discuss how this was answered in completing the Problem.

Reflecting on Student Learning

Use the following questions to assess student understanding at the end of the lesson.

- What evidence do I have that students understand the Focus Question?
  - Where did my students get stuck?
  - What strategies did they use?
  - What breakthroughs did my students have today?
- How will I use this to plan for tomorrow? For the next time I teach this lesson?
- Where will I have the opportunity to reinforce these ideas as I continue through this Unit? The next Unit?

ACE Assignment Guide

- **Applications:** 1–2
- **Connections:** 17–18

Which Team Is Most Successful?
Using the MAD to Compare Samples

▼ Problem Overview

> *Focus Question* What strategies might you use to evaluate numerical outcomes and judge success?

Problem Description

In Problem 1.2, students explore the properties of the mean. They also explore the relationship of the mean to other measures of center and to measures of variability. They look for ways to determine fairly which group had the best performance in a fundraising contest.

Problem Implementation

Have students work in pairs on this Problem.

Materials

- **Labsheet 1.2:** Fundraising Money Collected
- **Labsheet 1ACE:** Exercises 3–7 (accessibility)
- **Teaching Aid 1.2:** Line Plots of Fundraiser Data

Using Technology

Your students may benefit from completing the calculations for MAD by hand or with a calculator as a review. If, however, your students do not need this computational review, they can use the MAD calculator in the **Data and Graphs** tool to help them solve this Problem and some of the ACE Exercises.

Vocabulary

The following vocabulary terms are included in the Glossary as review but are not defined within the exposition of the Student Edition.

- distribution
- line plot

Mathematics Background

- The Process of Statistical Investigation
- Reviewing Measures of Center and Measures of Spread
- Exploring Variation
- Representing Data With Graphical Displays

At a Glance and Lesson Plan

- At a Glance: Problem 1.2 Samples and Populations
- Lesson Plan: Problem 1.2 Samples and Populations

▼ Launch

Connecting to Prior Knowledge

Problem 1.2 continues with the same focus as Problem 1.1. Students should be familiar with the concepts of center and spread from *Data About Us*. In particular, the mean absolute deviation (MAD) is explored as a way to evaluate variability in data distributions. Not only do students find the MAD, but they now also evaluate how many MADs each data value is away from the mean. In Investigation 3, students will use the MAD as a measurement unit in order to decide if one sample is markedly different from another sample.

Presenting the Challenge

Pose the fundraising context faced by the Hiking Club. Have students examine the table of data.

Suggested Questions

- In this Problem, you have a larger number of samples with more data values. It makes sense to represent the data on a graph. What kind of graph might you choose? (Students will almost certainly say a line plot or bar graph. Encourage the use of a line plot.)

- How do you make a line plot? (This will raise the issue of scale. Discuss the need for a common scale in all plots.)

- What might you observe on a line plot that helps you make comparisons? (clusters, gaps, and spread)

Have students brainstorm strategies they might use in order to decide how to answer the question posed. Resist actually carrying out strategies during this stage—the intent is to get ideas out. Some strategies students are likely to suggest are: find which of the six groups collected the most money, find the mean or the median, find a way to measure the contributions of individual members in terms of how "equal" they are, and so on.

Once you have brainstormed a list of strategies, you can have students start the Problem.

Have students work in pairs on Problem 1.2. **Labsheet 1.2: Fundraising Money Collected** contains a table version of the team data displayed on a bulletin board in the Student Edition. You can give this labsheet to students so they can use the team data to calculate the medians and other measures.

▼ Explore

Providing for Individual Needs

Question A involves students making line plots for each set of data; this allows them to look at the distributions differently.

In Question B, students interpret other students' thinking. In each of the three parts, different alternative approaches are proposed. Each one is designed to highlight key strategies that can be used.

Students might be puzzled as they work through parts (1)–(3). In part (1), they discover that all teams raised the same amounts of money, but one team has five people, and the rest have six people each. In part (2), all teams except Team 5 have the same mean; Team 5 has a higher mean, yet it also has fewer team members.

Suggested Questions

- How can Team 5 have a higher mean when all teams raised the same amount of money? (To find the mean, even out all data values to make them the same. For Team 5, the same total will be spread over fewer data values (five members, not six).)

- Do the means help you compare the teams? (No. The four teams with six members have the same means. Team 5 has a different mean, but it has fewer members.)

In Question B, part (3), students will calculate the MADs for each team.

- What does the MAD represent in each case? (The MAD is the average distance each data value is from the mean.)

- How do the MADs help you compare teams? (The smaller the MAD, the more consistent the team is in having all members contribute fairly equally to the total.)

Question C asks students to use any other strategies not yet tried to see how the results will help them answer the question.

Question D engages students in examining locations of data values in relation to MADs. Help students locate the markers on each distribution. Also, students might not know what to do when a data value is on a marker. Remind them that they are finding the number of data values within one MAD (or two MADs). Data values that fall on a MAD marker should not be counted as within, since they are not less than one MAD (or two MADs) from the mean. Students may want to use a calculator at this point.

Going Further

Ask students why it seems impossible to construct a data set with data values further than three MADs from the mean. Challenge them to identify a data set that has data values further than three MADs from the mean. They will soon realize that adding extreme values to the data set increases the MAD because the new data values are far from the mean. So, the unit of measurement MAD increases with the addition of extreme values, making three MADs an even greater distance from the mean.

Planning for the Summary

What evidence will you use in the summary to clarify and deepen understanding of the Focus Question?

What will you do if you do not have evidence?

Summarize

Orchestrating the Discussion

Look at the six line plots. You may use **Teaching Aid 1.2: Line Plots of Fundraiser Data**, which displays the line plots of the team data. Students will need to use the same scale for each graph in order to compare the distributions. It is easier to see which distributions are more variable and which are less variable in terms of data being spread out around the mean of the distribution. Teams 1, 2, and 6 seem to have less variability than the other three teams.

Have students discuss each of the strategies posed in Question B. In terms of identifying the most successful team, Jonah's strategy of using the MADs is probably the one that can help students focus on performance among group members.

For Question C, have students discuss any other strategies not considered in Question B. Students may focus on locating medians. This statistic is different for each group. Students might want to consider which statistic—the median or MAD—best characterizes groups working "fairly" together to raise money.

Question D engages students in thinking about how the data values relate both to the mean and to the MADs of a distribution.

Suggested Questions

- It looks like it is quite unusual for data to be more than two MADs from the mean. Does this give us a way to measure whose contributions may be considered unusual? Was any contribution unusually high? Low? (Data values more than two MADs from the mean may be considered unusual. Team 3's data value of 100 is unusually high. Even though Team 4's data value of 0 seems low, it falls within two MADs of the mean, so it is not unusual for that group.)

Have students look back at each distribution.

- Are all the data values within three MADs of the mean? If not, do you think a data value greater than three MADs from the mean is unusual, when compared to other data values? (All data values are within three MADs of the mean. A data value greater than three MADs from the mean would be highly unusual.)

Finally, you can return to the Focus Question and discuss how this was answered in completing this Problem.

Reflecting on Student Learning

Use the following questions to assess student understanding at the end of the lesson.

- What evidence do I have that students understand the Focus Question?
  - Where did my students get stuck?
  - What strategies did they use?
  - What breakthroughs did my students have today?
- How will I use this to plan for tomorrow? For the next time I teach this lesson?
- Where will I have the opportunity to reinforce these ideas as I continue through this Unit? The next Unit?

ACE Assignment Guide

- **Applications:** 3–7
- **Connections:** 19–20
- **Labsheet 1ACE:** Exercises 3–7 (accessibility)

This labsheet contains a table version of the team data displayed on a bulletin board in the Student Edition. You may wish to provide students with the table so that they can easily access the team data and mark up any values as they calculate the medians, etc.

Pick Your Preference
Distinguishing Categorical Data From
Numerical Data

▼ Problem Overview

> *Focus Question* How might you compare results to see if each sample
> responded to a survey in a similar way? How can using
> percentages help you make comparisons?

Problem Description

Problem 1.3 uses the context of an ongoing, interactive online survey of responses
to questions about roller-coaster rides. Students are provided with survey-
response data from two different groups and are asked to add their own data to
make a third group. Students use bar graphs and (eventually) relative frequencies
to represent these data and to decide if the three groups responded in similar
ways to the survey. This Problem involves using categorical data versus numerical
data and also using different-sized data sets.

Problem Implementation

Have students work in groups of three on this Problem.

Materials

• **Labsheet 1.3:** Roller Coaster Survey Responses
• **Teaching Aid 1.3:** Bar Graphs for Roller Coaster Survey Responses

Vocabulary

• relative frequency

The following vocabulary terms are included in the Glossary as review but are not
defined within the exposition of the Student Edition.

• bar graph
• categorical data
• frequency
• mode
• numerical data

Mathematics Background

- The Process of Statistical Investigation
- Reviewing Types of Data and Attributes
- Reviewing Measures of Center and Measures of Spread
- Exploring Variation
- Representing Data With Graphical Displays
- Comparing Distributions

At a Glance and Lesson Plan

- At a Glance: Problem 1.3 Samples and Populations
- Lesson Plan: Problem 1.3 Samples and Populations

▼ Launch

Connecting to Prior Knowledge

Students were introduced to the distinction between categorical and numerical data in *Data About Us*. While not emphasized, there are different kinds of categorical data:

- **Nominal data** has no order, and the assignment of numbers to categories is purely arbitrary (ex. 1 = East, 2 = North, 3 = South; colors: red, green, blue, etc.). Due to the lack of order or equal intervals, one cannot perform arithmetic ($+$, $-$, $\div$, $\times$) or logical operations ($>$, $<$, $=$) on nominal data.

- **Ordinal data** has order, but the intervals between scale points may be uneven. Rank data, such as students' class rank, are usually ordinal. For example, the interval between the top student to the second-highest student may be great, but the interval between the second-ranked student and the third-ranked may be very close. Given the lack of equal distances, arithmetic operations cannot be performed with ordinal data; however, it is possible to use logical operations (more than, less than, equal to) to "order" ordinal data.

Generally, in *Connected Mathematics*, nominal data are used. The mode is the only viable measure of center since no numerical calculations are possible.

In this Problem, students will compare different-sized data sets and use bar graphs to display these data. In *Data About Us*, students used counts, or frequencies. Now, in order to make data sets "comparable," students see that the data sets need to be the "same size." This can be done by reporting percentages, not counts. In statistics, this is called *relative frequency*. By using percents, students report responses "out of one hundred" to compare three sets of data.

Presenting the Challenge

Give students **Labsheet 1.3: Roller Coaster Survey Responses**, which contains the two tables of Roller Coaster Seating Preferences and Other Roller Coaster Preferences. The tables are like the ones found in the Student Edition, but with an added column for "Votes From Your Class." Introduce the students to the surveys on roller-coaster preferences. Collect and tally the total responses from the class to each question. Add class data in the column "Votes From Our Class(es)."

Look at the three sets of data.

Suggested Questions

- Is it OK to just say that more people online want to sit up front than 7th-grade students? (No. The comparison 97 versus 27 is not fair. The sample sizes are different.)

- Do more 7th-grade students like to sit up front than the people in our class? (27 versus X (class number) is also not a fair comparison. The sample sizes are different.)

- How can you make comparisons when the sample sizes are different? (You can use percents.)

- How do you calculate the percent of each group that like to sit up front? (Review the percent calculation briefly.)

Pose this situation to students:

- Suppose you go online, respond to a survey, and then see a set of graphs dynamically updated to show the latest results of the survey once you have taken it. What kinds of graphs would be easiest to use? (Answers will vary; bar graphs would be a reasonable choice.)

- How would you set up the graphs? (Answers will vary. It is important for students to consider the fact that there are different numbers of data in each group.)

Students are introduced to the distinction between using counts or percents to record frequencies. The latter is called *relative frequency*. Percents (as proportions) make it possible to compare different-size groups

- We have results of the survey from three different sample groups. How might you compare these results to see if each group responded to the survey in a similar way? (Answers will vary. Possible solution: make graphs of each group's data in order to compare the data.)

Note: If needed, there is a discussion about use of frequencies and relative frequencies in the student text that can be of assistance at this point as well.

▼ Explore

Providing for Individual Needs

Teachers have completed this activity in one of two ways. One option is to work through the making of the graphs as a class. This means that the activity takes a short amount of time. It also takes away the opportunity for students to decide whether percents or counts are the better way to represent these data.

Another way is to organize students in teams of three. Students may prepare their solutions on chart paper so that they can present and post their solutions. The class discusses the variety of solutions.

As you visit groups, focus on using the same frequency scales for different graphs and on displaying frequencies using percents vs. counts.

Note: Bar graphs of the Internet responses and 7th-grade responses are displayed on **Teaching Aid 1.3: Bar Graphs for Roller Coaster Survey Responses**.

Suggested Questions

For Question A, once data are collected, you might ask:

• How might you compare our class responses with the other two sets of data? (The sizes of each sample are different. You can eyeball whether the class responses are similar to the other two data sets. However, since the numbers in each sample are different, you need to compare across samples to see how much more or less the responses vary.)

For Question B, you might ask:

• How could you determine percents for each data set? For example, you know that 97 out of 165 respondents from the Internet survey voted for sitting at the front of a roller coaster. What percent of the votes is this? (To determine a percent, write a fraction. The number of votes is the numerator; the number of total responses is the denominator. Divide the numerator by the denominator. For example, $\frac{97}{165} = 59\%$.)

• How does reporting relative frequencies help you compare the three sets of data? (Relative frequencies allow you to compare the responses from the three groups as if the groups were all the same size.)

Question C is important. Since these are categorical data, only one measure of center may be used—the mode. Students may have trouble realizing that the median or mean will not work. Often, they will try to report the mean frequency or median frequency. Help them to see that the actual data are the responses to the survey; they are not numerical data.

For Question D, part (2), you might ask:

- Did you find any differences between groups?

- Did these differences surprise you, or do you have explanations for differences?

- If you wanted to make a general statement about how people responded to the first survey question, what might you say based on the data?

Continue with the remaining Question. Students can look at their graphs and the modes for each survey question. If the modes for each of the three sets of data are the same, they can note that "all groups chose. . ." If they are not, they might note that "two out of the three groups chose. . ." Or, if there is no clear pattern in modes, they might note that the groups were not similar in their choices.

For Question E, you might ask:

- How do you use statistics to help the manager predict how many people want to sit at the front of the roller coaster?

Students may want to use the percents from the larger sample. If they want to use their own data, you can approach the idea that maybe one class of 7th-grade students is not similar in tastes to the varied age levels that the manager is thinking about. If they want to combine data sets, ask why—perhaps they intuitively think that a larger set is a more reliable predictor.

Planning for the Summary

What evidence will you use in the summary to clarify and deepen understanding of the Focus Question?

What will you do if you do not have evidence?

▼ Summarize

Orchestrating the Discussion

Teaching Aid 1.3 displays the relative frequency bar graphs from the online survey and the group of 7th-grade students. With the students, look at the two different bar graphs for the first survey question (the one about seating preferences). For comparison, include a bar graph of your own class data from the survey.

Specifically, consider why relative frequencies as opposed to actual frequencies are needed to make the data sets appear as if they each are the same size. (Each data set is redefined as "out of 100." It is as if each survey had been given to exactly 100 people in that survey group. For example:

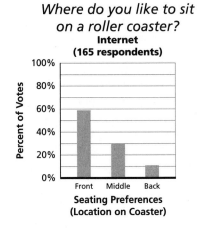

Suggested Questions

- What percent of the votes from the online-survey respondents like to ride up front in a roller coaster? How does this percent compare with that of the 7th graders? (59% of the online-survey voters preferred riding up front, which is 16% more than the 7th graders (43% of whom preferred to ride up front).)

- How do the other seat locations compare for the two groups? (About 30% of the online respondents vs. 35% of the 7th graders prefer to sit in the middle location. About 11% of the online voters vs. about 22% of the 7th graders prefer the back of the roller coaster.)

You can have a similar conversation about the second survey question (about roller-coaster characteristics).

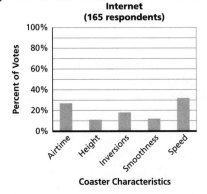

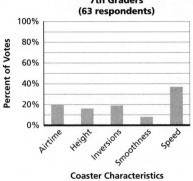

Finally, you can return to the Focus Question and discuss how this was answered in completing this Problem.

Reflecting on Student Learning

Use the following questions to assess student understanding at the end of the lesson.

- What evidence do I have that students understand the Focus Question?
  - Where did my students get stuck?
  - What strategies did they use?
  - What breakthroughs did my students have today?
- How will I use this to plan for tomorrow? For the next time I teach this lesson?
- Where will I have the opportunity to reinforce these ideas as I continue through this Unit? The next Unit?

ACE Assignment Guide

- **Applications:** 8
- **Connections:** 21
- **Extensions:** 27–33

Are Steel-Frame Coasters Faster Than Wood-Frame Coasters?

Using the IQR to Compare Samples

▼ Problem Overview

> *Focus Question* How might you decide whether steel-frame coasters or wood-frame coasters are faster?

Problem Description

Problem 1.4 opens with a census table showing the counts of different kinds of roller coasters worldwide. Students use two samples (30 steel-frame coasters and 30 wood-frame coasters) selected from roller coasters listed as part of the census. Students use the data from these samples and a variety of strategies to make comparisons between speeds of steel-frame and wood-frame coasters.

Problem Implementation

Have students work in pairs on this Problem.

Materials

- **Labsheet 1.4A:** Sample of 30 Steel-Frame Roller Coasters
- **Labsheet 1.4B:** Sample of 30 Wood-Frame Roller Coasters
- **Labsheet 1.4C:** Dot Plots of Top-Speed Data (accessibility)

Using Technology

Your students can use the **Data and Graphs** tool to help them identify the measures of center and spread for this Problem. If your students need a review of any of these measures, you may suggest that they calculate those measures by hand or with a calculator.

Vocabulary

- census
- population

The following vocabulary terms are included in the Glossary as review but are not defined within the exposition of the Student Edition.

- box-and-whisker plot (box plot)
- interquartile range (IQR)
- outlier
- quartile

Mathematics Background

- The Process of Statistical Investigation
- Reviewing Types of Data and Attributes
- Reviewing Measures of Center and Measures of Spread
- Exploring Variation
- Representing Data With Graphical Displays
- Comparing Distributions

At a Glance and Lesson Plan

- At a Glance: Problem 1.4 Samples and Populations
- Lesson Plan: Problem 1.4 Samples and Populations

▼ Launch

Launch Video

In this animation, students will see a real-life example of how variable a population's data can be. The scenario is of a 5k race with two groups of runners—adults and kids. There is variability in race times, and the two groups have some overlap. Even though the adults generally seem faster than the kids, some kids can run faster than the slowest adults. You can ask your students about other places where and times when they've noticed such great variability. You can also use this animation to have your students begin to think about the Focus Question. How might students decide whether, in this case, adults or kids are faster? Visit Teacher Place at mathdashboard.com/cmp3 to see the complete video.

Connecting to Prior Knowledge

As with earlier Problems, looking at measures of spread may provide better insights into ways to answer the question posed. Students look at the IQR and are asked to represent data with box plots, in addition to line plots or histograms. Using the median as a measure of center is explored, as well as variability centered about the median.

Presenting the Challenge

Continue discussing roller coasters. Have students examine the data on **Labsheet 1.4A: Sample of 30 Steel-Frame Roller Coasters** and **Labsheet 1.4B: Sample of 30 Wood-Frame Roller Coasters**. Have a discussion about how to read the tables and what information can be obtained from them.

Suggested Questions

- Is there any information in the tables that surprises you? Why or why not? (Answers will vary. Some students may be surprised that roller coasters have been around since the early 1900s. Other students might be surprised that the top speed of the slowest wood-frame roller coaster is faster than the top speed of the slowest steel-frame roller coaster (in this sample).)

- What other information might you want to collect about roller coasters? (Possible answer: You can collect information about how fast a coaster can travel, the park and state location, the number of people who can ride it, the tallest height, and so on.)

- How might you go about collecting this information about several coasters? (You can collect the information from the theme parks or amusement parks where coasters are located or from Web sites on the Internet.)

▼ Explore

Providing for Individual Needs

Question A familiarizes students with the two samples of 30 roller coasters. It helps students focus specifically on the attribute of top speed. Pay attention to the prompt in part (1). Teachers have found that it is important for students to think about what might be considered a fast speed for a roller coaster *before* analyzing the data. We suggest that students do this with their partners in order NOT to create a whole-class definition of fast initially. Students don't necessarily have a good notion of speed. This question provides an opportunity for them to wrestle with the idea. Part (2) helps students think about whether they use speed as a criterion when choosing to ride a roller coaster. Again, it is designed to help the students become more familiar with the data set being explored.

Students will need time to explore the data on **Labsheet 1.4A: Sample of 30 Steel-Frame Roller Coasters** and **Labsheet 1.4B: Sample of 30 Wood-Frame Roller Coasters** in order to answer Question B. Also, **Labsheet 1.4C: Dot Plots of Top-Speed Data** (accessibility) displays the dot plots of the top-speed data as shown in the Student Edition. Here are some questions you can ask students as they review the graphs:

Suggested Questions

- Do you need the same scale for each graph? Why or why not? (Although it is not required, the same scale does help make visual comparisons between the two sets of data.)

- Look at the shapes of the two distributions. What do you notice? (The distribution for the wood-frame roller coasters seems to cluster between 45 mi/h and 65 mi/h. It is quite symmetric, except for a few slow coasters. The distribution for the steel-frame roller coasters is more spread out.)

- What statistics might you use to compare the two distributions?
  (measures of center (mean, median) and measures of spread (range,
  IQR, and MAD))

Students can identify that the means are not the same, but the difference between
the two (~2.43 mi/h) is not important in this context. The same is true for the
difference between the two medians (~1.5 mi/h). Interestingly, the measures of
center for these data are similar, and there is not much difference between means
and medians of each distribution. The magnitude of the differences is minimal, so
you can't claim that steel-frame roller coasters are faster than wood-frame roller
coasters when comparing measures of center.

- The measures of center differ by about 2 to 3 miles per hour. Do you think
  you would notice that difference if you were riding a roller coaster? (The
  differences are not large enough to be important; it would be hard to tell
  the difference riding on the roller coaster.)

As students complete Question B, parts (2) and (3), focus their attention on the
measures of variability and how they are displayed in the graphs. The box plots
highlight how the speeds vary. Steel-frame roller coasters have a much greater
spread in speeds, including several very fast roller coasters. Wood-frame roller
coasters' speeds are less variable and do not have roller coasters with speeds that
would be found in the upper quartile of the steel-frame roller coaster speeds.
Encourage students to try to sort this out.

Going Further

It is possible to give students other opportunities to explore the data presented in
Labsheets 1.4A and 1.4B using the inquiries in Problem 1.4, Question B. Below is
a version of Question B that addresses *maximum heights*. Similar problems can be
created dealing with duration of rides or *track length*.

Ask the students:

*How might you decide which have greater maximum heights, steel-frame coasters
or wood-frame coasters?*

1. *Identify and compare the minimum and maximum values, ranges, medians,
   and means of the distributions of data for each type of roller coaster. Does this
   information help you write any responses to the question?*

2. *Identify and compare the IQR (interquartile range) for each distribution.
   Remember that this shows the spread of the middle 50% of the data. Does this
   information help you write any responses to the question?*

3. *Make a box-and-whisker plot for each distribution (use the same scale for each
   graph). Show outliers as part of your displays. Remember that you can identify
   the top 25% of the speeds for each type of coaster by looking at the graphs.
   Does this information help you write responses to the question?*

Planning for the Summary

What evidence will you use in the summary to clarify and deepen understanding of the Focus Question?

What will you do if you do not have evidence?

▼ Summarize

Orchestrating the Discussion

One way to summarize Problem 1.4 would be to ask each group of students to prepare a short report, no more than five sentences, explaining how they would answer the question about which type of roller coaster is faster. Have each group share their report with the class. After each report is made, the other groups are allowed to point out one important point they think was omitted (if there was such a point), and whether they agree with the overall report.

Then return to Question D with Charlie's and Rosa's reports.

Suggested Questions

- For Question D, do you agree with Charlie's overall conclusion? (It is possible to agree with Charlie's report while still criticizing his lack of attention to measures of spread. He is correct to point out that outliers affect the mean but not the median. Charlie is also correct to say that, if you just look at measures of center, the speeds are very similar. He does not, however, pay any attention to measures of spread.)

- Do you agree with Rosa's overall conclusion that steel-frame roller coasters are faster, but not all steel-frame roller coasters are faster? (Again, students might agree with Rosa while still wanting to clarify her language a bit.)

The point is to have students realize that comparisons of samples have to take both centers and spread into account.

Reflecting on Student Learning

Use the following questions to assess student understanding at the end of the lesson.

- What evidence do I have that students understand the Focus Question?
  - Where did my students get stuck?
  - What strategies did they use?
  - What breakthroughs did my students have today?
- How will I use this to plan for tomorrow? For the next time I teach this lesson?
- Where will I have the opportunity to reinforce these ideas as I continue through this Unit? The next Unit?

ACE Assignment Guide

- **Applications:** 9–16
- **Connections:** 22–26

Labsheet 1.4C: Dot Plots of Top-Speed Data can be used for ACE Exercise 14. It contains the two dot plots of top speeds for steel-frame and wood-frame roller coasters. Students may find it helpful to have the dot plots in order to mark up the data values while finding the medians.

Note: ACE Exercise 24 shows a dot plot. Because of the large number of dots over two of the values, the dots overlap. You may want to explain this to students before they complete the Exercise, as it may be unfamiliar to them.

▼ Mathematical Reflections

Possible Answers to Mathematical Reflections

1. **a.** A *part* of the population is called a **sample**. It is a portion or slice of the population.

    Note: At this stage, students will have only a vague idea of "sample." They might answer that we use samples to say something about a whole population. Students are unlikely to raise other issues such as size, representativeness, or lack of bias. These refinements will come later.

   b. **i.** Mode can be used to summarize categorical data (favorite movie). Measures of center (mean, median) and spread (range, MAD, and IQR) can be used to summarize numerical data (number of movies watched per week).

    ii. You can find the percent of students in the sample who say they watch two movies per week. Use this percentage, or relative frequency, to find the total number of students in the 7th grade who would say they watch two movies per week. Multiply the relative frequency from the sample by the total number in the population.

2. **a.** Using the same types of graphs with the same scales lets you look at and compare shapes of distributions; looking for symmetry or skewness is often one way to use graphs. Different graphs highlight different features of the data distributions.

   b. Depending on the variability in a sample, the measure of center can be a good way to describe what is typical of a data set. You can compare different measures of center to decide if the distributions are similar or different in terms of what is typical.

   c. You can compare different measures of spread to decide if they are similar or different in terms of variability.

3. The choice to use counts or percents is influenced by whether you are comparing distributions with equal numbers of data values or comparing distributions with unequal numbers of data values. When the data sets are not the same size, then using percents (relative frequencies) permits you to make all data sets "out of one hundred" so that they can be considered the same size. You may also report relative frequencies when you are using large data sets.

Possible Answers to Mathematical Practices Reflections

Students may have demonstrated all of the eight Common Core Standards for Mathematical Practice during this Investigation. During the class discussion, have students provide additional Practices that the Problem cited involved and identify the use of other Mathematical Practices in the Investigation.

One student observation is provided in the Student Edition. Here is another sample student response.

In Problem 1.4, I looked at a number of measures of spread in order to compare the speeds of steel-frame and wood-frame roller coasters. Besides identifying which measure is more than another, it often helps to describe *how much more* one is than the other. For example, I know that the range of speeds for the sample of steel-frame coasters is 38 mph and the range of speeds for the sample of wood-frame coasters is 10 mph. So, the ranges indicate that the spread for wood-frame coasters is less than the spread for steel coasters. The question is, "How much less?" One way to answer this is to say that the range of speeds for wood-frame coasters is about $\frac{1}{4}$ the range of speeds for steel-frame coasters.

I did the same thing in comparing spreads measured by the IQR. The IQR for speeds for steel-frame coasters is 28.5 mph; the IQR for speeds for wood-frame coasters is 11.25 mph. The IQR for steel-frame coasters is more than twice the IQR for wood coasters. This information highlights that the middle 50% of the speeds for steel-frame coasters may be as much as twice as variable as those for wood-frame coasters.

Finally, when I displayed these data on two box plots, I noticed that at least 25% of the steel-frame coasters have speeds that are faster than those of wood-frame coasters.

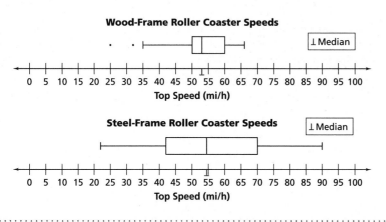

MP1: Make sense of problems and persevere in solving them.

Notes

Making Sense of Samples

People often want to know what is typical in a given situation. For example, you might want to find out your typical math test score. You may investigate the typical number of text messages sent by students in a middle-school class. You can gather information to determine the typical batting average of a baseball player. You can collect and examine data to analyze situations such as these.

All data sets include some *variability*. Not all math scores are the same. Not all students send the same number of texts. Not all baseball players perform the same at bat. Statistical investigations pose questions with variable outcomes.

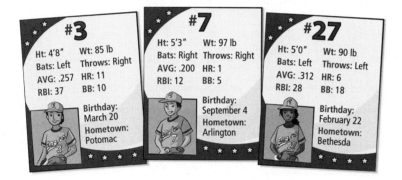

Common Core State Standards

7.SP.B.4 Use measures of center and measures of variability for numerical data from random samples to draw informal comparative inferences about two populations.

Essential for 7.SP.B.3 Informally assess the degree of visual overlap of two numerical data distributions with similar variabilities, measuring the difference between the centers by expressing it as a multiple of a measure of variability.

Also 7.NS.A.1 and 7.NS.A.1b, essential for 7.SP.A.1 and 7.SP.A.2

Investigation 1   **Making Sense of Samples**   7

1.1 Comparing Performances
Using Center and Spread

 The spreadsheet below shows the math test scores earned by two students, Jun and Mia, in the first quarter of 7th grade.

| File | Edit | Tool | View | Chart | Class | Help |

Math Test Scores | Math Homework

Class	Name	Student Number	Test 1	Test 2	Test 3	Test 4	Test 5	Test 6	Test Average
001	Jun	09	80	60	100				
001	Mia	22	75	80	85				

The math test scores are *samples* of the math test scores for each student throughout the school year. You can use data from samples to make general statements about overall performance.

- Who performs better on math tests, Jun or Mia? Explain.

In Problem 1.1, you will use measures of center and measures of variability, or spread, to determine who performs more consistently on tests.

Problem 1.1

A 1. Find the *mean* and *median* of Jun's scores. What do you notice?

2. Find the mean and median of Mia's scores. What do you notice?

3. Use the measures of center you found in parts (1) and (2). Compare Jun's and Mia's test performances.

Notes _____

_____

_____

Problem 1.1 continued

B **1.** Determine the *range* and *mean absolute deviation (MAD)* of Jun's test scores.

   2. Determine the range and MAD of Mia's test scores.

   3. Use the measures of spread you found in parts (1) and (2). Compare Jun's and Mia's test performances.

C Do you have enough data to make any general statements about Jun's or Mia's overall math test performance? Explain.

D The spreadsheet below shows Jun's and Mia's test scores at mid-year.

File	Edit	Tool	View	Chart	Class	Help			

| | Math Test Scores | | | | Math Homework | | | | |

Class	Name	Student Number	Test 1	Test 2	Test 3	Test 4	Test 5	Test 6	Test Average
001	Jun	09	80	60	100	80	80	80	
001	Mia	22	75	80	85	80	80	100	

   1. Find the median and mean of Jun's test data and of Mia's test data. Use each measure of center to compare Jun's scores and Mia's scores.

   2. Find the range and MAD of Jun's test data and of Mia's test data. Use each measure of variability to compare Jun's scores and Mia's scores.

   3. Decide whether you agree or disagree with each statement below. Use the statistics you found in parts (1) and (2). Explain your reasoning.

   • One student is a stronger math student than the other.

   • One student is more consistent than the other.

   • The two students perform equally well on math tests.

   • You can make better comparisons using the larger data set.

A C E Homework starts on page 20.

Notes _____

_____

_____

1.2 Which Team Is Most Successful?
Using the MAD to Compare Samples

A middle school's Hiking Club holds a fundraiser each spring. The club sells granola bars and packages of trail mix. The 35 club members form six fundraising teams. Each team is a *sample* of students from the club. The most successful team receives a prize.

The faculty advisor posts the money the teams raised on a bulletin board.

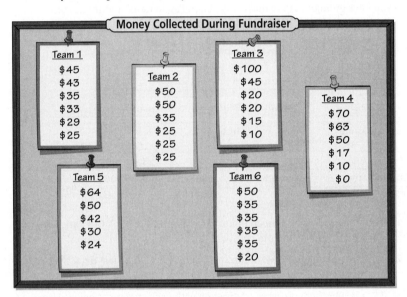

Money Collected During Fundraiser

Team 1	Team 2	Team 3	Team 4	Team 5	Team 6
$45	$50	$100	$70	$64	$50
$43	$50	$45	$63	$50	$35
$35	$35	$20	$50	$42	$35
$33	$25	$20	$17	$30	$35
$29	$25	$15	$10	$24	$35
$25	$25	$10	$0		$20

- Which team is the most successful and deserves to win the prize?
  Explain.

Notes

Problem 1.2

A Make a *line plot* of each team's data. Use a scale that makes it easy to compare results among teams. Write three sentences that compare the *distributions*.

B The Hiking Club's organizers must decide which team is awarded the prize. Each organizer has a different strategy for determining the most successful fundraising team.

For each strategy below, explain whether or not the strategy helps determine the most successful team. If the strategy helps determine the most successful team, determine who will win the prize.

1. Bianca

For each team, just add up all the money raised by its members. Then compare the team totals.

2. Gianna

Find the mean number of dollars raised by each team. Then compare the team averages.

3. Jonah

Compare the money raised by each member to the team's average. On average, how far does each member's amount differ from the team's mean amount? For each team, find the MAD. Then compare the MADs of the six teams.

C What other strategies might you use? How does your strategy help you determine which team was most successful?

continued on the next page >

Investigation 1   **Making Sense of Samples**   11

Notes _____

Problem 1.2 *continued*

D In Question A, you made line plots of the six sets of data. In Question B, part (3), you found the mean absolute deviation (MAD) of each of the six distributions.

The dot plot below shows Team 1's fundraising amounts. The red lines indicate the distances of one MAD and two MADs from the mean on either side. Count the data points located closer than, but not including, the distance of one MAD from the mean. (The △ indicates the mean, 35.)

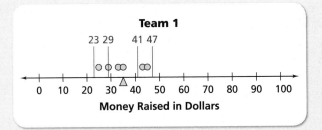

Team 1

23 29   41 47

Money Raised in Dollars

1. How many of Team 1's data values are located *within one MAD* (both less than and greater than the mean)? Write this number as a percent.

2. How many of Team 1's data values are located *within two MADs* of the mean? Write this number as a percent.

3. How many of Team 1's data values are located *more than two MADs* away from the mean? Write this number as a percent.

4. Repeat parts (1)–(3) for each of the other teams' data. For each team, use the team's MAD to analyze the distribution.

5. Use the MAD locations from parts (1)–(4) to describe how each team's data values spread around the mean of the data.

ACE Homework starts on page 20.

12 Samples and Populations

Notes

_____

_____

_____

1.3 Pick Your Preference
Distinguishing Categorical Data From Numerical Data

In this Unit, you have worked with *numerical data,* which are counts or measures. Sometimes, however, the answers to survey questions can be sorted into categories or groups, such as your birth month, favorite movie, or eye color. These answers are *categorical data.* You can count categorical data, but you cannot place them in numerical order.

A survey about roller coasters asks these questions:

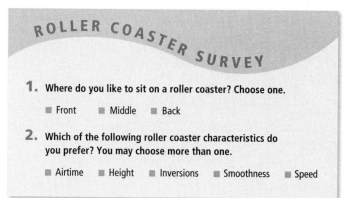

ROLLER COASTER SURVEY

1. Where do you like to sit on a roller coaster? Choose one.

 ■ Front   ■ Middle   ■ Back

2. Which of the following roller coaster characteristics do you prefer? You may choose more than one.

 ■ Airtime   ■ Height   ■ Inversions   ■ Smoothness   ■ Speed

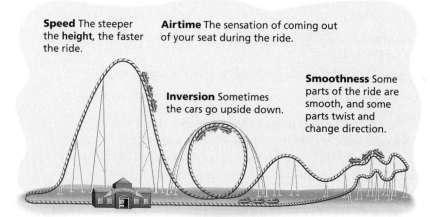

Speed The steeper the **height,** the faster the ride.

Airtime The sensation of coming out of your seat during the ride.

Inversion Sometimes the cars go upside down.

Smoothness Some parts of the ride are smooth, and some parts twist and change direction.

Investigation 1   **Making Sense of Samples**   13

Notes

The tables below show the Roller Coaster Survey responses collected from Internet respondents and from a group of 7th-grade students.

Roller Coaster Seating Preferences

Preference	Votes From Internet	Votes From 7th Graders
Front	97	27
Middle	50	22
Back	18	14
Total Votes	**165**	**63**

Other Roller Coaster Preferences

Preference	Votes From Internet	Votes From 7th Graders
Airtime	88	31
Height	36	24
Inversions	59	29
Smoothness	39	12
Speed	105	57
Total Votes	**327**	**153**

Notice the four different *samples* reported:

- Answers to the first Roller Coaster Survey question from Internet respondents

- Answers to the second Roller Coaster Survey question from Internet respondents

- Answers to the first Roller Coaster Survey question from 7th graders

- Answers to the second Roller Coaster Survey question from 7th graders

The table shows that 165 people responded to the Internet survey about seating. Of those, 97 people prefer to sit at the front. The *frequency* of the response "front" is 97.

- What is the frequency of 7th graders who prefer to sit at the front of a roller coaster?

Suppose you want to find out which group includes more people who prefer to sit at the front.

The sample sizes of Internet respondents and 7th graders are different. You can use **relative frequencies**—frequencies based on percentages—to compare samples of different sizes. For example, $\frac{97}{165} \approx 0.59$, so about 59% of the people who voted online prefer to sit at the front of a roller coaster.

Relative Frequency
$\frac{97}{165} \approx 59\%$

Survey Responses

	Internet	7th Graders
Prefers Front	97	27
Total	165	63

- How can you compare the results of a survey to see whether each group responded to the questions in a similar way?

Problem 1.3

A As a class, answer the two Roller Coaster Survey questions. On a copy of the tables on the previous page, record your class data.

B For each survey question, make *bar graphs* of the three data sets: the Internet data, the 7th-grade data, and your class data. Use percents to report relative frequencies on your bar graphs.

C Which measure(s) of center—*mean, median,* or *mode*—can you use to describe these results? Explain.

D 1. For each survey question, write two statements comparing results from the three data sets.

2. Write two statements to summarize the data collected from the Roller Coaster Survey. How are the summaries useful?

E Suppose 400 people ride a roller coaster in one day. How many of them would you predict want to sit at the front? Explain.

A C E Homework starts on page 20.

STUDENT PAGE

Notes

1.4 Are Steel-Frame Coasters Faster Than Wood-Frame Coasters?

Using the IQR to Compare Samples

 Have you ever wondered how many roller coasters there are in the world? The table below displays data from a **census.** It shows information about the **population**, or entire collection, of roller coasters worldwide. About 95% of the coasters are steel-frame coasters; about 5% are wood-frame coasters.

Roller Coaster Census

Roller Coaster Count				Some Types of Steel-Frame Coasters			
Continent	Total	Wood	Steel	Inverted	Stand Up	Suspended	Sit Down
Africa	59	0	59	3	0	0	56
Asia	1,455	13	1,442	47	4	16	1,362
Australia	24	3	21	2	0	0	19
Europe	822	35	787	28	1	12	733
North America	764	122	642	50	10	5	561
South America	142	1	141	3	0	4	134
Total	3,266	174	3,092	133	15	37	2,865

SOURCE: *Roller Coaster DataBase*

- How do you think the roller-coaster census data were collected?

Notes _____

_____

_____

In this Problem, you will use data from a sample of 30 steel-frame roller coasters and data from a sample of 30 wood-frame roller coasters. The table below shows some data from the samples.

Roller-Coaster Sample Data

Steel-Frame Roller Coasters	Top Speed (mi/h)	Duration (min)
Steel-Frame Coaster A	22	1.50
Steel-Frame Coaster B	40	1.53
Steel-Frame Coaster C	50	2.00
Steel-Frame Coaster D	70	0.55
Wood-Frame Roller Coasters	**Top Speed (mi/h)**	**Duration (min)**
Wood-Frame Coaster A	50	1.75
Wood-Frame Coaster B	50	1.83
Wood-Frame Coaster C	55	2.00
Wood-Frame Coaster D	62	2.50

 How might you decide which are faster, steel-frame roller coasters or wood-frame roller coasters? Explain.

Problem 1.4

Use the samples of roller-coaster data provided by your teacher for Questions A–D.

A 1. What do you consider to be a fast speed for a roller coaster? Explain.

2. Suppose you want to ride the faster of two roller coasters. Does knowing each roller coaster's top speed help you make the decision? Explain.

3. Do you think steel-frame roller coasters are faster than wood-frame roller coasters? Use the top-speed data to justify your answer.

continued on the next page >

Notes _____

_____

_____

Problem 1.4 *continued*

B The dot plots below show the top-speed data from the sample of 30 steel-frame coasters and 30 wood-frame coasters. The mean is marked with a blue triangle (△). Use the dot plots to answer parts (1)–(3).

Steel-Frame Roller Coaster Speeds

Mean = 55.03 mi/h
MAD = 14.64 mi/h

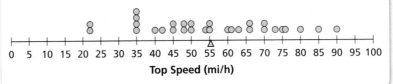

Top Speed (mi/h)

Wood-Frame Roller Coaster Speeds

Mean = 52.6 mi/h
MAD = 7.47 mi/h

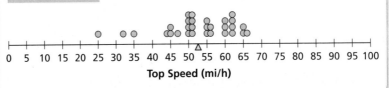

Top Speed (mi/h)

1. Identify the minimum and maximum values, ranges, and means of each distribution. Use these statistics to compare the speeds of steel-frame and wood-frame roller coasters.

2. Identify the median and the *interquartile range (IQR)* of each distribution. Use the medians and IQRs to compare the speeds of steel-frame and wood-frame roller coasters.

3. Make a *box-and-whisker plot*, or box plot, of each distribution. Use the same scale for each graph. Use the box plots to compare the speeds of steel-frame and wood-frame roller coasters.

Notes _____

_____

_____

Problem 1.4 continued

C Compare your answer to Question A, part (3) with your answers to Question B. Are steel-frame roller coasters faster than wood-frame roller coasters? Explain your reasoning.

D Charlie and Rosa wrote the reports below. They used the two distributions of data to compare steel-frame roller coasters and wood-frame roller coasters. Do you agree with Charlie or with Rosa? Explain your reasoning.

Charlie

I found that the means and medians are about the same for each distribution. If I looked at the box plots and the statistics, I would say that steel-frame roller coasters are slightly faster than wood-frame roller coasters.

When I made the box plots, I noticed that the data distribution for wood-frame roller coasters has two outliers. I know that low or high data values shift the mean. In this case, the outliers made the mean speed of the wood-frame roller coasters shift down below the median.

So keeping the outliers in mind, I concluded that steel-frame roller coasters and wood-frame roller coasters have similar speeds.

Rosa

The measures of center were all pretty close, so i looked at the measures of spread. The IQR helped me see that there is greater variability in the steel-frame roller coasters than in the wood-frame roller coasters.

I looked at the top 25% of all roller-coaster speeds. The top speeds for wood-frame roller coasters are around 60–66 mi/h and steel-frame roller coasters have top speeds around 70–90 mi/h.

Steel-frame roller coasters have faster speeds than wood-frame roller coasters, but not all steel-frame roller coasters are faster than all wood-frame roller coasters.

A C E Homework starts on page 20.

Notes

 ## Applications

For all Exercises, use your calculator when needed.

For Exercises 1 and 2, use the table below.

Diving Scores

Diver	Dive 1	Dive 2	Dive 3	Dive 4	Dive 5
Jarrod	8.5	8.1	6.4	9.5	10.0
Pascal	9.3	7.5	8.0	8.5	9.2

1. **a.** Find the mean and the median of Jarrod's diving scores. Compare the mean and the median.

   b. Find the mean and the median of Pascal's diving scores. Compare the mean and the median.

   c. Use measures of center to compare Jarrod's and Pascal's diving results. What can you say about their performances?

2. **a.** Find the range and the MAD of Jarrod's scores.

   b. Find the range and the MAD of Pascal's scores.

   c. Use measures of spread to compare Jarrod's and Pascal's diving results. What can you say about their performances?

Notes _____

_____

_____

The Soccer Club holds a flavored-popcorn fundraiser each fall. The
23 club members form four teams. The most successful team receives
a prize. For Exercises 3–7, use the data in the table below.

Money Collected During Fundraiser
(dollars)

Team 1	Team 2	Team 3	Team 4
55	56	100	80
53	53	50	73
44	50	40	44
44	38	40	38
39	37	25	35
35	36	15	

3. Find the total amount of money collected by each team. Do the totals
   help you determine the most successful team? Explain.

4. a. What is the mean amount of money collected by each team? The
      median?

   b. Do either of these measures of center help you determine the
      most successful team? Explain.

5. a. For each team, find the range and MAD.

   b. Do either of these measures of spread help you determine the
      most successful team? Explain.

**For Exercises 6 and 7, use the table above. Answer each question for
Teams 1–4.**

6. a. How many of the team's data values are located *within one MAD*
      of the mean (both less than and greater than the mean)? Write
      this number as a percent.

   b. How many of the team's data values are located *within two MADs*
      of the mean? Write this number as a percent.

   c. How many of the team's data values are located *more than two
      MADs* away from the mean? Write this number as a percent.

7. Use your calculations from Exercise 6. Does any team have a
   member who raised much more (or much less) money than the
   other team members? Explain your reasoning.

Notes _____

_____

_____

8. The following question was asked in a survey:

What is your favorite amusement-park ride?

▪ Roller Coaster   ▪ Log Ride   ▪ Ferris Wheel   ▪ Bumper Cars

The tablet below shows the results from an Internet survey and from surveys of 7th-grade students at East Jr. High and West Jr. High.

Favorite Amusement Park Rides

Favorite Ride	Votes From the Internet	Votes From East Jr. High	Votes From West Jr. High
Roller Coaster	92	42	36
Log Ride	26	31	14
Ferris Wheel	22	3	6
Bumper Cars	20	4	4
Total Votes	**160**	**80**	**60**

a. Make bar graphs for each of the three data sets: the Internet survey data, the data from East Jr. High, and the data from West Jr. High. Use percents to show relative frequencies.

b. Write three or more statements comparing the data sets.

For Exercises 9–13, use the Roller Coaster Census from Problem 1.4 to complete the statements below.

9. For every one wood-frame roller coaster there are about ▪ steel-frame roller coasters.

10. North America has about ▪ times as many roller coasters as South America.

11. Asia has about ▪ times as many roller coasters as North America.

12. North America has ▓ % of all the wood-frame roller coasters in the world.

13. Write two of your own comparison statements.

14. Use the dot plots below. For each part (a)-(c), answer the questions for each distribution.

Steel-Frame Roller Coaster Speeds

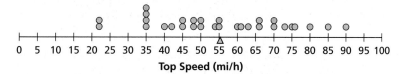

Mean = 55.03 mi/h
MAD = 14.64 mi/h

Top Speed (mi/h)

Wood-Frame Roller Coaster Speeds

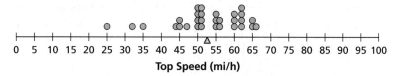

Mean = 52.6 mi/h
MAD = 7.47 mi/h

Top Speed (mi/h)

a. How many roller coasters have speeds within one MAD of the mean (both less than and greater than the mean)? Write this number as a percent.

b. How many roller coasters have speeds within two MADs of the mean? Write this number as a percent.

c. How many roller coasters have speeds more than two MADs away from the mean? Write this number as a percent.

Investigation 1   Making Sense of Samples   **23**

Notes

The three pairs of dot plots below show data for 50 wood-frame roller coasters. Each mean is marked with a △. Each median is marked with a ⊥. Use the dot plots to answer Exercises 15 and 16 on the next page.

Maximum Drop for Each Wood-Frame Roller Coaster

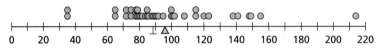

Years: 1960–2004

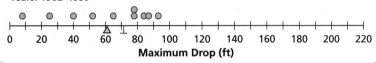

Years: 1902–1959

Maximum Drop (ft)

Maximum Height for Each Wood-Frame Roller Coaster

Years: 1960–2004

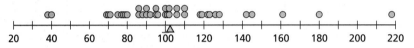

Years: 1902–1959

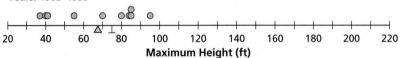

Maximum Height (ft)

Top Speed for Each Wood-Frame Roller Coaster

Years: 1960–2004

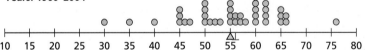

Years: 1902–1959

Top Speed (mi/h)

Notes _____

_____

_____

15. **a.** Write three statements comparing wood-frame roller coasters built before 1960 with wood-frame roller coasters built in 1960 or later.

   b. Hector said there are too few roller coasters to make comparisons. Do you agree with Hector? Explain.

16. **Multiple Choice** Most of the data values in a distribution will be located—

   A. more than two MADs away from the mean.

   B. within two MADs of the mean.

   C. within one MAD of the mean.

Connections

17. **Multiple Choice** Suppose the data value 27 is added to the set of data 10, 29, 15, 29, 35, and 2. Which statement is true?

   F. The mean would increase by 4.

   G. The mode would decrease by 10.

   H. The median would decrease by 1.

   J. None of the above.

18. **Multiple Choice** The mean of six numbers is 25. If one of the numbers is 15, what is the mean of the other five numbers?

   A. 15   **B.** 25   **C.** 27   **D.** 40

19. **Multiple Choice** Jasper's test scores for eight exams are below.

   $$84, 72, 88, 84, 92, 94, 78, \text{ and } x$$

   If the median of his scores is 86, what is a possible value for x?

   F. 68   **G.** 84   **H.** 86   **J.** 95

20. **Multiple Choice** In Mr. Ramirez's math class, there are three times as many girls as boys. The girls' mean grade on a recent quiz was 90. The boys' mean grade was 86. What was the mean grade for the class altogether?

   A. 88   **B.** 44   **C.** 89   **D.** 95

Notes _____

_____

_____

21. The tables below show the results of a survey of children ages 5 to 15. Use the data to answer the questions on the next page.

**Table 1:
Years Lived in
Current Home**

Years	Children	Percent
<1	639	7.9%
1	776	9.6%
2	733	9.0%
3	735	■
4	587	7.2%
5	612	7.5%
6	487	6.0%
7	431	5.3%
8	442	5.4%
9	412	5.1%
10	492	6.0%
11	520	6.5%
12	508	6.3%
13	339	4.1%
14	225	2.8%
15	176	2.2%
Total	8,114	100%

SOURCE: *National Geographic*

**Table 2:
Apartments or Houses
Lived in Since Birth**

Number of Apartments or Houses	Children	Percent
1	1,645	20.7%
2	1,957	24.7%
3	1,331	16.8%
4	968	■
5	661	8.3%
6	487	6.1%
7	291	3.7%
8	184	2.3%
9	80	1.0%
10	330	4.2%
Total	7,934	100%

**Table 3:
Cities or Towns Lived in Since Birth**

Number of Cities or Towns	Boys	Girls	Ages 5–12	Ages 13–15
1	■	42.2%	42.1%	40.9%
>1	58.9%	57.8%	■	59.1%
Total	100%	100%	100%	100%

Notes _____

_____

_____

a. Find the missing percents in each table. Explain how you found them.

b. Make a bar graph to display the information in the third column of Table 2.

c. Write a summary paragraph about Table 2.

d. What percent of children have lived in the same home for 10 or more years? Justify your answer.

e. What percent of children have lived in only one home since they were born? Justify your answer.

f. About what fraction of the boys have lived in the same city or town all their lives? Explain.

22. The titles of the two circle graphs below are not shown. Use the data from the Roller Coaster Census in Problem 1.4. Which title goes with which graph? Explain.

Title 1: Wood-Frame Roller Coasters by Continent

Title 2: Steel-Frame Roller Coasters by Continent

a.
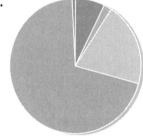

b.
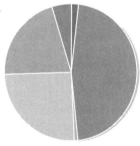

Key:
■ Africa		░ Europe	
▨ Asia		▧ North America	
▦ Australia		■ South America	

For Exercises 23 and 24, use the dot plot below. The dot plot shows the amount of sugar per serving in 47 cereals.

Sugar in Cereals

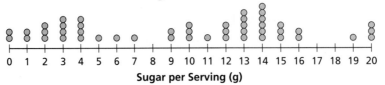

Sugar per Serving (g)

23. Describe the shape of the distribution above.

24. Estimate the locations of the mean and the median. How does the shape of the distribution influence your estimates?

For Exercises 25 and 26, use the dot plot below. The dot plot shows the serving sizes of 47 cereals.

Serving Sizes of Cereals

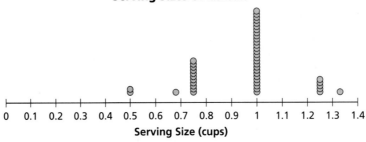

Serving Size (cups)

25. Describe the distribution of serving sizes.

26. Estimate the locations of the mean and the median. How does the shape of the distribution influence your estimates?

Notes _____

_____

_____

Extensions

For Exercises 27–32, use the dot plots and box plots below. The dot plots show the resting and exercise heart rates for a 7th-grade class.

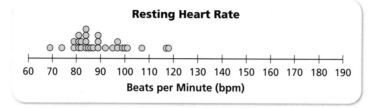

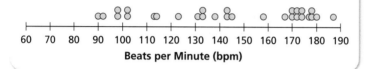

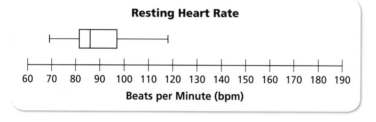

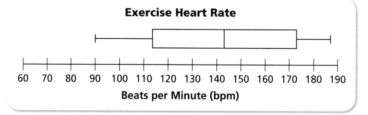

Notes _____

For Exercises 27–32, use the dot plots and box plots on the previous page.

27. Suppose you were given two means: 143.3 bpm and 89.4 bpm. Which mean is for the distribution of resting heart rates? Exercise heart rates? Explain.

28. Suppose you were given two MADs: 27.3 bpm and 8.9 bpm. Which MAD is for the distribution of resting heart rates? Exercise heart rates? Explain.

29. How does knowing the MADs help you compare resting and exercise heart rates?

30. Suppose you were given two IQRs: 15.5 bpm and 59.5 bpm. Which IQR is for the distribution of resting heart rates? Exercise heart rates? Explain.

31. How does knowing the IQRs help you compare resting and exercise heart rates?

32. Write three statements comparing resting and exercise heart rates.

33. The frequency table below shows the numbers of students who earned each grade in a teacher's math classes.

Letter Grade	Number of Students
A	8
B	15
C	20
D	5
F	2

a. Make a bar graph that shows the frequency of each letter grade.

b. Compute the *relative frequency* of each letter grade.

c. Make a bar graph that shows the relative frequencies.

d. Compare the two bar graphs. What do you notice about the shapes of the two distributions?

e. The teacher wants to predict about how many students might earn a letter grade of C in another math class. Should the teacher use frequency or relative frequency to help her make a prediction? Explain.

Mathematical Reflections 1

In this Investigation, you developed strategies to compare two or more distributions with equal or unequal amounts of data. The following questions will help you summarize what you have learned.

Think about these questions. Discuss your ideas with other students and your teacher. Then write a summary of your findings in your notebook.

1. **a.** A new term is used in this Investigation: *sample*. **What** do you think *sample* means?

   b. Suppose you have data from a 7th-grade class. The data are answers to the questions:

   • What is your favorite movie?

   • How many movies do you watch per week?

   i. Which statistics can you use to summarize the results of the data?

   ii. How could you use the data to predict the number of students in the entire 7th grade who would say they watch two movies per week?

2. **a. How** do graphs of distributions help you compare data sets?

   b. How do measures of center help you compare data sets?

   c. How do measures of spread help you compare data sets?

3. **When** does it make sense to compare groups using counts, or frequencies? When does it make sense to compare groups using percents, or relative frequencies? Explain.

Notes _____

Common Core Mathematical Practices

As you worked on the Problems in this Investigation, you used prior knowledge to make sense of them. You also applied Mathematical Practices to solve the Problems. Think back over your work, the ways you thought about the Problems, and how you used Mathematical Practices.

Sophie described her thoughts in the following way:

> Sometimes, knowing the mean is not enough when you want to compare data sets. You have to get MAD!
>
> The MAD (mean absolute deviation) is how much, on average, data values in a data set differ from the mean. When there are only a few data values, you can do the work by hand.
>
> In Problem 1.2, the mean amount collected by Team 1 was $35. We found the difference between each member's amount and the mean. We added the differences (10 + 6 + 2 + 0 + 8 + 10 = 36). Then we divided the sum by the total number of team members (36 ÷ 6 = 6). The MAD for Team 1 was $6. So, on average, the data values were $6 less than or greater than the mean of $35.
>
> For larger data sets, you can use special calculators. We noticed that more consistent data sets had smaller MADs.
>
> **Common Core Standards for Mathematical Practice**
> **MP6** Attend to precision.

- What other Mathematical Practices can you identify in Sophie's reasoning?

- Describe a Mathematical Practice that you and your classmates used to solve a different Problem in this Investigation.

Notes _____

_____

_____

Choosing a Sample From a Population

▼ Investigation Overview

Investigation Description

In Investigation 2, students consider the statistical distinctions between samples and populations. They also use results of data analyses from samples to draw conclusions about characteristics or behaviors of a population. First, students consider the implications of making estimates about the entire U.S. population based on an Internet survey involving a few thousand people. The survey raises the issue of projecting the results collected from a sample to an entire population.

Next, students consider the differences among different types of sampling methods: convenience, voluntary-response, systematic, and random. They explore techniques for choosing samples randomly from a population—such as using spinners, number cubes, and random-number generators on calculators—and consider why random samples are often preferable to other types of sampling methods. Then, they investigate the relationship between sample size and accuracy of population estimates. Students study sampling distributions of means and medians, noticing that the means or medians from larger samples (e.g., 30 values) taken from the same population are less variable than those from smaller samples (e.g., 5 or 10 values). This helps students realize that measures of center from larger samples are more similar; it is possible to use the mean from a large sample to draw reliable conclusions about the given population.

Note: The Introduction to Investigation 2 is longer than usual. It is designed to engage students' thinking about what distinguishes a sample from a population. Please see the real-world examples under the header called, "Consider this information." The examples are intended to provoke such questions as these: "Can we really use information from a sample to generalize about an entire population?" and "How do they get this information anyway?" The following focus questions may be helpful:

- What is the situation being described? Who is it about? (Each case talks about cell phone usage of teenagers. The first statistic talks about cell phone and smart phone ownership of teens. The second statistic involves the number of texts teens send per day.)

- Do you think that the entire population was surveyed? (In each case, the entire population was not surveyed; it would be too difficult and costly to do this.)

- How can the report make this claim if not all the people in that population were surveyed? (Answers will vary. The data were probably collected using some type of random sampling strategy; most statistical reports provide data from a sample.)

- If we collected information about this topic from the students in our class, could we use our answers to make predictions about the entire U.S. population? (Answers will vary. The class may not be representative of all people in the U.S. population.)

Take time to read through the specific examples provided, thinking about the above ideas. There is no need to bring closure now, but these points help students see how sampling is an important statistical concept. Notice that some of the examples report results and then make comparisons to past (earlier) similar studies so that their results provide trend data. The examples really can help students see statistics in action and serve as an "advanced organizer" for the work in this Investigation.

Investigation Vocabulary

- convenience sampling
- random sampling
- representative sample
- sample
- sampling distribution
- sampling plan
- systematic sampling
- voluntary-response (or self-selected) sampling

The following vocabulary term is included in the Glossary as review but is not defined within the exposition of the Student Edition.

- five-number summary

Mathematics Background

- The Process of Statistical Investigation
- Reviewing Types of Data and Attributes
- Reviewing Measures of Center and Measures of Spread
- Exploring Variation
- Representing Data With Graphical Displays
- Comparing Distributions
- Variability Across Samples: Expected From Natural Variability or Due to Meaningful Differences Between Samples?
- Sampling Plans

Planning Charts

Content	ACE	Pacing	Materials	Resources
Problem 2.1	1–4, 18–19, 39	1 day		**Teaching Aid 2.1** Honesty Survey
Problem 2.2	5–9, 20–24, 40	1 day	**Labsheet 2ACE:** Exercises 20–22 (accessibility)	• Data and Graphs • Expression Calculator
Problem 2.3	10–14, 25–31	1 day	**Labsheet 2.3A** Responses to Grade 7 Movie and Sleep Survey **Labsheet 2.3B** Blank Number Lines for Movies Watched Line Plots **Labsheet 2.3C** Blank Number Lines for Hours Slept Box Plots • 10-Section Spinners 10-sided solids paper clips or bobby pins (optional)	**Teaching Aid 2.3** Graphs for Grade 7 Survey (Whole Population) • Probability • Data and Graphs
Problem 2.4	15–17, 32–38, 41	2 day	**Labsheet 2.3A** Responses to Grade 7 Movie and Sleep Survey **Labsheet 2.4A** Blank Number Lines for Movies Watched Last Week (Means) **Labsheet 2.4B** Blank Number Lines for Movies Watched Last Week (Medians) **Labsheet 2.4C** Blank Number Lines for Hours of Sleep Last Night (Means) **Labsheet 2.4D** Blank Number Lines for Hours of Sleep Last Night (Medians) **Labsheet 2.4E** Group Organizer for Sample-Size Statistics **Labsheet 2.4F** Class Organizer for Sample-Size Statistics • 10-Section Spinners 10-sided solids (optional) paper clips or bobby pins (optional)	**Teaching Aid 2.3** Graphs for Grade 7 Survey (Whole Population) • Probability • Data and Graphs

continued on next page

Planning Charts *continued*

Content	ACE	Pacing	Materials	Resources
Mathematical Reflections		½ day		
Assessment: Partner Quiz		1 day		• Partner Quiz

▼ Goals and Standards

Goals

The Process of Statistical Investigation Deepen the understanding of the process of statistical investigation and apply this understanding to samples

- Pose questions, collect data, analyze data, and interpret data to answer questions

Analysis of Samples Understand that data values in a sample vary and that summary statistics of samples, even same-size samples, taken from the same population also vary

- Choose appropriate measures of center (mean, median, or mode) and spread (range, IQR, or MAD) to summarize a sample

- Choose appropriate representations to display distributions of samples

- Compare summary statistics of multiple samples drawn from either the same population or from two different populations and explain how the samples vary

Predictions and Conclusions About Populations Understand that summary statistics of a representative sample can be used to gain information about a population

- Describe the benefits and drawbacks to various sampling plans

- Use random-sampling techniques to select representative samples

- Apply concepts from probability to select random samples from populations

- Explain how sample size influences the reliability of sample statistics and resulting conclusions and predictions

- Explain how different sampling plans influence the reliability of sample statistics and resulting conclusions and predictions

- Use statistics from representative samples to draw conclusions about populations

- Use measures of center, measures of spread, and data displays from more than one random sample to compare and draw conclusions about more than one population

- Use mean and MAD, or median and IQR, from random samples to assess whether the differences in the samples are due to natural variability or due to meaningful differences in the underlying populations

Mathematical Reflections

Look for evidence of student understanding of the goals for this Investigation in their responses to the questions in *Mathematical Reflections*. The goals addressed by each question are indicated below.

1. Why are data often collected from a sample rather than from an entire population?

Goals

- Explain how sample size influences the reliability of sample statistics and resulting conclusions and predictions

- Use statistics from representative samples to draw conclusions about populations

2. Describe four plans for selecting a sample from a population. Discuss the advantages and disadvantages of each plan.

Goals

- Describe the benefits and drawbacks to various sampling plans

- Explain how different sampling plans influence the reliability of sample statistics and resulting conclusions and predictions

3. a. How are random samples different from convenience, voluntary-response, and systematic samples?

b. Why is random sampling preferable to the other sampling plans?

c. Describe three plans for selecting a random sample from a given population. What are the advantages and disadvantages of each plan?

Goals

- Use random-sampling techniques to select representative samples

- Apply concepts from probability to select random samples from populations

4. Suppose you select several random samples of size 30 from the same population.

a. When you compare the samples to each other, what similarities and differences would you expect to find among the measures of center and spread?

b. When you compare the samples to the larger population, what similarities and differences would you expect to find among the measures of center and spread?

Goals

- Choose appropriate measures of center (mean, median, or mode) and spread (range, IQR, or MAD) to summarize a sample

- Choose appropriate representations to display distributions of samples

- Use measures of center, measures of spread, and data displays from more than one random sample to compare and draw conclusions about more than one population

- Compare summary statistics of multiple samples drawn from either the same population or from two different populations and explain how the samples vary

5. How has your idea of the term *sample* changed from what you wrote in Mathematical Reflections, Investigation 1?

Goal

- Pose questions, collect data, analyze data, and interpret data to answer questions

Standards

Common Core Content Standards

7.SP.A.1 Understand that statistics can be used to gain information about a population by examining a sample of the population; generalizations about a population from a sample are valid only if the sample is representative of that population. Understand that random sampling tends to produce representative samples and support valid inferences. *Problems 1, 2, 3, and 4*

7.SP.A.2 Use data from a random sample to draw inferences about a population with an unknown characteristic of interest. Generate multiple samples (or simulated samples) of the same size to gauge the variation in estimates or predictions *Problems 1, 3, and 4*

7.SP.C.7 Develop a probability model and use it to find probabilities of events. Compare probabilities from a model to observed frequencies; if the agreement is not good, explain possible sources of the discrepancy. *Problems 3 and 4*

7.SP.C.7a Develop a uniform probability model by assigning equal probability to all outcomes, and use the model to determine probabilities of events. *Problems 3 and 4*

Facilitating the Mathematical Practices

Students in *Connected Mathematics* classrooms display evidence of multiple Common Core Standards for Mathematical Practice every day. Here are just a few examples of when you might observe students demonstrating the Standards for Mathematical Practice during this Investigation.

Practice 1: Make sense of problems and persevere in solving them.

Students are engaged every day in solving problems and, over time, learn to persevere in solving them. To be effective, the problems embody critical concepts and skills and have the potential to engage students in making sense of mathematics. Students build understanding by reflecting, connecting, and communicating. These student-centered problem situations engage students in articulating the "knowns" in a problem situation and determining a logical solution pathway. The student-student and student-teacher dialogues help students not only to make sense of the problems, but also to persevere in finding appropriate strategies to solve them. The suggested questions in the Teacher Guides provide the metacognitive scaffolding to help students monitor and refine their problem-solving strategies.

Practice 5: Use appropriate tools strategically.

In Problem 2.3, students use various tools in order to randomly select 30 numbers, 1–100. Those tools may include: 10-sided solids, a 10-section spinner, a random-number generator on a calculator, or the *Connected Mathematics* "Interactive Math Tools" online spinner. Students need to strategize how to determine two-digit numbers and the number 100, and select again in the case of duplicates.

Practice 7: Look for and make use of structure.

Throughout this Investigation, students explore how samples are chosen from a population. In Problem 2.4, students take sample sizes of 5, 10, and 30 students out of the 100-student database. They then combine their samples with those of their classmates to analyze the data. This method treats the smaller and individual samples as building blocks to the larger and collective samples. Thus, students are better able to make predictions about the whole population.

Students identify and record their personal experiences with the Standards for Mathematical Practice during the Mathematical Reflections at the end of the Investigation.

Asking About Honesty
Using a Sample to Draw Conclusions

▼ Problem Overview

Focus Question What is a population? What is a sample? What is a sampling Plan?

Problem Description

Students consider the implications of making estimates about the entire U.S. population based on a magazine survey involving a few thousand people. The survey raises issues about drawing conclusions about an entire population using data collected from a sample.

Problem Implementation

Have students work in pairs on this Problem.

Materials

• **Teaching Aid 2.1:** Honesty Survey

Vocabulary

• sample
• sampling plan

Mathematics Background

• The Process of Statistical Investigation
• Reviewing Types of Data and Attributes
• Representing Data With Graphical Displays
• Comparing Distributions
• Sampling Plans

At a Glance and Lesson Plan

- At a Glance: Problem 2.1 Samples and Populations
- Lesson Plan: Problem 2.1 Samples and Populations

▼ Launch

Connecting to Prior Knowledge

Students have reviewed several important ideas from *Data About Us* in Investigation 1. Take time to assess where your students are, and who might need additional support going forward. The emphasis on measures of variability will continue into Investigation 2, where a major theme is that the data collected in a sample will show variability, and that samples from the same population will also vary from each other.

Presenting the Challenge

Explain that we can often study a large population by analyzing only part of the population—a sample. We can use data about a sample to help us draw conclusions about an entire population.

Introduce the survey about honesty, which is reproduced as **Teaching Aid 2.1: Honesty Survey**. Ask students to read the survey and to consider how it describes honest behavior. They may mention other ways to pursue the question of what constitutes honest behavior.

Suggested Questions

- If you wanted to use this survey to study the honesty of the students in our school, how would you go about collecting the data? (Students will offer a variety of strategies from doing a census to collecting data from some smaller group of students.)

- In order to draw conclusions about the students in our school, is it necessary to ask everyone in the school to complete the survey? (Answers will vary. No; it is not necessary.)

Explain what a sampling plan is. Essentially, a sampling plan involves identifying the population that is to be described (in the case of the magazine survey, the population is the United States) and identifying the sample of the population that will be involved in the survey (in this case, the sample is anyone who reads the magazine and completes the survey).

- If you wanted to gather information from a sample of students in our school, how would you decide whom to ask? In other words, what would your sampling plan be?

Have students work in pairs to complete Problem 2.1.

▼ Explore

Providing for Individual Needs

Circulate as groups work. Remind students to be prepared to present their answers and to describe the strategies they used.

Students may need help constructing a graph in Question C. Since the data are categorical, students should represent the data using a bar graph reporting percent frequencies. Placing bars for "honest" and "dishonest" answers next to each other allows for comparisons across questions.

Look for different strategies in Question D. Students have opportunities to apply concepts they learned in *Decimal Ops* and *Comparing and Scaling.*

Suggested Questions

- How might you scale up the results of the survey to try to predict something about the whole U.S. population? (You can use percentages or ratios.)

- Why would percentages help? (Each sample would be represented "out of 100," so all the samples can be evaluated as if they were the same size.)

Look for different student strategies to share in the Summarize. Make sure to focus students' attention on Question E, which addresses the question of *representativeness*. Do the results of the analysis of these data predict the population behavior? Is this sample *representative* of the population? When you have a representative sample, this means that you have surveyed a smaller group of people whose characteristics accurately reflect those of the larger population from which they were chosen. This is a point that is addressed explicitly in Problem 2.2. Discussing the idea informally at the end of Problem 2.1 gives students an opportunity to think about the issue of representative samples.

Planning for the Summary

What evidence will you use in the summary to clarify and deepen understanding of the Focus Question?

What will you do if you do not have evidence?

▼ Summarize

Orchestrating the Discussion

Questions B, C, and D are rather straightforward mathematically and offer a brief review of percents. However, take time to discuss students' solution strategies. If more than one answer is presented, resolve any questions about working with percents.

In Question C, students compare responses across questions. You might ask:

Suggested Questions

- Why are percentages useful in Question C? (They make comparisons between the proportion of honest and dishonest responses clear.)

- What differences do you see? (Sample answer: The percentage of "honest" answers is higher in some situations than in others. Perhaps the more personal the interaction, the more likely the person is to act honestly.)

Have students share their responses to Question E, which asks why the results of this survey may not apply to all Americans. Any *reader response* survey runs the risk of gathering the views of an atypical collection of people: those who read certain kinds of newspapers or magazines; those who are willing to invest money and time going online to express their opinions; and, generally, those who feel strongly about the issue being considered. Though we might assume that the magazine has a national circulation, we don't know what type of magazine it is and so we cannot identify the audience. There are other things we don't know about the characteristics of the people in the sample; students might discuss the problem of drawing valid generalizations from such surveys. If so, they are identifying questions related to what makes a sample "representative" of a population, which will be considered later in this Investigation.

Students will have a variety of ideas about revising the sampling plan in response to Question E, part (2). Ask them to provide reasons for how they propose to revise the plan and to identify the problems they are trying to remedy by using a plan other than the one developed by the magazine. Gently challenge each suggestion by asking the following:

- Is that sampling plan more likely to give results that represent the entire population (i.e., the sample has characteristics that accurately reflect those of the larger population from which they were chosen)?

Once completed, have students consider the Focus Question. If need be, have them look back at the set of examples in the Investigation's introduction to make sense of these questions.

Reflecting on Student Learning

Use the following questions to assess student understanding at the end of the lesson.

- What evidence do I have that students understand the Focus Question?
  - Where did my students get stuck?
  - What strategies did they use?
  - What breakthroughs did my students have today?
- How will I use this to plan for tomorrow? For the next time I teach this lesson?
- Where will I have the opportunity to reinforce these ideas as I continue through this Unit? The next Unit?

ACE Assignment Guide

- **Applications:** 1–4
- **Connections:** 18–19
- **Extensions:** 39

PROBLEM
2.2

Selecting a Sample
Different Kinds of Samples

▼ Problem Overview

> *Focus Question* How could you select a sample of your school population to survey?

Problem Description

Students consider a variety of sampling methods. They analyze the advantages and disadvantages of each and determine which would produce a sample most representative of the population.

Problem Implementation

Have students work in groups of 2–4 on this Problem.

Materials

• **Labsheet 2ACE:** Exercises 20–22 (accessibility)

Using Technology

If your students have access to computers, they can use the **Expression Calculator** tool to help them find summary statistics for ACE Exercises 20 and 23.

Vocabulary

• convenience sampling
• random sampling
• representative sample
• systematic sampling
• voluntary-response (or self-selected) sampling

Mathematics Background

• The Process of Statistical Investigation
• Exploring Variation
• Comparing Distributions
• Sampling Plans

At a Glance and Lesson Plan

• At a Glance: Problem 2.2 Samples and Populations
• Lesson Plan: Problem 2.2 Samples and Populations

▼ Launch

Launch Video

In this animation, a school principal wants to collect data on whether or not students would like to begin school one hour earlier. Two students collect data from other students as they enter the school at the beginning of the day. The students conducting the survey begin collecting data an hour before school begins; they stop collecting data about five or ten minutes ahead of the school's start time. Show this animation to your students to have them begin thinking about how different data-collection methods can be baised. Visit Teacher Place at mathdashboard.com/cmp3 to see the complete video.

Connecting to Prior Knowledge

Problem 2.2 expands upon the previous one. It raises further issues about sampling and surveying. Students consider four sampling plans, analyzing the advantages and disadvantages of each and determining which method is more likely to produce the sample most representative of the population under investigation.

Presenting the Challenge

Introduce the topic by reading, or having students read, the two questions in the hypothetical research project.

Suggested Questions

• How might you word each of these as a survey question to ask students? The questions might be phrased as follows:
  • How many hours of sleep do you get each night?
  • How many movies do you watch in a week?
• Do you think your questions are clear? What would happen if you asked students in your school each question?

If students do not see that some of the questions might be ambiguous, point out that asking how many hours of sleep a student gets each night raises issues about including weekends or how many nights' data are needed in order to determine what is typical. Also, students might not realize the ambiguity of the general term *movies*—does it refer to watching movies in a theater, on television, on an MP3 player, or on DVD? In the table of data, the question students answered did include all those movies options. Additionally, there may be more than one person collecting the data, which may bias the survey results if the questions are unclear. The respondents all need to understand the question in the same way, too.

- What sampling plan might you design to conduct this research? (Answers will vary. Possible answer: collecting lists of students per home room and randomly selecting a certain number of students from each)

- Suppose there are more students in one grade than another and you want to represent both grades. How will you address this in your sampling plan? (Answers will vary. Students will offer different ideas as to whether they want each grade to be represented by the same number of students or by a number proportional to the number of students in the grade. Or, you may just want to ignore grade level and give each student the same chance of being picked.)

- What are some of the ways you might represent and analyze your data? (Answers will vary. Students will offer ideas about graphs, such as bar graphs, and statistics.)

- When you are finished with the research project, what might you be able to say about how students in the school spend their time? (Answers will vary. Students will offer different ideas. They could find out how many hours a typical student sleeps on a school night or how many movies a typical student watches in a week. They might also see a relationship between the two.)

It is not necessary to bring closure to these questions; they are simply provided to help students think about the many issues that must be considered in such a study.

▼ Explore

Providing for Individual Needs

If students have trouble understanding a particular sampling method, ask them to focus on the name of the strategy. Each title—convenience sampling, systematic sampling, voluntary-response sampling, and random sampling—is descriptive of the important feature of that method.

Pay particular attention to Questions A, B, and D. Questions B and D address the issue of representativeness. Help students think about what *representativeness* means and how each sampling method would or would not result in a representative sample by asking for each plan:

Suggested Questions

- Will group X's plan result in a sample that is representative of the whole school? Explain.

- For Group 1, is it possible that students have some common characteristic that is more usual for bus riders than for students in the whole school? (The bus might carry younger students, students from the same subdivision, or so on.)

- For Group 2, is it possible that this method systematically skips some groups of students? (This is certainly not the same as deliberately choosing a biased sample by skipping a particular group of students, but neither is it a completely random sample, because it probably ensures that two best friends cannot both be chosen if they meet in the lunch line.)

- For Group 3, is it possible that having surveys from only students who want to respond distorts the results? (Most likely; people who volunteer have a particular opinion or interest that motivates them to take the survey. This method is also referred to as self-selected sampling.)

- For Group 4, is it possible that each student in the school has an equally likely chance of being included in the sample? Would this make the sample representative? (This does give each student the same chance of being chosen and is therefore a random sample.)

  Students may want to be more deliberate about making a sample representative, but any interference by the sampler might constitute an unconscious and unintended bias. The discussion around this plan should bring out that it is unbiased, and that, with larger samples, it is likely to be representative of the population.

They may want to make a list advantages and disadvantages that can be considered in a class discussion later.

Planning for the Summary

What evidence will you use in the summary to clarify and deepen understanding of the Focus Question?

What will you do if you do not have evidence?

▼ Summarize

Orchestrating the Discussion

One way to summarize the sampling methods used by the four groups of students in Problem 2.2 is to post four large sheets of paper at the front of the classroom. Divide each sheet into two halves titled "Advantages" and "Disadvantages." Add to the charts as students share their ideas about each sampling method.

After the class has reviewed the four sampling plans used by the groups, ask students to share their ideas about which plan would give the most *representative* sample. Make reference to the summary notes that the class has developed. Ask students to explain their ideas and to critique the ideas of the other students.

As you review Question C, add the name of each sampling method to the appropriate chart.

For Question D, review ideas about what a representative sample is.

When we say the results from a sample are representative, we mean that the characteristics of the sample we have selected are like those—or represent—the population from which the sample was chosen. For example, surveying only 6th graders and then making a prediction about the response of all students in the 6th, 7th, and 8th grades would not be a representative sample. The sample of 6th graders is not representative of the population.

Educational research has shown that students will often evaluate a situation for representativeness from a fairness perspective. They will think about whether a particular sample will be fair—*fair* meaning that all members of the population have a chance to be a part of a sample. If so, it makes sense to use sample data to draw conclusions about all members of the population.

The second part of question D raises a variation on the types already mentioned. Students are likely to think this is fair, because each sample will have an equal number of students from each grade and an equal number of boys and girls. Randomness should play a part in student selection. Students might point out that there could be different numbers of students in each grade or unequal numbers of each gender in a class, and that the plan does not account for this. They might also point out that having the teacher ask the questions might add bias.

Note: This kind of sampling plan is called a *stratified* random sample. You can think of the sample as being composed of layers, or strata, comprised of eight students from each grade. The composition of the sub-sample in each layer should be random.

Reflecting on Student Learning

Use the following questions to assess student understanding at the end of the lesson.

- What evidence do I have that students understand the Focus Question?
  - Where did my students get stuck?
  - What strategies did they use?
  - What breakthroughs did my students have today?
- How will I use this to plan for tomorrow? For the next time I teach this lesson?
- Where will I have the opportunity to reinforce these ideas as I continue through this Unit? The next Unit?

ACE Assignment Guide

- **Applications:** 5–9
- **Connections:** 20–24
- **Extensions:** 40
- **Labsheet 2ACE:** Exercises 20–22 (accessibility) contains the two dot plots of minutes spent on homework. Students may find it helpful to have the dot plots in order to mark up the data values while finding the medians.

Choosing Random Samples
Comparing Samples Using Center and Spread

▼ Problem Overview

> *Focus Question* How could you use statistics of a random sample of data to make predictions about an entire population?

Problem Description

Students explore variability as it relates to sample data and statistics. They select random samples of 30 from a population of 100, and they analyze the samples to help them draw conclusions about the population. By comparing graphs and summary statistics of different samples, students learn about how random samples vary, how some may be more representative of the population than others, and how sampling is a good technique in general, but can occasionally lead to drawing poor conclusions.

Problem Implementation

Have students work in groups of three on this Problem. Each student will draw his or her own random sample, so a group of three will have three different distributions to compare. These distributions get compared to sample distributions created by other groups.

Materials

- **Labsheet 2.3A:** Responses to Grade 7 Movie and Sleep Survey
- **Labsheet 2.3B:** Blank Number Lines for Movies Watched Line Plots
- **Labsheet 2.3C:** Blank Number Lines for Hours Slept Box Plots
- **10-Section Spinners**
- **Teaching Aid 2.3:** Graphs for Grade 7 Survey (Whole Population)

10-sided solids (as many as available)

paper clips or bobby pins (optional)

Using Technology

If your students have access to computers, they can use the **Probability** tool to help them choose random samples. They can also use the **Data and Graphs** tool to help them calculate summary statistics.

Vocabulary

The following vocabulary term is included in the Glossary as review but is not defined within the exposition of the Student Edition.

• five-number summary

Mathematics Background

• The Process of Statistical Investigation
• Reviewing Types of Data and Attributes
• Reviewing Measures of Center and Measures of Spread
• Exploring Variation
• Representing Data With Graphical Displays
• Comparing Distributions
• Sampling Plans

At a Glance and Lesson Plan

• At a Glance: Problem 2.3 Samples and Populations
• Lesson Plan: Problem 2.3 Samples and Populations

▼ Launch

Connecting to Prior Knowledge

Problem 2.3 continues with the idea of random sampling and connects back to *What Do You Expect?* It may be helpful to review the big ideas in probability with students: What is probability? What does it mean for outcomes to be equally likely? How might using what we know from probability help us choose a sample from a population?

Presenting the Challenge

Introduce your students to **Labsheet 2.3A: Responses to Grade 7 Movie and Sleep Survey**, which is a copy of the table in the Student Edition. Talk about the idea of selecting a random sample of students to study rather than calculating statistics and making statistical representations for the entire set of data, or population.

Have students look back at the four sampling plans from Problem 2.2. Group 4's strategy reflects a way to choose a random sample of students. Have students explain why each of the other strategies is not a random sampling plan. Refer back to the discussion of each of the strategies in Problem 2.2.

The Student Edition proposes three methods for choosing a random sample from the data set: spinning two spinners, rolling two number cubes, and using a calculator to generate random numbers. Students can use the online **Probability** tool to help generate random numbers.

Ask students for their ideas about how to use two spinners to generate 2-digit numbers. (By spinning the spinners a total of two times you could generate the numbers from 00 to 99. If you count 00 as 100, then each of the 100 students has an equally likely chance of being included in the sample.)

Talk with students about the desirability of sampling plans that produce random samples, samples in which each member of a population has the same chance of being selected.

Have students work in groups of three on the Problem. You might consider doing Question C after the summary of Questions A and B.

▼ Explore

Providing for Individual Needs

For Question A, every student in each group of 3 should select a random sample of 30 students from the table of 100 7th-grade students found in the Student Edition. The fact that each sample will be different allows students to explore variability as it relates to sample data statistics.

For Question B, have groups draw the line plots of the three distributions on **Labsheet 2.3B: Blank Number Lines for Movies Watched Line Plots.** Look to see if students are paying attention to scaling in order to compare line plots. Prompt students to describe how the data are spread out around a measure of center. They might recall that a data set is *symmetric* when data are balanced, or nearly balanced, around the mean. Data that are spread out on one side of the mean are skewed. Students may wish to use a MAD calculator to generate the MADs from their sample of 30. Have them complete their analyses, responding to Question B, parts (2) and (3). Together, each group can prepare a response for part (4) of the problem, which they will present when they display their line plots in the class discussion. If they complete their work early, encourage them to respond to part (5) in relation to their three samples and, again, when they have a class discussion.

Note: Hold off working on Question C. Discuss Questions A and B first (see the Summarize section), and then have students complete Question C.

For Question C, have groups draw the box plots of the three distributions on **Labsheet 2.3C: Blank Number Lines for Hours Slept Box Plots.** Look to see if students are paying attention to scaling in order to compare box plots. Have them complete their analyses, responding to Question C, parts (2) and (3). Together, each group can prepare a response for part (4), when they will present when they display their box plots in the class discussion. If they complete their work early, encourage them to respond to part (5) in relation to their three samples and, again, when they have a class discussion.

Planning for the Summary

What evidence will you use in the summary to clarify and deepen understanding of the Focus Question?

What will you do if you do not have evidence?

▼ Summarize

Orchestrating the Discussion

This summary should take place after students complete Questions A and B. As the class views sets of line plots generated by various groups of students in this problem, ask students to evaluate the plots from the perspective below.

Suggested Questions

- Are there any apparent differences in the variability among the three samples drawn by each group of students? (There will be differences in variability, but with samples of 30 these will not be marked.)

- Now that you have seen the line plots produced by other students, how would you answer the question asked in Question B, part (4)? (The line plots are all different, but most seem to center around approximately the same number of movies. Some samples have centers quite unlike the majority of samples.)

  Note: This is a great lesson in why mathemeticians never claim that a prediction from one sample is infallible.

- For Question B, part (5), what can you conclude about the movie-watching behavior of the population based on the patterns you have seen in the samples selected by the various groups? (Students will probably use the mean to make a statement about a typical student's movie-watching behavior. Having seen that sample statistics vary they may state this as an interval, rather than as a single number.)

Once students have considered the results from several samples, choose data from a single sample and use just the one line plot. Have students think about what they might be able to say about the population based on using the results from a single sample, that is, how *representative* is this sample?

- What might you be able to say about the population if we had data from only one sample? (You may want to have students describe how confident they are that they can draw this conclusion using just their sample data.)

- What can you conclude about the movie-watching behavior of the population? (The samples were all chosen from a single population. The goal is to have students recognize that, while there may be variation among the samples, the resulting statistics and line plots are similar for the majority of the samples.)

A similar summary can take place after students explore Question C (refer to the Explore). Distribute **Labsheet 2.3C: Blank Number Lines for Hours Slept Box Plots** to each group. They will use a similar sampling process for the hours-slept data as they used for the movies-watched data.

Have students share their answers to the important ideas addressed in Question C.

- What can you conclude about the hours of sleep of the population of 100 students based on the patterns in the samples selected by your group? (Allow students to share ideas for better ways to phrase the question about determining the number of movies watched and hours slept, and conclude with a discussion of the difficulties that can arise in surveys.)

- Why might it be difficult to gather accurate data on topics like these? (Discuss the fact that acquiring accurate data about such topics as hours slept and number of movies watched is tricky because it can be hard for people to remember such numbers for very long. In addition, people are sometimes tempted to report numbers that are not a true measure of their behavior.)

To tie things up, you may want to display **Teaching Aid 2.3: Graphs for Grade 7 Survey (Whole Population)**, which shows a dot plots and box plots of the data for all 100 students in the database. Then ask:

- How well did you estimate the mean number of movies from a single sample? The median number of hours of sleep? (Answers will vary based on the summary statistics of the samples the students used. Since the samples are of 30 students, many of the samples will give good estimates of the typical student for the entire population. In Problem 2.4, students will see how sample size changes the accuracy of conclusions drawn.)

- Would some samples give better estimates than others? (Some samples may give better estimates than others. Choosing any random sample, however, gives a good chance of gathering information on a representative sample. If all groups in your class choose random samples, a group who chooses a more representative sample than other groups has done so purely by chance.)

- Does a line plot or box plot of your sample help you make a better estimate? (Either works well, but the box plot predicts the median, not the mean. Additionally, the box plot sometimes makes students think of reporting an interval for a prediction, which is not a bad idea.)

- Would any of the samples have given a very poor estimate? (Some samples may have given poor estimates. Again, however, this would be by chance if students used random sampling plans.)

- If there is a sample that would have given a very poor estimate, was this because the sample was chosen incorrectly? (Random sampling plans can also provide poor estimates, as all samples vary from sample to sample, even when sampling is done using proper methods.)

  Note: Make the point that a random sample resulting in a poor estimate is not anyone's fault. This rarely happens.

Reflecting on Student Learning

Use the following questions to assess student understanding at the end of the lesson.

- What evidence do I have that students understand the Focus Question?
  - Where did my students get stuck?
  - What strategies did they use?
  - What breakthroughs did my students have today?
- How will I use this to plan for tomorrow? For the next time I teach this lesson?
- Where will I have the opportunity to reinforce these ideas as I continue through this Unit? The next Unit?

ACE Assignment Guide

- **Applications:** 10–14
- **Connections:** 25–31

Growing Samples
What Size Sample to Use?

▼ Problem Overview

Focus Question Can you make good statistical estimates with less work by selecting smaller samples? How does sample size relate to the accuracy of statistical estimates?

Problem Description

Continuing with the data set from Problem 2.3, students explore and compare conclusions drawn from samples of size 5, 10, and 30. They make distributions of sample medians/means and discuss which sample sizes seem to have medians/means that are most similar to the population median/mean. They also look at measures of spread and how variability changes as the sample size increases.

Problem Implementation

Have students work in groups of three on this Problem. Each student will be collecting movie and sleep data from their own three random samples—of size 5 and 10, and the size-30 sample that was already collected in Problem 2.3. They will calculate the mean, median, MAD, and IQR for the number of movies watched and hours slept for each sample. This information will be shared by the whole class and compiled in a class chart. Consistent organization will be crucial.

Labsheet 2.4E: Group Organizer for Sample-Size Statistics will help each group organize their statistics for each of the three sample sizes. For Question B, part (2), record the statistics found by each student on the board. Students can use **Labsheet 2.4F: Class Organizer for Sample-Size Statistics** to compile the statistics from all the students, as well.

Students can use copies of Labsheets 2.4A–2.4D to help them draw their line plots.

You might consider doing Question C after the summary of Questions A and B. For Question C, have students work in groups for part (1). Then, discuss part (2) as a class.

Materials

- **Labsheet 2.3A:** Responses to Grade 7 Movie and Sleep Survey
- **Labsheet 2.4A:** Blank Number Lines for Movies Watched Last Week (Means)
- **Labsheet 2.4B:** Blank Number Lines for Movies Watched Last Week (Medians)
- **Labsheet 2.4C:** Blank Number Lines for Hours of Sleep Last Night (Means)
- **Labsheet 2.4D:** Blank Number Lines for Hours of Sleep Last Night (Medians)
- **Labsheet 2.4E:** Group Organizer for Sample-Size Statistics
- **Labsheet 2.4F:** Class Organizer for Sample-Size Statistics
- **10-Section Spinners**
- **Teaching Aid 2.3:** Graphs for Grade 7 Survey (Whole Population)

10-sided solids (optional)

paper clips or bobby pins (optional)

Using Technology

If your students have access to computers, they can use the **Probability** tool to help them choose random samples. They can also use the **Data and Graphs** tool to help them calculate summary statistics.

Vocabulary

- sampling distribution

Mathematics Background

- The Process of Statistical Investigation
- Reviewing Types of Data and Attributes
- Reviewing Measures of Center and Measures of Spread
- Exploring Variation
- Representing Data With Graphical Displays
- Comparing Distributions

At a Glance and Lesson Plan

- At a Glance: Problem 2.4 Samples and Populations
- Lesson Plan: Problem 2.4 Samples and Populations

▼ Launch

Connecting to Prior Knowledge

The completion of Problem 2.3 lays the groundwork for Problem 2.4. Problem 2.4 also connects with probability concepts learned in *What Do You Expect?*

Presenting the Challenge

Introduce the Problem by asking students if they think their statistical estimates from 30 students will be similar to the estimates they will make by taking smaller samples from the database of 100 7th-grade students.

Suggested Questions

• In Problem 2.3, you analyzed samples of 30 students. Do you think you would get similar results from smaller sample sizes? (Answers will vary. Some students will intuitively know that, with smaller samples, the estimates will be influenced more by specific data values chosen.)

After Question B, part (2), record your students' statistics on the board. At this point, you may want to do a mini-summary with your class. Hand out Labsheets 2.4A–2.4D to each student. Explain to students what they will be plotting in Question C.

Have students work in their groups to complete Questions D and E. Save Questions F and G until after the Problem Summarize.

▼ Explore

Providing for Individual Needs

Allow students to choose methods for generating random samples. Designate sections of the board for groups to record the movie data (means/medians they find for samples of 5, 10, and 30 students) and the hours-slept data (means/ medians they find for samples of 5, 10, and 30 students). For each sample size, let the class know when all groups have recorded their results so that they can draw line plots. You may want to post the statistics for the entire population of 100 students: mean (4.22 movies) and median (3 movies) number of movies and the mean (7.7 hours) and median (8 hours) number of hours slept. If you have room on the board, you can also record the MADs and IQRs.

Some students will need help understanding that the data values in the line plots are not single pieces of data about a student; each data value is a mean. For Question C, ask:

Suggested Questions

- What does each point in your line plot represent? How is this the same as or different from the line plot you made in Problem 2.3? (Each point on the line plot in Problem 2.3 represented a number of movies seen by one student. Each point in this line plot in Problem 2.4 represents a mean number of movies for a sample.)

- When you found the mean in Problem 2.3, what did it tell you? (the mean number of movies seen by a sample of students)

- If you were to find the mean of the data you graphed in Question C, what would it tell you? (the mean of all the mean numbers of movies from samples)

- Compare the line plot you made for your single sample of 30 in Problem 2.3 and the line plot of means from samples of 30 in Problem 2.4, Question C. What do you notice? (Both should be centered on or around the mean of the population, but the distribution of means will be more tightly clustered. This illustrates that one sample may or may not give a good predictor of the mean of the population. However, over the long haul, predicting from samples of 30 works well.)

- What do you observe about the overall distribution of the means? How do the three distributions of means for each sample size compare? (The means for larger sample sizes cluster more closely around the population's mean; the means for smaller sample sizes are more spread out.)

- What does this tell you about using samples to draw conclusions about the mean of a population? (This indicates that larger samples are usually more reliable for drawing conclusions about the mean of the population. A smaller proportion of the larger samples will result in inaccurate conclusions.)

The procedure of collecting samples of different sizes, finding sample statistics for each sample, and then creating a line plot (with mean number of movies in Question C) is quite tricky to understand. But after doing this once for the three sampling distributions of mean number of movies, Questions D and E should go more smoothly. You can ask the same questions in relation to the sampling distributions of median number of movies, mean number of hours slept and median number of hours slept.

Planning for the Summary

What evidence will you use in the summary to clarify and deepen understanding of the Focus Question?

What will you do if you do not have evidence?

▼ Summarize

Orchestrating the Discussion

For Questions A, B, and C you may have done a summary mid-Problem. The important questions to discuss as a class are the same as in the Explore:

- For Question C, what does each point in your line plot in represent? How is this similar to or different from the points in the line plot you made in Problem 2.3?

- When you found the mean in Problem 2.3, what did it tell you?

- If you were to find the mean of the data you graphed in Question C, what would it tell you?

- What do you observe about the overall distribution of the means? How do the three distributions of sample means for each size compare?

- What does this tell you about using samples to draw conclusions about the mean of a population?

For Question D, display class line plots of the distributions of sample medians of the movie data for sample sizes of 5, 10, and 30.

Once the class data are displayed, students can discuss their observations about the three line plots. Compare the distributions of medians for the different-sized samples to each other. Then, compare the medians of these distributions of samples to the population median.

Suggested Questions

- What do you observe about the overall distributions of the medians? (They are all centered on the median of the population.)

- How do the three distributions of sample medians for each sample size compare? (The medians for larger sample sizes will probably cluster more closely around the population median; for smaller sample sizes, the medians will be more spread out.)

Do the same for Question E as a class. Display three line plots—one for each of the medians for the sleep data that students found for samples of 5, 10, and 30 students—and find the median. Below are examples of three line plots for median hours of sleep:

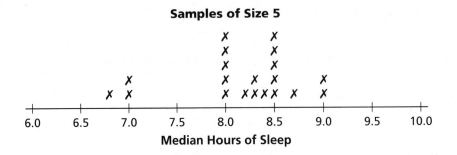

Samples of Size 5

Median Hours of Sleep

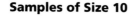

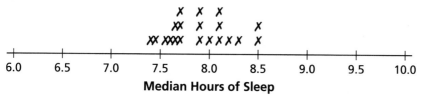

Samples of Size 10

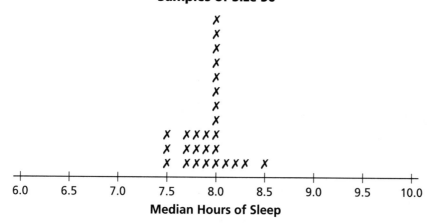

Samples of Size 30

Repeat the same process of reporting and discussing for the mean hours slept. Answer Question F as a class. Help students think about the fact that because 50 is a larger sample size than 30, it is reasonable to expect that there will be less variation among the means and medians of samples of 50, and that the means and medians of samples of 50 will cluster more closely around the mean and median of the population.

For Question G, bring the class back to the initial collection of data and statistics.

- What do you notice about the MADs for the samples about movies watched?

- What do you notice about the IQRs for the samples about movies watched?

- What do you notice about the MADs for the samples about hours slept?

- What do you notice about the IQRs for the samples about hours slept? (In each case students might say these measures vary. They may note that small samples have larger measures of variability than large samples, and they vary more from each other. They may also say that the measures for large samples are more like the equivalent measures for the population.)

Note: Students do not calculate MAD for sampling distributions, but if they did, they would find that the sampling distributions of means or medians have lower measures of variability than the population. That is, the sample means are more closely clustered around the mean of the population than the raw data are.

Consider the Focus Question. Have your students summarize their responses to these questions.

Reflecting on Student Learning

Use the following questions to assess student understanding at the end of the lesson.

- What evidence do I have that students understand the Focus Question?
  - Where did my students get stuck?
  - What strategies did they use?
  - What breakthroughs did my students have today?
- How will I use this to plan for tomorrow? For the next time I teach this lesson?
- Where will I have the opportunity to reinforce these ideas as I continue through this Unit? The next Unit?

ACE Assignment Guide

- **Applications:** 15–17
- **Connections:** 32–38
- **Extensions:** 41

Mathematical Reflections

Possible Answers to Mathematical Reflections

1. Collecting data from a sample rather than from an entire population simplifies the task. If the sample is chosen wisely, you can tell a lot about what is true for the population. Doing this is especially helpful when the population is very large. Collecting data from an entire large population can be difficult.

2. Convenience sampling is selecting a sample of people who are easy to reach; however, the easiest sample to reach might not be representative of the entire population. Systematic sampling is a regular procedure for choosing from a population. While it may be a fairer method than convenience sampling, one must be careful that the systematic procedure does not bias selection toward or away from some sector of the population. Voluntary-response (or self-selected) sampling produces data from people who choose to respond. It may be easy to implement, but the data can be misleading because you get reports from either those who are atypically responsible or those who care strongly about an issue. Random sampling is a system that gives every member of a population an equal chance of being selected. It can be more difficult to implement, but it may give the best results.

3. **a.** In a random sample, every individual in a population has the same chance of being selected. With the other three types—convenience, in which people who are present are sampled; voluntary-response, in which people choose to respond; and systematic in which some rule is used to select the sample—everyone does not have an equally likely chance to be a part of the sample.

   b. Random sampling is less likely to produce a biased sample—a sample that is not representative.

   c. Answers will vary. You could identify each individual with a code number, letter, or name, then select the sample by generating random numbers (using spinners, a calculator or computer, or number cubes). Or, you could draw names or numbers from a bowl without looking.

   Using a calculator or a computer to generate random numbers is probably the most efficient method. Using spinners or number cubes will work, but it is more time-consuming. Drawing names from a bowl may be even more time-consuming because you must first write each value on a slip of paper.

4. **a.** Several samples of the same size from the same population should have similar distributions (as shown in box plots and line plots) and summary statistics (measures of center and spread). **Note:** Measures of center and spread are likely to vary more, from sample to sample, for small samples than for large samples.

   b. As the sizes of the random samples get larger (up to about 30 cases generally), the measure of center and spread for a sample is more likely to be representative of the population. It is unlikely the statistics will be identical, but they do permit statisticians to make predictions about the population.

5. Answers will vary. Students should now understand that sampling method and sample size are important in finding reliable results.

Note: Choosing a sample size of 30 is a "rule of thumb." The measures of center and spread are likely to vary from one small sample to another. At a sample size of about 30, the variation from one sample to another is reduced. The measures of center and spread from a sample of size 30 are good indicators of the measures of center and spread for the population.

Possible Answers to Mathematical Practices Reflections

Students may have demonstrated all of the eight Common Core Standards for Mathematical Practice during this Investigation. During the class discussion, have students provide additional Practices that the Problem cited involved and identify the use of other Mathematical Practices in the Investigation.

One student observation is provided in the Student Edition. Here is another sample student response.

Problem 2.4 asked if it was possible to make good estimates with less work by selecting smaller samples. In order to answer this question, I needed to generate different-sized samples and combine the results from my samples with everyone else's in my class. Together, we had to make graphs and compute statistics. As a class, we actually made graphs of the distributions of the means for the different size samples we all got and of the medians. This was fun even though it seems like a lot of work.

The distribution of the means for small samples was more spread out—more variable than the distribution of the means for the larger sample. So, if I want to use samples in the future, I need to think about the size of the sample I choose. It matters to have more cases than fewer. And it helped to see that 30 cases may be a good "rule of thumb" about how many to choose.

MP1: Make sense of problems and persevere in solving them.

Investigation 2

Choosing a Sample From a Population

Collecting information about the students in your math class, such as their favorite foods or activities, would be fairly easy. On the other hand, collecting information about all the middle-school students in your state would be very difficult.

To make collecting information on a large group, or *population*, easier, you can collect data from a small part, or **sample**, of that population. Depending on how the sample is selected, it may be possible to use the data to make predictions or draw conclusions about an entire population. The challenge is to choose a sample that accurately represents the population as a whole.

another sample of the population

a sample of the population

·······················

Common Core State Standards

7.SP.A.1 Understand that statistics can be used to gain information about a population by examining a sample of the population; generalizations about a population from a sample are valid only if the sample is representative of that population. Understand that random sampling tends to produce representative samples and support valid inferences.

7.SP.A.2 Use data from a random sample to draw inferences about a population with an unknown characteristic of interest. Generate multiple samples (or simulated samples) of the same size to gauge the variation in estimates or predictions.

Also 7.RP.A.3, 7.SP.C.7, 7.SP.C.7a

Notes _____

_____

_____

Consider this information:

In the United States, over 75% of teens have cell phones. Almost half of the teens who own cell phones own smartphones. So, more than 35% of all teens own smartphones, compared to 23% in 2011.

From 2009 to 2011, the median number of daily texts teens sent rose from 50 to 60. Texting among older teens, ages 14–17, increased from 60 texts to 100 texts per day during that two-year span.

• How could the groups reporting this information know about the activities of all the teenagers in the United States?

• Do you think these facts were gathered from every teenager in the population? Why or why not?

Did You Know?

Thirty years ago, the first "mobile" phones were car phones that weighed over 20 pounds. Early cell phones weighed just under two pounds and cost almost $4,000 (that's roughly $9,200 in today's dollars). Today, smartphones generally weigh about 4 ounces and cost less than $1,000.

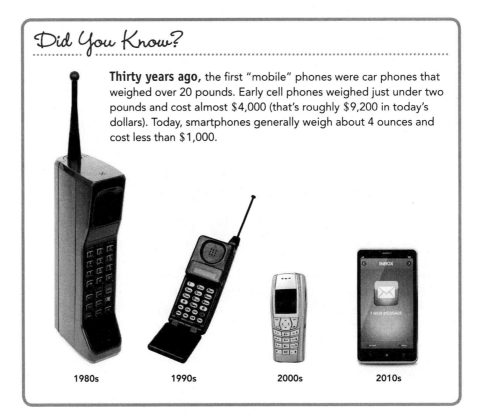

| 1980s | 1990s | 2000s | 2010s |

Notes

2.1 Asking About Honesty
Using a Sample to Draw Conclusions

Suppose a national magazine asks its readers to respond to the questions below about honesty. Readers take the survey on the magazine's Web site.

HONESTY SURVEY

If This Happened to You

1. What would you do if you found someone's wallet on the street?
   a. Try to return it to the owner
   b. Return it, but keep the money
   c. Keep the wallet and the money

2. What would you do if a cashier mistakenly gave you $10 extra in change?
   a. Tell the cashier about the error
   b. Say nothing and keep the cash

3. Would you cheat on an exam if you were sure you wouldn't get caught?
   a. Yes   b. No

4. Would you download music from the Internet illegally instead of buying the music?
   a. Yes   b. No

5. Do you feel that you are an honest person in most situations?
   a. Yes   b. No

- What is the population for the Honesty Survey?

- Is asking readers to volunteer their answers a good way for the magazine to draw conclusions about the honesty of the population? Why or why not?

STUDENT PAGE

Notes _____

_____

_____

Problem 2.1

Ⓐ A **sampling plan** is a strategy for choosing a sample from a population. What is the population for the Honesty Survey? What is the sample? How was the sample chosen from the population?

Ⓑ Suppose 5,280 people completed the survey.

1. For the first question: 3,960 people said they would try to return the wallet to the owner; 792 said they would return the wallet but keep the money; and 528 said they would keep the wallet and the money. What is the relative frequency of each response?

2. For the second question: 4,752 said they would tell the cashier about the error. What is the relative frequency of respondents who said they would tell the cashier about the error?

3. For the third question: 4,224 people answered "No." What is the relative frequency of respondents said they would *not* cheat on an exam?

4. For the fourth question: 1,584 people answered "Yes." What is the relative frequency of respondents who said they would *not* download music illegally from the Internet?

Ⓒ 1. Make a table or graph that shows the relative frequencies of "honest" and "dishonest" answers for each of the first four questions of the Honesty Survey.

2. Use your table or graph to analyze the responses to the four survey questions. What conclusions can you draw about people's behavior? Explain.

Ⓓ Use the survey results in Question B and your answers to Question C. Suppose the United States population is about 314 million.

1. Estimate how many people in the United States would say that they would not cheat on an exam.

2. Estimate how many people in the United States would say that they would not download music illegally from the Internet.

Notes

Problem 2.1 *continued*

E 1. Do you think this sample of 5,280 people accurately represents the population of the United States? Why or why not?

2. Suppose you were asked to revise the sampling plan for this survey. How could you make sure that the sample more accurately represents the U.S. population?

A C E Homework starts on page 45.

2.2 Selecting a Sample
Different Kinds of Samples

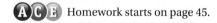

Drawing accurate conclusions about a population based on a sample can be complicated. When you choose a sample, it should be *representative* of the population. This means the sample must have characteristics similar to those of the population. Not all samples are **representative samples.**

Suppose you are doing research on students at your school. You plan to ask these questions:

> • How many hours of sleep do you get each school night?
>
> • How many movies do you watch each week?

If your school has many students, it might be difficult to gather and analyze data from every student.

- Are these questions clear enough to allow you to collect good data? Why or why not?

- How might you select a sample of your school population to survey?

Problem 2.2

Ms. Ruiz's class is conducting a survey about the number of hours students spend sleeping and the number of hours they spend watching movies. The class divides into four groups. Each group devises a plan for sampling the school population.

Group 1

Group 2

Group 3

Group 4

Notes

_____

_____

_____

Problem **2.2** *continued*

(A) What are the advantages and disadvantages of each sampling plan?

(B) Which plan do you think will collect the most accurate data to represent students in the whole school? Explain.

(C) The four sampling plans are examples of common sampling methods.

1. Group 1's plan is an example of **convenience sampling**. What do you think convenience sampling is? Describe another sampling plan using convenience sampling.

2. Group 2's plan is an example of **systematic sampling**. What do you think systematic sampling is? Describe another sampling plan using systematic sampling.

3. Group 3's plan is an example of **voluntary-response sampling**. What do you think voluntary-response sampling is? Describe another sampling plan using voluntary-response sampling.

4. Group 4's plan is an example of **random sampling**. What do you think random sampling is? Describe another sampling plan using random sampling.

(D) 1. Jahmal thinks that Group 1, Group 2, and Group 3 devised sampling plans that might not give representative samples. Do you agree or disagree? Explain.

2. Jahmal comes up with a new plan. He thinks each teacher should select one boy and one girl and ask them the survey questions. There are four teachers for each grade (Grades 6–8), so they would end up with a sample of 24 students.

    i. What type of sampling plan is this?

    ii. Will it give a representative sample?

    iii. Do you like Jahmal's plan? Explain. If you do not like Jahmal's plan, how would you change it?

 Homework starts on page 45.

Notes

2.3 Choosing Random Samples
Comparing Samples Using Center and Spread

In most cases, a good sampling plan is one that gives each member of the population the same chance of being selected. To do this, you may use concepts from probability, such as *equally likely* outcomes.

A random sampling plan gives each member of a population an equally likely chance of being included in the sample. The resulting sample is called a random sample.

To select a random sample from a population of 100 students, you can use spinners to generate pairs of random digits.

- How does using the two spinners help you select a random sample from a population of 100 students?

- What two-digit numbers can you generate with the spinners?

- How can you make sure Student 100 has an equally likely chance of being included in your sample?

- What ideas from probability are you using?

There are many other ways to select a random sample of students. For example, you could roll two 10-sided numbered solids or generate random numbers with your calculator.

- What other strategies could you use?

The table on the next page shows data collected from a 7th-grade class. The data include the number of hours of sleep each student got the previous night and the number of movies each student watched the previous week.

- How can you use statistics from a random sample to draw conclusions about the entire population of 7th-grade students in the school?

Notes

_____

_____

_____

Responses to Grade 7 Movie and Sleep Survey

Student	Sleep Last Night (h)	Movies Last Week (no. of)	Student	Sleep Last Night (h)	Movies Last Week (no. of)	Student	Sleep Last Night (h)	Movies Last Week (no. of)
01	11.5	14	35	6.5	5	68	5.5	0
02	2.0	8	36	9.3	1	69	10.5	7
03	7.7	3	37	8.2	3	70	7.5	1
04	9.3	1	38	7.3	3	71	7.8	0
05	7.1	16	39	7.4	6	72	7.3	1
06	7.5	1	40	8.5	7	73	9.3	2
07	8.0	4	41	5.5	17	74	9.0	1
08	7.8	1	42	6.5	3	75	8.7	1
09	8.0	13	43	7.0	5	76	8.5	3
10	8.0	15	44	8.5	2	77	9.0	1
11	9.0	1	45	9.3	4	78	8.0	1
12	9.2	10	46	8.0	15	79	8.0	4
13	8.5	5	47	8.5	10	80	6.5	0
14	6.0	15	48	6.2	11	81	8.0	0
15	6.5	10	49	11.8	10	82	9.0	8
16	8.3	2	50	9.0	4	83	8.0	0
17	7.4	2	51	5.0	4	84	7.0	0
18	11.2	3	52	6.5	5	85	9.0	6
19	7.3	1	53	8.5	2	86	7.3	0
20	8.0	0	54	9.1	15	87	9.0	3
21	7.8	1	55	7.5	2	88	7.5	5
22	7.8	1	56	8.5	1	89	8.0	0
23	9.2	2	57	8.0	2	90	7.5	6
24	7.5	0	58	7.0	7	91	8.0	4
25	8.8	1	59	8.4	10	92	9.0	4
26	8.5	0	60	9.5	1	93	7.0	0
27	9.0	0	61	7.3	5	94	8.0	3
28	8.5	0	62	7.3	4	95	8.3	3
29	8.2	2	63	8.5	3	96	8.3	14
30	7.8	2	64	9.0	3	97	7.8	5
31	8.0	2	65	9.0	4	98	8.5	1
32	7.3	8	66	7.3	5	99	8.3	3
33	6.0	5	67	5.7	0	100	7.5	2
34	7.5	5						

Notes

STUDENT PAGE

Problem 2.3

In this Problem, you will choose a sample and then represent the data with a line plot and with a box plot. You will compare your sample's distribution with your classmates' distributions. Your class should decide on a scale for the line plot and box plot before starting.

A 1. Select a random sample of 30 students from the table on the previous page. Your sample should include 30 different students. If you select a student who is already in your sample, select another.

2. For each student in your sample, record the number of hours slept and the number of movies watched.

B 1. Make a line plot showing the number of movies watched by your sample.

2. **a.** Locate the mean.

   b. Describe the shape of the distribution.

3. Find the range and MAD. Describe the variability of the number of movies watched by students in your sample.

4. Compare your sample distribution with those of your classmates. Describe any similarities or differences.

5. What can you conclude about the number of movies the population of 7th-grade students watched last week based on all the samples selected by your class? Explain.

C 1. Find the *five-number summary* of the number of hours slept for your sample. Make a box-and-whisker plot of the data in your sample.

2. Describe the shape of the distribution.

3. Find the range and IQR. Describe the variability of the number of hours slept for the students in your sample.

4. Compare your sample distribution with those of your classmates. Describe any similarities or differences.

5. What can you conclude about the number of hours the population of 7th-grade students slept last night based on all the samples selected by your class? Explain.

ACE Homework starts on page 45.

Notes

2.4 Growing Samples
What Size Sample to Use?

In Problem 2.3, you used statistics from random samples to estimate the number of hours slept and the number of movies watched by 100 students.

> ❓ • Are you able to make good estimates with less work by selecting smaller samples?
>
> • How does sample size relate to the accuracy of statistical estimates?

Problem 2.4

Ⓐ Use the population of 100 students from Problem 2.3. Select a random sample of 5 students and a random sample of 10 students. Record the number of hours slept and the number of movies watched for each student. **Note:** You should select a new set of students for each sample, but one or more students may happen to appear in both samples.

Ⓑ Use all three samples (the 5-student sample and the 10-student sample from Question A, and the 30-student sample from Problem 2.3) to answer the questions below.

 1. For each sample size (5, 10, and 30), find the mean and median number of hours slept. Find the mean and median number of movies watched. Find the IQR and the MAD of each data set.

 2. Record the means, the medians, the IQRs, and the MADs in a class chart. Record the summary statistics of your classmates' samples as well.

continued on the next page >

Notes _____

STUDENT PAGE

Problem **2.4** *continued*

C **1.** Use the class data about the mean number of movies watched. For each sample size (5, 10, and 30 students), make a line plot displaying the *means* of the samples. You will have three line plots, each showing how the means vary across the samples. These are called **sampling distributions**. Compare the three sampling distributions by describing the variability in each distribution.

2. The mean number of movies watched for the population of 100 students is 4.22 movies. Write a paragraph describing how close the means of samples of different sizes are to the mean of the population.

D **1.** Use the class data about the median number of movies watched. For each sample size, make a line plot displaying the *medians* of the samples. You will have three line plots, each showing how the medians vary across the samples. Compare the three sampling distributions by describing the variability in each distribution.

2. The median number of movies watched for the population of 100 students is 3 movies. Write a paragraph describing how close the medians of samples of different sizes are to the median of the population.

E For the population of 100 students, the mean number of hours slept is 7.96 hours, and the median is 8 hours.

Follow the steps you used in Questions C and D to analyze the distribution of means and medians of samples of different sizes. Discuss how close the means and medians of samples of different sizes are to the mean and median of the whole population for the number of hours slept.

F Suppose each student in your class chose a sample of 50 students and found the means and medians of the data for the number of hours slept and the number of movies watched. What would you expect the line plots of these means and medians to look like? Explain.

G Use the class chart of summary statistics. What patterns do you see in the measures of spread for the three different sample sizes? Explain why these patterns make sense.

A C E Homework starts on page 45.

Notes

_____

_____

_____

Applications

For Exercises 1–4, describe the *population*, the *sampling plan*, and the *sample*.

1. A magazine for teenagers asks its readers to write in with information about how they solve personal problems.

2. An 8th-grade class wants to find out how much time middle-school students spend on the telephone each day. Students in the class keep a record of the amount of time they spend on the phone each day for a week.

3. Ms. Darnell's class wants to estimate the number of soft drinks middle-school students drink each day. They obtain a list of students in the school and write each name on a card. They put the cards in a box and select the names of 40 students to survey.

4. The newspaper below gives information about how adults feel about global warming. The editors of the school paper want to find out how students feel about this issue. They select 26 students for their survey—one whose name begins with A, one whose name begins with B, one whose name begins with C, and so on.

Notes

A middle school has 350 students. One math class decides to investigate how many hours a typical student in the school spent doing homework last week. Several students suggest sampling plans. For Exercises 5–8, name the type of sampling plan. Then tell whether you think the sampling plan would give a representative sample.

5. Zak suggests surveying every third student on each homeroom class list.

6. Kwang-Hee suggests putting 320 white beans and 30 red beans in a bag. Each student would draw a bean as he or she enters the auditorium for an assembly. The 30 students who draw red beans will be surveyed.

7. Ushio suggests that each student in the class survey everyone in his or her English class.

8. Kirby suggests putting surveys on a table at lunch and asking students to return completed questionnaires at the end of the day.

9. A radio host asked her listeners to call in to express their opinions about a local election. What kind of sampling plan is she using? Do you think the results of this survey could be used to describe the opinions of all the show's listeners? Explain.

Manufacturers often conduct quality-control tests on samples of their products. For Exercises 10–13, describe a random sampling plan you would recommend to the company. Justify your recommendation.

10. A toy company produces 5,000 video-game systems each day.

11. A music company manufactures a total of 200,000 compact discs for about 100 recording artists each day.

12. A fireworks company produces over 1,500 rockets each day.

13. A bottling company produces 25,000 bottles of spring water each day.

Notes

14. Use the table from Problem 2.3.

   a. Suppose you select the first 30 students for a sample. A second student selects the next 30 students for a different sample, and so on. Will these samples be representative? Explain.

   b. You select students 1, 5, 9, 13, 17, 21, 25, . . . for your sample. A second student chooses students 2, 6, 10, 14, 18, 22, 26, . . . for his sample. A third student chooses students 3, 7, 11, 15, 19, 23, 27, . . . for her sample, and so on. Will this result in representative samples? Explain.

15. a. The homecoming committee wants to estimate how many students will attend the homecoming dance. It does not, however, want to ask every student in the school. Describe a method the committee could use to select a sample of students to survey.

   b. Describe how the committee could use the results of its survey to predict the number of students who will attend the dance.

16. Use the graph below. About how many more hours per day does a typical newborn sleep than a typical 10- to 13-year-old?

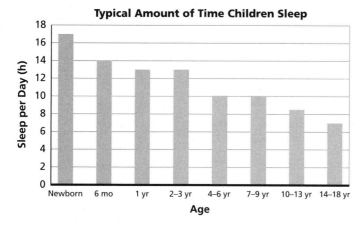

Typical Amount of Time Children Sleep

17. Suppose you want to survey students in your school to find out how many hours they sleep each night. Which would be the best sample size: 5 students, 10 students, or 30 students? Explain.

Notes

STUDENT PAGE

Applications   Connections   Extensions

Connections

18. The scoreboard below displays Ella's diving scores from a recent
competition. One score cannot be read.

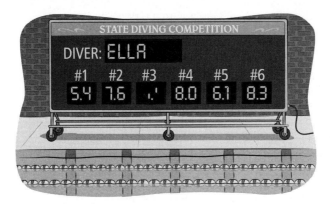

These statistics summarize Ella's diving scores:

mean = 6.75 points   median = 6.85 points   range = 3.2 points

What was Ella's missing score for the competition? Explain.

19. Between ages 5 and 18, the average student eats 1,500 peanut butter
and jelly sandwiches. You can make about 15 sandwiches from an
18-ounce jar of peanut butter.

  a. How many 18-ounce jars of peanut butter would you need to
make 1,500 sandwiches? Explain.

  b. From age 5 to age 18, about how many 18-ounce jars of peanut
butter does an average student eat each year?

  c. How many peanut butter sandwiches does a student need to eat
each week to consume the number of jars per year from part (b)?

48   Samples and Populations

148   Samples and Populations   Investigation 2   Choosing a Sample From a Population

For Exercises 20–22, use the two dot plots below. The dot plots show the number of hours students spent doing homework on Monday.

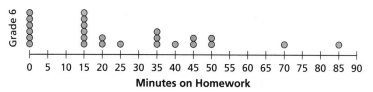

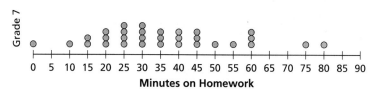

20. Find the median homework times. Copy and complete the table below.

Time Spent on Homework (minutes)

Grade	Mean	Median	MAD
6	25.8	▦	18.56
7	36.13	▦	14.53

21. a. For each grade, describe the variability in the distribution of homework times. Use what you know about the distribution's shape and the MAD.

b. Use statistics to compare the times 6th graders spent doing homework to the times 7th graders spent doing homework.

22. Could these data be used to describe the time spent on homework on a typical school night by a typical student in each grade? Explain.

STUDENT PAGE

Notes _____

_____

_____

23. Consider the following data set: 20, 22, 23, 23, 24, 24, and 25.

   a. Find the mean and the range of the values.

   b. Add three data values to the data set so that the mean of the new data set is greater than the mean of the original data set. What is the range of the new data set?

   c. Add three data values to the original data set so that the mean of the new data set is less than the mean of the original data set. What is the range of the new data set?

   d. How do the ranges of the three data sets compare? Why do you think this is so?

24. Multiple Choice Suppose you survey 30 students from a population of 150 students in the 7th grade. Which statement is *false*?

   A. The ratio of those sampled to those not sampled is 30 to 120.

   B. One out of every five people in the population was sampled.

   C. Twenty-five percent of the students in the population were sampled.

   D. One-fifth of the students in the population were sampled.

25. There are 350 students in a school. Ms. Cabral's class surveys two random samples of students to find out how many went to camp last summer. The results are below.

   Sample 1: 8 of 25 attended camp.

   Sample 2: 7 of 28 attended camp.

   a. Use the results from Sample 1. What fraction of the students in the school do you think attended camp? How many students attended camp?

   b. Use the results from Sample 2. What fraction of the students in the school do you think attended camp? How many students attended camp?

   c. Which sample concludes that the greater fraction of students attended camp?

   d. One of Ms. Cabral's students says, "We were careful to choose our samples at random. Why did the two samples give us different conclusions?" How would you answer the student's question?

Notes

Use the following information for Exercises 26–31.

Annie's teacher starts each class with the names of all the students in a container. There are 12 girls and 6 boys in the class.

The teacher pulls out names at random to choose students to present answers. After choosing a name, the teacher sets the name aside. At the end of class, the teacher replaces all the names in the container. So, each student's name has a chance of being chosen the next day.

26. What is the probability Annie will be the first student chosen on Monday?

27. What is the probability Annie will be the first student chosen on Tuesday?

28. What is the probability Annie will be the first student chosen on both Monday and Tuesday?

29. What is the probability the first student chosen on a given day will be a girl?

30. Suppose Annie is chosen first. What is the probability that the next student selected will be another girl?

31. Suppose the teacher plans to choose six students during one class. Would you be surprised if only two girls were chosen? Explain.

Notes

Use the following information for Exercises 32 and 33. Alyssa wants to know what students think about replacing the candy in two vending machines in the cafeteria with more healthful snacks. Alyssa obtains a list of student names, grouped by grade, with the girls listed first in each grade.

There are 300 6th graders, 300 7th graders, and 200 8th graders. Half of the students in each grade are girls.

32. Alyssa chooses 3 different students at random from the list of 800 students.

 a. What is the probability that the first choice is a girl? The second choice is a girl? The third choice is a girl?

 b. What is the probability that Alyssa chooses three girls?

33. Alyssa decides to choose one person *from each grade* at random.

 a. What is the probability that the 6th-grade choice is a girl?

 b. What is the probability that she chooses three girls?

For Exercises 34–38, use the table below. Alyssa chooses one girl and one boy from each grade. She asks each, "Which would you prefer, a machine with healthful snacks or a machine with candy?"

Vending Machine Preferences

	Grade 6	Grade 7	Grade 8
Girl	healthful snack	healthful snack	healthful snack
Boy	candy	candy	healthful snack

34. How many 6th-grade students do you think prefer a machine with healthful snacks?

35. How many students in the whole school do you think prefer a machine with healthful snacks?

36. What is the probability that a student chosen at random from the whole school is an 8th grader who prefers a machine with healthful snacks?

37. What advice would you give Alyssa's principal about Alyssa's data and the two vending machines? Explain.

Notes

38. Alyssa's principal polls all 800 students and finds that 600 prefer a machine with healthful snacks.

    a. What is the probability that a student selected at random prefers a machine with healthful snacks?

    b. What is the probability that a student selected at random is a girl who prefers a machine with healthful snacks?

    c. What is the probability that a student selected at random is a boy who prefers a machine with healthful snacks?

    d. What advice would you give the principal about the data collected and the vending machines?

Extensions

39. Television stations, radio stations, and newspapers often use polls to predict the winners of elections long before the votes are cast. What factors might cause a pre-election poll to be inaccurate?

40. Political parties often write and then conduct their own pre-election polls to find out what voters think about their campaign and their candidates. How might such a poll be biased?

41. a. Polls conducted prior to presidential elections commonly use samples of about 1,000 eligible voters. Suppose there are 207 million eligible voters in the United States. About what percent of eligible voters are in a sample of 1,000?

    b. How do you think this small sample is chosen so that the results will predict the winner with reasonable accuracy? Consider which groups within the total population need to be represented, such as adults 65 years or older.

> ### Did You Know?
>
> **How do pollsters** decide whom to contact? When pollsters take phone polls, they use random sampling techniques to choose voters from the total voting population. Internet polls, in most cases, exclude households without Internet access. Most online polls are also completed by people who choose to participate.

Notes _____

_____

_____

STUDENT PAGE

Mathematical Reflections 2

In this Investigation, you learned about sampling techniques. You also drew conclusions about a population by examining data from random samples. The following questions will help you summarize what you have learned.

Think about these questions. Discuss your ideas with other students and your teacher. Then, write a summary of your findings in your notebook.

1. **Why** are data often collected from a sample rather than from an entire population?

2. **Describe** four plans for selecting a sample from a population. Discuss the advantages and disadvantages of each plan.

3. a. **How** are random samples different from convenience, voluntary-response, and systematic samples?

   b. **Why** is random sampling preferable to the other sampling plans?

   c. **Describe** three plans for selecting a random sample from a given population. **What** are the advantages and disadvantages of each plan?

4. Suppose you select several random samples of size 30 from the same population.

   a. When you compare the samples to each other, **what** similarities and differences would you expect to find among the measures of center and spread?

   b. When you compare the samples to the larger population, **what** similarities and differences would you expect to find among the measures of center and spread?

5. **How** has your idea of the term *sample* changed from what you wrote in Mathematical Reflections, Investigation 1?

Notes

Common Core Mathematical Practices

As you worked on the Problems in this Investigation, you used prior knowledge to make sense of them. You also applied Mathematical Practices to solve the Problems. Think back over your work, the ways you thought about the Problems, and how you used Mathematical Practices.

Nick described his thoughts in the following way:

In Problem 2.4, I was able to use data from all of the samples that my classmates had gathered. Instead of collecting multiple samples myself, we compiled all of our class data in one big chart.

I could use the information from all of the samples to draw conclusions about the means and medians of the larger population's data. The more data I could use, the more confident I was that my conclusions about the whole population were accurate.

••

Common Core Standards for Mathematical Practice
MP7 Look for and make use of structure.

- What other Mathematical Practices can you identify in Nick's reasoning?

- Describe a Mathematical Practice that you and your classmates used to solve a different Problem in this Investigation.

Notes _____

_____

_____

Using Samples to Draw Conclusions

▼ Investigation Overview

Investigation Description

Students apply what they have learned about samples and populations to engaging real-world problems in Investigation 3.

First, they analyze measurements of Native American arrowheads found at six different archeological sites. Scientists know the approximate time periods during which four of the sites were settled. The time periods for two newer sites are unknown. Students explore how data from the known sites may be used to draw conclusions about the newer sites.

In Problem 3.2, students determine whether the differences found between two samples of basketball player heights (one sample from a male professional basketball player population and the other from a female professional basketball player population) are most likely due to naturally occurring variability or meaningful differences between the distributions of heights in the two populations. They base this analysis on the relationship of the samples' means and MADs.

Next, students use a sampling procedure to investigate how many chocolate chips must be added to a batch of cookie dough to ensure that each cookie in the batch will contain at least five chips. They use concepts that they have learned about sampling techniques and probability to solve this real-world quality control problem.

Last, in Problem 3.4, students simulate the **capture–tag–recapture method** that scientists and policymakers often use to sample and draw conclusions about the sizes of wildlife populations. In this Problem, students use containers of beans to represent deer populations.

Investigation Vocabulary

• capture–tag–recapture

• simulate

The following vocabulary term is included in the Glossary as review but is not defined within the exposition of the Student Edition.

• histogram

Mathematics Background

- The Process of Statistical Investigation
- Reviewing Types of Data and Attributes
- Reviewing Measures of Center and Measures of Spread
- Exploring Variation
- Representing Data With Graphical Displays
- Comparing Distributions
- Variability Across Samples: Expected From Natural Variability or Due to Meaningful Differences Between Samples?
- Sampling Plans

Planning Chart

Content	ACE	Pacing	Materials	Resources
Problem 3.1	1–2, 15–17	1½ days	**Labsheet 3.1A** Arrowhead Data **Labsheet 3.1B** Blank Tables for Arrowhead Summary Statistics **Labsheet 3.1C** Arrowhead Summary Statistics **Labsheet 3.1D** Box Plots for Arrowhead Data • Graph Paper calculators	• Data and Graphs
Problem 3.2	3–7, 24–28	1 day	**Labsheet 3.2** Heights of Basketball Players **Labsheet 3ACE:** Exercises 3–6 (accessibility) **Labsheet 3ACE:** Exercise 7 (accessibility) calculators	• Data and Graphs

continued on next page

Planning Charts *continued*

Content	ACE	Pacing	Materials	Resources
Problem 3.3	8–10, 18–23, 30	1½ days	**Labsheet 3.3** Cookie Simulation Tables **Labsheet 3ACE** Exercises 8 and 9 • 12-Section Spinners • Graph Paper spinners (optional) number cubes (optional) coins (optional) calculators	• Probability • Coordinate Grapher
Problem 3.4	11–14, 29	1½ days	**Labsheet 3.4** Capture–Tag–Recapture Table **Labsheet 3ACE:** Exercise 11 (accessibility) • Graph Paper containers of beans (one container per group; about 250 beans per container; each container should have the same number of beans) markers or pens calculators	• Probability
Mathematical Reflections		½ day		
Looking Back		½ day		
Assessment: Self-Assessment		Take-home		• Self-Assessment • Notebook Checklist
Assessment: Unit Test		1 day		• Unit Test

Goals and Standards

Goals

The Process of Statistical Investigation Deepen the understanding of the process of statistical investigation and apply this understanding to samples

- Pose questions, collect data, analyze data, and interpret data to answer questions

Analysis of Samples Understand that data values in a sample vary and that summary statistics of samples, even same-size samples, taken from the same population also vary

- Choose appropriate measures of center (mean, median, or mode) and spread (range, IQR, or MAD) to summarize a sample

- Choose appropriate representations to display distributions of samples

- Compare summary statistics of multiple samples drawn from either the same population or from two different populations and explain how the samples vary

Design and Use of Simulations Understand that simulations can model real-world situations

- Design a model that relies on probability concepts to obtain a desired result

- Use the randomly generated frequencies for events to draw conclusions

Predictions and Conclusions About Populations Understand that summary statistics of a representative sample can be used to gain information about a population

- Describe the benefits and drawbacks to various sampling plans

- Use random-sampling techniques to select representative samples

- Apply concepts from probability to select random samples from populations

- Explain how sample size influences the reliability of sample statistics and resulting conclusions and predictions

- Explain how different sampling plans influence the reliability of sample statistics and resulting conclusions and predictions

- Use statistics from representative samples to draw conclusions about populations

- Use measures of center, measures of spread, and data displays from more than one random sample to compare and draw conclusions about more than one population

- Use mean and MAD, or median and IQR, from random samples to assess whether the differences in the samples are due to natural variability or due to meaningful differences in the underlying populations

Mathematical Reflections

Look for evidence of student understanding of the goals for this Investigation in their responses to the questions in *Mathematical Reflections*. The goals addressed by each question are indicated below.

1. **a.** How can you use statistics to compare samples? How can you use samples to draw conclusions about the populations from which they are selected?

    b. In what ways might the data distribution for a sample be similar to or different from the data distribution for the entire population?

    Goals
    - Compare summary statistics of multiple samples drawn from either the same population or from two different populations and explain how the samples vary

    - Use statistics from representative samples to draw conclusions about populations

    - Use measures of center, measures of spread, and data displays from more than one random sample to compare and draw conclusions about more than one population

2. **a.** How can you use box plots, medians, and IQRs to compare samples? Give an example.

    b. How can you use means and MADs to compare samples? Give an example.

    c. How can you use statistics to decide whether differences between samples are expected due to natural variability or reflect measurable differences in underlying populations?

    Goals
    - Compare summary statistics of multiple samples drawn from either the same population or from two different populations and explain how the samples vary

    - Use statistics from representative samples to draw conclusions about populations

    - Use measures of center, measures of spread, and data displays from more than one random sample to compare and draw conclusions about more than one population

    - Explain how sample size influences the reliability of sample statistics and resulting conclusions and predictions

    - Explain how different sampling plans influence the reliability of sample statistics and resulting conclusions and predictions

    - Use mean and MAD, or median and IQR, from random samples to assess whether the differences in the samples are due to natural variability or due to meaningful differences in the underlying populations

3. **a.** How can you use simulations to generate samples?

    b. How can you use data from a capture–tag–recapture simulation to estimate the actual size of a population?

Goals

- Design a model that relies on probability concepts to obtain a desired result

- Use the randomly generated frequencies for events to draw conclusions

- Use random-sampling techniques to select representative samples

- Apply concepts from probability to select random samples from populations

- Explain how sample size influences the reliability of sample statistics and resulting conclusions and predictions

- Explain how different sampling plans influence the reliability of sample statistics and resulting conclusions and predictions

- Pose questions, collect data, analyze data, and interpret data to answer questions

4. The process of statistical investigation involves posing questions, collecting and analyzing data, and making interpretations to answer the original questions. Choose a Problem from this Investigation. Explain how you used the process of statistical investigation to solve the Problem.

Goals

- Compare summary statistics of multiple samples drawn from either the same population or from two different populations and explain how the samples vary

- Use statistics from representative samples to draw conclusions about populations

- Pose questions, collect data, analyze data, and interpret data to answer questions

Standards

Common Core Content Standards

7.NS.A.1 Apply and extend previous understandings of addition and subtraction to add and subtract rational numbers; represent addition and subtraction on a horizontal or vertical number line diagram. *Problem 2*

7.NS.A.1b Understand $p + q$ as the number located a distance $|q|$ from p, in the positive or negative direction depending on whether q is positive or negative. . . Interpret sums of rational numbers by describing real-world contexts. *Problem 2*

7.RP.A.2 Recognize and represent proportional relationships between quantities. *Problem 4*

7.SP.A.1 Understand that statistics can be used to gain information about a population by examining a sample of the population; generalizations about a population from a sample are valid only if the sample is representative of that population. Understand that random sampling tends to produce representative samples and support valid inferences. *Problems 1, 2, 3, and 4*

7.SP.A.2 Use data from a random sample to draw inferences about a population with an unknown characteristic of interest. Generate multiple samples (or simulated samples) of the same size to gauge the variation in estimates or predictions. *Problems 3 and 4*

7.SP.B.3 Informally assess the degree of visual overlap of two numerical data distributions with similar variabilities, measuring the difference between the centers by expressing it as a multiple of a measure of variability. *Problem 2*

7.SP.B.4 Use measures of center and measures of variability for numerical data from random samples to draw informal comparative inferences about two populations. *Problems 1 and 2*

7.SP.C.5 Understand that the probability of a chance event is a number between 0 and 1 that expresses the likelihood of the event occurring. Larger numbers indicate greater likelihood. A probability near 0 indicates an unlikely event, a probability around 1/2 indicates an event that is neither unlikely nor likely, and a probability near 1 indicates a likely event. *Problem 3*

7.SP.C.7 Develop a probability model and use it to find probabilities of events. Compare probabilities from a model to observed frequencies; if the agreement is not good, explain possible sources of the discrepancy. *Problem 3*

7.SP.C.7a Develop a uniform probability model by assigning equal probability to all outcomes, and use the model to determine probabilities of events. *Problem 3*

Facilitating the Mathematical Practices

Students in *Connected Mathematics* classrooms display evidence of multiple Common Core Standards for Mathematical Practice every day. Here are just a few examples of when you might observe students demonstrating the Standards for Mathematical Practice during this Investigation.

Practice 1: **Make sense of problems and persevere in solving them.**

Students are engaged every day in solving problems and, over time, learn to persevere in solving them. To be effective, the problems embody critical concepts and skills and have the potential to engage students in making sense of mathematics. Students build understanding by reflecting, connecting, and communicating. These student-centered problem situations engage students in articulating the "knowns" in a problem situation and determining a logical solution pathway. The student-student and student-teacher dialogues help students not only to make sense of the problems, but also to persevere in finding appropriate strategies to solve them. The suggested questions in the Teacher Guides provide the metacognitive scaffolding to help students monitor and refine their problem-solving strategies.

Practice 2: **Reason abstractly and quantitatively.**

Throughout Investigation 3, students rely on statistics and data displays to draw conclusions about samples and populations

Practice 4: Model with mathematics.

In Problems 3.3 and 3.4, students use simulations to solve problems. These simulations are models of real-world situations, which can help students to understand what might happen if they encountered that scenario in real life.

Practice 5: Use appropriate tools strategically.

Throughout Investigation 3, students use calculators. Rather than spending too much time calculating statistics, students can use calculators or other tools to find summary statistics more efficiently. Additionally, when students need to generate numbers at random, they use appropriate probability tools (such as spinners, number cubes, and coins in Problem 3.3) to generate these numbers.

Practice 6: Attend to precision.

In Problem 3.2, students compare the means of one distribution to the values within one and two MADs of another distribution. In comparing these values, students need to pay attention to precision. A misstep in precision could potentially lead to incorrect conclusions.

Practice 8: Look for and express regularity in repeated reasoning.

Students complete simulations in Investigation 3, which mimic real-world situations. During these simulations, students repeat trials multiple times and modify their conclusions after each repetition.

Students identify and record their personal experiences with the Standards for Mathematical Practice during the Mathematical Reflections at the end of the Investigation.

▼ Problem Overview

> *Focus Question* How might you analyze samples from known and unknown
> populations to determine whether the unknown population has
> one or more attributes in common with the known population?

Problem Description

In Problem 3.1, students examine tables that list the measurements of Native
American arrowheads found at six different archeological sites. Students read about
archeologists who knew the approximate time periods during which four of the sites
were settled. The time periods for the two newly discovered sites were unknown.

In this Problem, students are asked to use statistics to draw conclusions about
when each of the unknown sites was settled. They compare the measurements of
the arrowheads from the known sites, thus making comparative inferences about
four samples of populations. Then they compare data from the four known sites to
data from the two unknown sites in order to estimate the time period during which
each unknown site was settled.

Problem Implementation

Have students work in groups of two or three on this Problem.

Labsheet 3.1C: Arrowhead Summary Statistics and **Labsheet 3.1D: Box Plots
for Arrowhead Data** show the box plots and statistics for the four known sites.
If you think your students would benefit from the practice of calculating statistics
for these four data sets, wait until the Summarize to display these labsheets. You
can hand out copies of **Labsheet 3.1B: Blank Tables for Arrowhead Summary
Statistics** instead so that students have a place to record their work.

If, however, you think your students will get enough practice in calculating
statistics and constructing box plots just from working with data from the two
unknown sites, you can distribute **Labsheet 3.1C: Arrowhead Summary Statistics**
and **Labsheet 3.1D: Box Plots for Arrowhead Data** at the beginning of the
Problem. They can fill in the missing statistics and box plots for Sites I and II.

Students may find it useful to use **Graph Paper** to help them construct their
box plots

Materials

- **Labsheet 3.1A:** Arrowhead Data
- **Labsheet 3.1B:** Blank Tables for Arrowhead Summary Statistics
- **Labsheet 3.1C:** Arrowhead Summary Statistics
- **Labsheet 3.1D:** Box Plots for Arrowhead Data
- **Graph Paper**

calculators

Using Technology

Students can use the **Data and Graphs tool** to help them calculate the median and IQR of the data for this Problem and for ACE Exercise 2.

Vocabulary

There are no new glossary terms introduced in this Problem.

Mathematics Background

- Reviewing Measures of Center and Measures of Spread
- Exploring Variation
- Representing Data With Graphical Displays
- Comparing Distributions

At a Glance and Lesson Plan

- At a Glance: Problem 3.1 Samples and Populations
- Lesson Plan: Problem 3.1 Samples and Populations

▼ Launch

Launch Video

This animation serves as an illustration to the Problem's introduction. Show this animation to your students before reading the Student Edition to help them understand the context of the Problem. Visit Teacher Place at mathdashboard.com/cmp3 to see the complete video.

Connecting to Prior Knowledge

In Problem 3.1, students extend the understanding they built in Investigation 2. In particular, students explored using data collected with random sampling to make inferences about a population. Investigation 3 extends this by asking students to draw conclusions by comparing more than one population. Students analyze data by calculating measures of center and variability, concepts that students learned about in *Data About Us* and used earlier in *Samples and Populations*.

Suggested Questions

- There are six tables showing data in this Problem. In each table, there are a lot of data listed. How might you make these large sets of data easier to compare? (Calculate statistics from the data. Display the data in a graph.)

- What statistics might be helpful in comparing these data? What displays might be helpful? (Possible answer: You can calculate means or medians to find a typical value for each table column. You can display the data in a frequency chart or a box plot to help you see how the data compare.)

Presenting the Challenge

You might introduce Problem 3.1 by discussing archeology with your students to provide context. You may ask students what they know about the methods people use to gather information about ancient civilizations.

Suggested Questions

- How do people gather information about ancient civilizations? (Possible answer: They search for artifacts from the ancient civilizations, often by digging at archeological sites. Then, they study those artifacts.)

Discuss the archeological digs described in Problem 3.1. Have students examine the tables of data, which list lengths, widths, and neck widths of Native American arrowheads that were unearthed at each of six sites. Give students time to familiarize themselves with the tables.

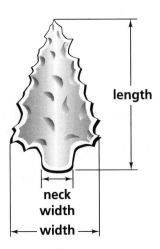

As a class, discuss how your students might approach this Problem.

- What does this Problem ask you to figure out? (Possible answer: Archeologists have found arrowheads at two sites, Site I and Site II. They want to find out when the sites were settled. In other words, they want to determine the time period in which these arrowheads were made.)

- What do you know that can help you with this Problem? (Possible answer: Data from four sites are listed. Archeologists know the time period during which these sites were settled. In other words, the measurements of the arrowheads from these sites are known, and the arrowheads have been dated already. The measurements of each sample are characteristic of the population for a particular known time period.)

- Which of the known sites are the oldest? (Laddie Creek/Dead Indian Creek and Kubold/Buffalo Creek are the oldest sites. They were settled between 4000 B.C. and A.D. 500. The other known sites were settled after A.D. 500.)

- How can you estimate the time period during which each of the two unknown sites was settled? (Calculate statistics for each of the six sets of data. Compare the statistics to look for similarities between the known sites and the unknown sites.)

- Do you have enough data to make good comparisons? (Note that the data sets have different numbers of data values. Laddie Creek/Dead Indian Creek has 18 arrowheads listed and Site I has 15 arrowheads listed. The other sets of data have more data values listed. This should be enough to draw good conclusions. Investigation 2 implied that students need about 30 data values, in general, to make good comparisons. Discuss with your class what they can do when they don't have at least 30 data values to work with. Statisticians often need to decide whether a data set of less than 30 values is sufficient to draw accurate conclusions.)

- What different graphs could you use to display these data and make comparisons? (These data are best displayed in some way that groups the data, rather than displaying the data as individual data values. Students should suggest using histograms or box plots instead of dot plots, line plots, or frequency bar graphs. Problem 3.1 tells students to use box plots.)

Give students a copy of **Labsheet 3.1A: Arrowhead Data** so that they can easily track the data values. Have them work in groups of two or three. You might point out that, in real-world situations, people often work in teams to solve problems. It would be too time-consuming for any one person to analyze these data; the task is much easier when it is shared.

▼ Explore

Providing for Individual Needs

The Problem is stated in an open-ended way. Students can develop their own strategies for determining when each unknown site was settled. For each site, students are asked to both calculate summary statistics and construct box plots to represent the data and make comparisons. They can rely on either the box plots or the statistics to draw conclusions about Sites I and II.

If students are using graphing calculators, they may want to calculate statistics with the calculator and then construct the box plot on paper to summarize their findings. If they are using statistical software, it may be possible to display all six box plots on one scale. Such a display can then be printed and analyzed.

Suggested Questions

- How do you construct box plots to display the data? (Find the minimum value, the lower quartile, the median, the upper quartile, and the maximum value for the data. Use these summary statistics to identify the box and whiskers. If there are any outliers, you can show those on a box plot as well.)

- How can you use summary statistics to determine when the unknown sites were settled? The box plots? (You can compare the summary statistics of the unknown sites with those from the known sites. If the statistics of an unknown site are similar to a known site, you can conclude that those sites were settled during the same time period. You can make the same comparison with a box plot.)

- Are the summary statistics for either of the unknown-site samples identical to the statistics for a known-site sample? If they are not identical, how can you decide what time period the unknown-site samples are from? (Samples vary, so you cannot expect two samples to have exactly the same summary statistics. You need to make a judgment about whether the statistics are close enough to say that an unknown sample comes from a particular time period.)

Note: In Problem 3.2, students use MAD to measure whether or not a difference in summary statistics is due to natural variability or a meaningful difference in populations. In this Problem, students simply make a judgment based on the visual evidence of box plots.

Planning for the Summary

What evidence will you use in the summary to clarify and deepen understanding of the Focus Question?

What will you do if you do not have evidence?

▼ # Summarize

Orchestrating the Discussion

Ask students to discuss their conclusions and justify their answers. The box plots students have drawn will yield two distinct groups of data, one with generally higher medians than the other. These data provide a way to identify the time periods during which the new sites may have been settled.

Ask questions to help students think about how to apply what they have learned.

Suggested Questions

- How confident are you about your predictions?

Have students support their answers with reasoning either from the summary statistics they calculated or the box plots they drew. It is important for students to understand that their answers need to be supported.

- You compared data sets with different sample sizes in this Problem. Are you able to make comparisons among samples of different sizes? (Possible answer: You can use box plots to make these comparisons because they display data in quartiles. 25% of data are reflected in each of the four quartiles. Knowing the actual number of data values is not necessary, as the box plot displays grouped data. Also, while the sample sizes were different, none of the sample sizes was too small. So, the conclusions can be considered reliable.)

- For the known sites, which populations can you group together? What similarities do you see between these sites? (Possible answer: You can group together the Big Goose Creek and Wortham Shelter sites. They were settled during the same time period. After analyzing the data, you can also see a that the measurements gathered from the two sites' arrowheads are similar. You can also group together the Laddie Creek/ Dead Indian Creek and Kobold/Buffalo Creek sites. These two sites were settled during the same time period, and the measurements collected from their arrowheads are similar. Additionally, the measurements from the Big Goose Creek and Wortham Shelter sites are rather different from the measurements from the Laddie Creek/Dead Indian Creek and Kobold/ Buffalo Creek sites. So it is clear that these four populations can be identified as belonging in two distinct groups.)

- What inferences can you make about the two unknown sites by comparing their data? What inferences can you make about the two unknown sites by comparing their data to the data from the known sites? (Possible answer: The two unknown sites most likely come from two different time periods. The summary statistics of their arrowhead measurements are not similar enough to imply that they were settled at the same time. Using the same idea, you can conclude which time period each of these unknown sites was settled during by comparing them to the known sites. Site I and Site II each have similar summary statistics to some of the known sites.)

Finally, you can return to the Focus Question and discuss how this was answered in completing this Problem.

Reflecting on Student Learning

Use the following questions to assess student understanding at the end of the lesson.

- What evidence do I have that students understand the Focus Question?
  - Where did my students get stuck?
  - What strategies did they use?
  - What breakthroughs did my students have today?
- How will I use this to plan for tomorrow? For the next time I teach this lesson?
- Where will I have the opportunity to reinforce these ideas as I continue through this Unit? The next Unit?

ACE Assignment Guide

- **Applications:** 1–2
- **Connections:** 15–17

PROBLEM 3.2

Comparing Heights of Basketball Players
Using Means and MADs

▼ # Problem Overview

> *Focus Question* How can you determine whether differences in sample data are large enough to be meaningful, or just due to naturally occurring variability from one sample to another?

Problem Description

In Problem 3.2, students focus on drawing comparative conclusions about two populations using samples. Students informally assess how much two numerical data distributions (a distribution of heights of male professional basketball players and a distribution of heights of female professional basketball players) with similar variability overlap.

Students examine the mean and the MAD of each distribution to identify whether or not the mean of one distribution is within one or two MADs of the other distribution. Students use this information to decide if the differences between samples are greater than expected from naturally occurring variability.

Problem Implementation

Have students work in pairs on this Problem. You may want to have students complete Question A during the Launch so that they can discuss the means of the two distributions before they continue on with the Explore.

You can give students copies of **Labsheet 3.2: Heights of Basketball Players** so that they can mark up the dot plots as they work.

Materials

- **Labsheet 3.2:** Heights of Basketball Players
- **Labsheet 3ACE:** Exercises 3–6 (accessibility)
- **Labsheet 3ACE:** Exercise 7 (accessibility)
calculators

Using Technology

Your students can use the **Data and Graphs tool** to help them calculate measures of center and spread for ACE Exercises 3–7.

Vocabulary

There are no new glossary terms introduced in this Problem.

Mathematics Background

- Reviewing Measures of Center and Measures of Spread
- Exploring Variation
- Representing Data With Graphical Displays
- Comparing Distributions
- Variability Across Samples: Expected From Natural Variability or Due to Meaningful Differences Between Samples?

At a Glance and Lesson Plan

- At a Glance: Problem 3.2 Samples and Populations
- Lesson Plan: Problem 3.2 Samples and Populations

▼ Launch

Connecting to Prior Knowledge

In Investigation 1, students learned that most of the data values in a distribution are usually located within two MADs from the mean of that distribution. Data values greater than two MADs from the mean (or less than two MADs from the mean) are generally few in number. They are, therefore, seen as unexpected values for the overall distribution.

Suggested Questions

- How might you determine which values are unexpected for a distribution of data? (Find the MAD of the distribution. Identify the values that are within one and two MADs from the mean. Any values that are outside of two MADs from the mean can be considered unexpected values.)

- In this Problem, you will be comparing two distributions of data that have similar variabilities. How can you tell whether two distributions of data have similar variabilities? (Find the MAD or IQR for each distribution. If the distributions have similar MADs or IQRs, they have similar variabilities.)

Presenting the Challenge

Discuss heights of basketball players as a class. The data values are given in centimeters. Make sure your students can visualize the magnitude of these heights. You may want to have students complete Question A at this point so that they can discuss the mean heights of the sample of male professional basketball players and the sample of female professional basketball players.

Suggested Questions

• Look at the two dot plots. What information does each dot plot give? (One dot plot gives the heights of 32 male professional basketball players measured in centimeters. The other gives the heights of 32 female professional basketball players in centimeters.)

• How much taller do you think these basketball players are than the students in our class?

Students need to develop a sense of how tall these players are, especially since they may not be familiar with measurements taken with the metric system. Ask students about the conversion rate from centimeters to inches (2.5 cm ≈ 1 inch). Consider having the students convert the maximum and minimum values of each dot plot. The lowest value on the dot plot is 168 centimeters, which is about 66 inches (or 5 feet 6 inches). You might relate this to your height, so that students can picture how tall the shortest player displayed is.

• Who is taller, the male basketball players or the female basketball players? How do you know?

Students will most likely note that the male players are taller than the female players. Have your students share their reasoning. If students focus on comparing the means, point out that there are portions of the two distributions that overlap.

• When you compare these two samples, can you tell me that, for these samples, the men are taller than the women? Or can you tell me, that for these two populations (professional male and female basketball players), the heights are distributed differently? (Push students to explain why they think they can leap from comparing samples to comparing the underlying populations. They should mention that the sample size makes it likely that the sample statistics are similar to the statistics for the underlying populations.)

• These two distributions have similar variabilities. Because of this, we can compare the means of the distributions rather accurately. The difference between the means is about 16 centimeters (or about 6 inches). Do you think this difference in means is just due to the fact that heights vary from sample to sample? Or do you think that you can say that male basketball players are generally taller than female basketball players? In other words, if you were given two other samples from the male basketball player and the female basketball player populations, might you find there is no difference in heights?

Let students talk about their opinions. Point out that these are samples. The Problem asks them to figure out if these sampled data are enough to prove that the difference in heights is true for the two entire populations of players.

- In this Problem, you need to find a way to show whether the sample means differ this much because of naturally occurring variability from one sample to another, or whether they differ this much because the population of male professional basketball players is measurably taller than the population of female professional basketball players.

Let students know that when they finish the Problem, they should be ready to discuss a strategy for deciding whether differences in samples are due to naturally variability or due to meaningful differences in the populations.

▼ Explore

Providing for Individual Needs

Give students copies of **Labsheet 3.2: Heights of Basketball Players** so that they can mark up the dot plots as they follow the directions in the Problem.

After students finish Question C, you may want to do a mini-summary. This will help your class to realize the connection between comparing the mean of one distribution with the values within one MAD or two MADs in the other distribution. After completing these Questions, students should discuss comparing the two distributions. If the mean of one distribution is placed on the second distribution and it does not fall within two MADs of the second distribution, you can assume that the difference between the two means is more than you could expect from naturally occurring variability. Instead, the difference implies a meaningful difference in the attributes of the populations.

Suggested Questions

- Where does the mean height of the male players fall on the dot plot of the heights of the female players? (to the right of the value that marks two MADs greater than the mean height of the female professional basketball players)

- What does this tell you about the mean male player height in comparison to the female player heights? (The mean male professional basketball player height is an unexpected height for female professional basketball players.)

- Where does the mean height of the female players fall on the dot plot of the heights of the male players? (almost at the value that marks two MADs less than the mean of the male basketball players)

- What does this tell you about the mean female player height in comparison to the male player heights? (The mean female professional basketball player height is within an expected range of values for the male professional basketball players, but at the very lower end.)

Students will likely think that the distribution shown in Question D is of male professional basketball player heights. Encourage them to justify their answer by explaining how they compared the distribution in Question D to each of the distributions discussed in the introduction.

Planning for the Summary

What evidence will you use in the summary to clarify and deepen understanding of the Focus Question?

What will you do if you do not have evidence?

▼ Summarize

Orchestrating the Discussion

During the Summarize, spend time making sure that students justify the reasoning behind their comparisons. First have the students provide answers to Problem 3.2. Then have them explain generally how they can discuss differences in sample data by addressing the Focus Question.

Suggested Questions

- For Question C, you compared the two sample distributions. The means are different. How did you measure this difference? (Each mean is compared to the distribution of values in the other sample. MADs are used to measure the difference. Data values that are 2 or 3 MADs from the mean of a distribution are unexpected for that distribution.)

- You compared samples in Question C, but you also drew conclusions about the heights of the populations of male and female basketball players. Why are you justified in doing this? (The samples are large, random samples, so they are likely to be representative of the underlying populations. When you say the mean of one sample is an unexpected value for the other sample, you are actually saying that the typical height for the population of male basketball players is different from the typical height for the population of female basketball players.)

- For Question D, how did you determine whether the sample data were taken from a male professional basketball player population or a female professional basketball player population? (The distribution in Question D has a mean that is about 2 centimeters less than the male player distribution, but about 14 centimeters greater than the female player distribution.

  The mean of the unknown distribution is also within one MAD of the male player distribution and within two MADs of the unknown distribution. This mean, therefore, is considered expected for either the male basketball player or female basketball player distributions.

While it is an expected mean, however, within either distribution, the distribution in Question D has a mean that is more similar to the male professional basketball player distribution, and within 1 MAD for the male professional basketball player distribution.)

- Do you think that the differences between the male basketball player sample heights and the female basketball player sample heights prove that there are meaningful height differences in those populations? Or, do the differences in the samples simply show naturally occurring variability? (From the data in this Problem, you can conclude that male professional basketball players are noticeably taller than female professional basketball players. The difference between the sample means is too great to be just the result of naturally occurring variability among samples from the same population.)

At the end of this Problem, students should understand that when they analyze two samples whose means seem very different from each other, they can use the MADs of the samples as measures of difference. Students can use these measures to conclude that the samples either represent two populations that share a similar attribute, and the size of the difference is caused by the natural variability among the samples, or they represent two populations whose measures on those attributes are distinctly different.

Reflecting on Student Learning

Use the following questions to assess student understanding at the end of the lesson.

- What evidence do I have that students understand the Focus Question?
  - Where did my students get stuck?
  - What strategies did they use?
  - What breakthroughs did my students have today?
- How will I use this to plan for tomorrow? For the next time I teach this lesson?
- Where will I have the opportunity to reinforce these ideas as I continue through this Unit? The next Unit?

ACE Assignment Guide

- **Applications:** 3–7
- **Connections:** 24–28
- **Labsheet 3ACE: Exercises 3–6** (accessibility) and **Labsheet 3ACE: Exercise 7** (accessibility) are optional. They give examples as to how to provide students with additional support for ACE Exercises.

PROBLEM

3.3

Five Chocolate Chips in Every Cookie

Using Sampling in a Simulation

▼ Problem Overview

> *Focus Question* How can you simulate a real-world problem? How can you analyze the data that you collect from that simulation to draw conclusions?

Problem Description

In Problem 3.3, students apply what they have learned about samples and populations to address a realistic quality-control problem. Your class will determine how many total chocolate chips should be mixed in the dough for a batch of 12 cookies so that each cookie gets at least 5 chips. They will rely on probability concepts to conduct a simulation that resembles the real-world problem.

Each group will conduct a simulation that ends when each "cookie" in their batch of 12 cookies has 5 "chocolate chips." Each group will then have a total number of chips (or *sample measurement*) that they can say results in each cookie having at least 5 chips. The class will use data collected by each group to help them determine how many chocolate chips should be added to the cookie dough to ensure 5 chips in each cookie.

Problem Implementation

Have students work in pairs on this Problem.

Students will need a way to generate random numbers between 1 and 12 to conduct the simulation. Many calculators have the capability to produce numbers at random. Students could also use **12-Section Spinners** or the **Probability** tool. Be sure to let students decide on their own how they will generate random numbers. They should be able to brainstorm methods on their own.

Within the **Probability** tool, students could roll a number cube to produce a number between 1 and 6. Using this method and a coin toss (where students could add 6 for one side of the coin, or leave the number as is for the other side of the coin) would give students an opportunity to generate the numbers 1 through 12. (Students could also use the physical manipulatives of a number cube and a coin.)

Last, students could use cards labeled 1 through 12. This, however, would necessitate a card shuffle after every drawing, which would be rather time-consuming.

Students can record their work on copies of **Labsheet 3.3: Cookie Simulation Tables**. This labsheet contains the tables found in the Student Edition. If your students complete the Going Further in the Explore, they may find it helpful to graph their data on **Graph Paper**.

Materials

- **Labsheet 3.3:** Cookie Simulation Tables
- **Labsheet 3ACE:** Exercises 8 and 9
- **12-Section Spinners**
- **Graph Paper**

spinners (optional)

number cubes (optional)

coins (optional)

calculators

Using Technology

Your students can use the **Probability** tool to generate numbers for their simulation, both in the Problem and in ACE Exercise 30. Students may want to use the **Coordinate Grapher** tool to graph data that they gather in the Going Further of the Explore.

Vocabulary

- simulate

The following vocabulary term is included in the Glossary as review but is not defined within the exposition of the Student Edition.

- histogram

Mathematics Background

- The Process of Statistical Investigation
- Reviewing Types of Data and Attributes
- Sampling Plans

At a Glance and Lesson Plan

- At a Glance: Problem 3.3 Samples and Populations
- Lesson Plan: Problem 3.3 Samples and Populations

▶ Launch

Connecting to Prior Knowledge

Problem 3.3 includes applications of probability in its structure, building upon Investigation 2 and *What Do You Expect?* In this Problem, students consider the number of total chocolate chips that should be mixed in the dough for a batch of 12 cookies so that each cookie gets at least 5 chips.

As groups collect data on the number of total chips their simulation requires to ensure that each cookie gets 5 chips, they begin to link the concepts of probability with the concepts of data analysis.

You may want to review the process of constructing a histogram before students work on their own. They are required to construct one for Question C.

Presenting the Challenge

Read through the introduction of Problem 3.3, which discusses Jeff and Hadiya's cookie business. While Jeff and Hadiya advertise that there are five chocolate chips in each of their cookies, a customer points out that this is not true. As a class, discuss the illustration of a sample batch of cookies in the Student Edition, which shows that the chocolate chips often will not be evenly distributed among 12 cookies.

Suggested Questions

- There are 60 total chips in this batch of cookies. Why does Jeff think that 60 chips should be added to the dough? (Jeff reasoned that if he adds 60 chips to a batch of dough, there will be an average of 5 chips per cookie: $60 \div 5 = 12$ chips. He didn't consider that the chips most likely would not be distributed evenly. An average of 5 chips per cookie means that some cookies may have fewer than 5 chips and some may have more than 5 chips. Some may have exactly 5 chips, but it is not likely that all will.)

- Does each cookie have five chips? (no)

- What does this Problem ask you to figure out? (How many chips Jeff and Hadiya must add to a batch of dough to be fairly certain that every cookie will contain at least five chips.)

Before discussing Hadiya's Simulation in the Student Edition, ask students to think about ways that they might explore this Problem. Students may or may not suggest that they need to simulate this situation.

After your class discusses ways to explore the Problem, read Hadiya's simulation. Tell your students that they will be combining the results of many simulations, each group's simulation, in order to predict the typical number of chips that are needed.

Remind your students about their exploration in Investigation 2. In Investigation 2, students generated several samples for a specific problem and then looked at the distribution of one or more sample measurements. Here, the sample measurement is the total number of chips to be added to a batch of dough for 12 cookies.

- Why is it important that you share your results with your classmates? Why is it important that you use your classmates' results to come up with a solution to the problem? (If you only use the single simulation that you complete, you will not have enough information to make a good estimate of how many total chocolate chips are needed. One simulation may use less chocolate chips than another. By collecting data from classmates, you get a lot of samples of information.)

Make sure the students understand the overall plan for how to simulate distributing chocolate chips among 12 cookies in a batch.

▼ Explore

Providing for Individual Needs

Students need to track the process of their simulations and data analysis as they complete the Problem. The data collection and analysis shifts throughout the Problem.

In Question A, students work on collecting individual data as they assign cookie numbers to each "chip" that they place in the batch of dough.

Suggested Questions

- How might you generate integers from 1 to 12 at random? (Possible answer: cards labeled with numbers 1–12 (which would need to be reshuffled after each trial); a combination of a number cube and a coin toss; a spinner with 12 sections)

The frequency table below shows the results of two actual simulations. In the first, it took 135 randomly selected numbers from 1 to 12 for each cookie to get at least 5 chips (Cookie 7 is the last cookie to receive a chip, so all have at least 5 chips). In the second, it took 102 randomly selected numbers for each cookie to get at least 5 chips per cookie (Cookie 11 is the last cookie to receive a chip, so all have at least 5 chips).

Chocolate Chip Cookie Simulations

Simulation 1			Simulation 2		
Cookie Number	Chip Tally	Number of Chips	Cookie Number	Chip Tally	Number of Chips
1	‖‖‖ ‖‖‖ ‖	11	1	‖‖‖ ‖‖‖‖	9
2	‖‖‖ ‖‖‖ ‖‖	12	2	‖‖‖ ‖‖‖ ‖‖‖‖	14
3	‖‖‖ ‖‖‖ ‖‖‖‖	14	3	‖‖‖ ‖‖‖	8
4	‖‖‖ ‖‖‖ ‖	11	4	‖‖‖ ‖‖	7
5	‖‖‖ ‖‖‖ ‖‖‖	13	5	‖‖‖ ‖‖‖ ‖‖	12
6	‖‖‖ ‖‖‖	10	6	‖‖‖	5
7	‖‖‖	5	7	‖‖‖ ‖‖‖	10
8	‖‖‖ ‖‖‖ ‖‖‖	15	8	‖‖‖	5
9	‖‖‖ ‖‖‖ ‖‖‖	13	9	‖‖‖ ‖	6
10	‖‖‖ ‖‖‖	8	10	‖‖‖ ‖	6
11	‖‖‖ ‖‖‖	8	11	‖‖‖	5
12	‖‖‖ ‖‖‖ ‖‖‖	15	12	‖‖‖ ‖‖‖ ‖‖‖	15

Notice that there is an overall average of approximately 10 chips per cookie, with the data varying from 5 to 15 chips per cookie in both cases.

- On average, how many chips are there per cookie? What do you think of Jeff's earlier reasoning based on your results?

Students can compare their answers to Jeff's earlier reasoning that 60 chips gives an average of 5 chips per cookie. As shown in the sample simulations above, Jeff's reasoning was not correct.

As students complete their simulations, they can record their results for the class in the same location. This should be large enough so it is visible to all students; they will use these results for Question C to make histograms and box plots.

In Questions B, C, and D, the data students work with are the total number of chips that should be added to a batch of dough. For these questions, the types of data being collected are different from those collected for Question A.

Students represent the data collected during Question C with both a histogram and a box plot. Consider telling the students to draw these on the same scale. They do not make comparative inferences about multiple populations or samples in this case. Rather, they use the graphs and measures of center to decide upon some total number of chips that should be added to a batch of dough.

- What does the box plot tell you about batches of cookies mixed with the median number of chips? What does the histogram tell you about batches of cookies mixed with the maximum number of chips? (Possible answer: If you use the median number of chips, it is likely that about half the batches of cookies will have enough chips in each cookie, and about half the batches of cookies will not have enough chips in each cookie. You should choose a number greater than the median value to put in each batch. If you choose the median number, then there is a good chance that not all cookies will have 5 chips. If you choose Quartile 3 as the number of chips to put in each batch, then about 25% of the batches will not have enough chips. If you look at the histogram, you can find a number greater than most of the data values. This ensures that your cookies will most likely all have 5 chips. You probably shouldn't choose the greatest value. Even though you will be almost guaranteed that every cookie will have enough chips, you might waste chocolate chips.)

Last, in Question E, the Problem shifts again. Students complete simulations with a set number of chips (decided upon by the class) to see whether or not each cookie in a batch of 12 contains 5 chips. Here, they collect categorical data of either "yes" or "no." This allows students to see whether their recommendation for the total number of chips to be added to a batch of 12 cookies will actually result in all cookies having at least 5 chocolate chips.

At any stage of the Problem (during Question A or E), students who are finished early can conduct an additional simulation. Having more sets of results by completing the simulations several times can only be beneficial. It is essential that students have enough samples to support their conclusions with confidence.

Suggested Questions

- How many chips should Jeff and Hadiya add to a batch of dough for four dozen cookies to be confident that each cookie will contain five chips?

Students will often suggest scaling up the number that they recommended for one dozen cookies by a factor of four. You may want to suggest that students test this reasoning. One way to test this is to conduct a number of trials for batches of various sizes.

- How many chips do you need, on average, to have at least five chips per cookie in a batch of two cookies? A batch of four cookies? A batch of eight cookies? A batch of sixteen cookies?

Students can test each batch size starting with two cookies. They should conduct multiple simulations for each batch size. Students can then graph the data they collect by relating the number of cookies in a batch to the median number of chips required per batch.

One class found the following data.

Chocolate Chip Cookie Trials

Batch Size	Results of 6 Trials (total number of chips)	Median
2 cookies	11, 12, 12, 13, 18, 18	12.5
3 cookies	17, 18, 19, 19, 25, 22	19
4 cookies	21, 24, 27, 29, 32, 34	28
5 cookies	31, 33, 34, 36, 47, 55	35
6 cookies	41, 49, 51, 55, 59, 78	53
7 cookies	46, 52, 57, 60, 68, 69	58.5
8 cookies	69, 72, 75, 82, 90, 91	78.5
9 cookies	64, 69, 70, 72, 82, 97	71
10 cookies	83, 85, 100, 103, 110, 120	101.5
11 cookies	76, 84, 94, 97, 111, 113	95.5
12 cookies	From Problem 3.2	

The coordinate graph of these data is shown below. More data points would make the linear pattern in the data more evident.

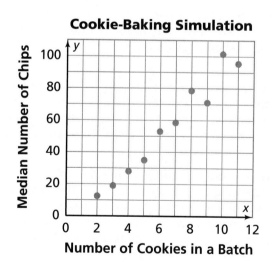

Cookie-Baking Simulation

Planning for the Summary

What evidence will you use in the summary to clarify and deepen understanding of the Focus Question?

What will you do if you do not have evidence?

▼ Summarize

Orchestrating the Discussion

Throughout the Problem, students should be sharing their data and responses so that all students can benefit from multiple samples of data. Ensure that students share their answers for Questions D and E in the Summarize.

For Question D, students should recognize that, to address this particular problem, finding the mean or the median is not sufficient. Students need to find the least number of chips needed in order to virtually guarantee five chips in each cookie.

Suggested Questions

- How did you decide on the number of chips to put in a batch? (Answers will vary greatly. Possible answer: I looked at the upper quartile value of the box plot and added 10 chips to that amount. I figured the value was greater than those produced by 75% of the simulations; then most batches with that many chips would guarantee 5 chips per cookie.)

- Did you use the simulation that results in the greatest number of chips, or did you choose a lesser number? Is adding this many chips to a batch of a dozen cookies practical? Why? (Answers will vary. Possible answer: I chose less than the greatest number of chips. As Question D states, if I chose the greatest number of chips, then I'd be wasting chips for most batches.)

- Were you surprised by the results of the simulations? (Answers will vary.)

- What is the average number of chips per cookie that would result from your recommendation? (Answers will vary based on the recommended number of chips. Students should divide their recommended number of chips by 12.)

- In each simulation, the cookie with the fewest chips contained 5 chips. How many chips did the cookie(s) with the most chips contain? Is this many chips in a cookie realistic? (Answers will vary. In the simulations shown in the Explore, some cookies had 15 chips. This number could be considered excessive for a normal-sized cookie.)

- What kinds of displays can you construct with these data? Which displays are most useful for addressing the Problem? Explain. (Box plots are helpful displays for this Problem. You can locate summary statistics to help you decide upon a recommendation. Histograms are also helpful. You can find a recommended number of chips by finding a number greater than that given in most simulations. Frequency charts and frequency bar graphs can be made, but they do not give a good overview of the data.)

Finally, you can return to the Focus Question and discuss how it was answered in completing this Problem. You can also ask students to extend their answer to the Focus Question beyond the context of Problem 3.3.

Reflecting on Student Learning

Use the following questions to assess student understanding at the end of the lesson.

- What evidence do I have that students understand the Focus Question?
  - Where did my students get stuck?
  - What strategies did they use?
  - What breakthroughs did my students have today?
- How will I use this to plan for tomorrow? For the next time I teach this lesson?
- Where will I have the opportunity to reinforce these ideas as I continue through this Unit? The next Unit?

ACE Assignment Guide

- **Applications:** 8–10
- **Connections:** 18–23
- **Extensions:** 30

You may want to give your students copies of **Labsheet 3ACE: Exercises 8 and 9** so that they can mark up the tables from the Student Edition.

Estimating a Deer Population
Using Samples to Estimate the Size of a Population

▼ Problem Overview

Focus Question How can you estimate the size of a large population?

Problem Description

Problem 3.4 provides students with an opportunity to further develop their understanding of sampling. It is relatively open-ended so that students can freely explore the Problem situation on their own, using the skills and knowledge that they have built throughout the Unit. If you wish, you can present this Problem as a project and evaluate it with the sample rubric in the Launch section.

Problem Implementation

Have students work in groups of three on this Problem.

Students can record their data on **Labsheet 3.4: Capture–Tag–Recapture Table**. You may want to pass out copies of **Graph Paper** so that they can more easily construct displays.

Note: In real-world investigations of this sort, scientists do not pre-determine sample sizes. You may want to discuss this with your students. The reason for pre-determining sample sizes in Problem 3.4 is to allow students to compare their data with their classmates' data.

Materials

- **Labsheet 3.4:** Capture–Tag–Recapture Table
- **Labsheet 3ACE:** Exercise 11 (accessibility)
- **Graph Paper**
- **Self-Assessment**
- **Notebook Checklist**
- **Unit Test**

containers of beans (one container per group; about 250 beans per container)

markers or pens

calculators

Note: Each group should have the same number of beans in their containers. Also, because students mark 100 beans in the capture–tag phase, the containers each need to have at least 250 beans. Otherwise, it would be fairly easy to estimate the number of beans in the container without doing the simulation.

Using Technology

Students can use the **Probability** tool to help them carry out their simulations in ACE Exercise 29.

Vocabulary

- capture–tag–recapture

Mathematics Background

- The Process of Statistical Investigation
- Sampling Plans

At a Glance and Lesson Plan

- At a Glance: Problem 3.4 Samples and Populations
- Lesson Plan: Problem 3.4 Samples and Populations

▼ Launch

Launch Video

In this animation, two birds discuss why animals may be tagged. This animation can serve as an introduction to the Problem so that your students understand the benefits of this tagging process. You can show this animation to your students before reading through the introduction in the Student Edition. Visit Teacher Place at mathdashboard.com/cmp3 to see the complete video.

Connecting to Prior Knowledge

This Problem is intended to help students make use of all their work in the three Investigations of this Unit. It also builds further connections with the importance of probability in sampling work, as well as refreshes proportional reasoning.

In Problem 3.4, students conduct a simulation. They mark 100 beans from a container of beans. They take a sample of the total beans in a container and count the number of marked beans. They use the information gathered from the sample to estimate the number of beans in the entire container. Through gathering information from different sample sizes, students give a final estimate of how many beans are in the entire container.

Students make use of proportional reasoning when estimating. When students take a sample, they know three values: the number of marked beans in the sample, the total number of marked beans in the population, and the number of total beans in the sample. They can estimate the number of total beans in the population by solving for the missing value in a proportion.

Suggested Questions

- How do you set up and solve a proportion? (You set up a proportion by setting two equivalent ratios equal to one another. The ratios can be part-to-part or part-to-whole. You can find the missing value in a proportion by using scaling strategies.)

Presenting the Challenge

Students conduct an experiment to simulate estimating the deer population in a specific region. If you know of a more appropriate local example, you may want to substitute it.

Introduce the topic by asking students what they know about estimating the size of populations that can't be easily counted.

Suggested Questions

- How do wildlife officials determine how many eagles there are in the United States? (Answers will vary. As students suggest possible methods, have other students in the class respond to the feasibility of these methods.)

- How do environmentalists decide whether an animal or plant should be on the endangered list? (Possible answer: They occasionally measure the population size of the plant or animal. If the population size is too small or is decreasing at too great of a rate, the plant or animal will be added to the endangered list.)

Review the steps of the bean experiment. You may want to model the experiment with a small container of beans:

- Take a sample of beans and mark them. Remember how many you marked.

- Return the marked beans to the container. Ask students what they should do now.

- Mix the marked and unmarked beans together. Ask your students how they might use the marked beans to estimate the total number of beans in the container.

- Take a new sample and count the marked and unmarked beans. Ask students how they can use the gathered information.

Students need to recognize that they now know the number of marked beans in the whole population, the number of marked beans in the sample, and the sample size.

- How can you use ratios to estimate the number of beans in the whole population? (You now know three of the four values that can be used to make a proportion: the number of marked beans in the whole population, the number of marked beans in the sample, and the sample size. You can solve for the missing value by scaling up the ratios.)

Have your students discuss how the experiment models the capture–tag–recapture method that people use in the real world.

- What difficulties might scientists or wildlife officials have when they use the capture–tag–recapture method? (The officials need to be sure to take a large enough sample of data, they need to ensure that they give the animals enough time to thoroughly mix with the entire population again, and they need to be sure to keep track of what regions they take samples from.)

Alternative Presentation

As mentioned in the Problem Description, this Problem can be used as a Unit Project. If you choose to assign this as a project, you can use the rubric below to grade the written reports.

This rubric employs a point scale from 0 to 4, with 4+ for work that goes beyond what has been asked for in some unique way. Use the rubric as presented here, or modify it to fit your needs and your district's requirements for evaluating and reporting students' work and understanding.

4+ Exemplary Response

- Complete, with clear, coherent work and explanations
- Shows understanding of the mathematical concepts and procedures
- Satisfies all essential conditions of the Problem and goes beyond what is asked for in some unique way

4 Complete Response

- Complete, with clear, coherent work and explanations
- Shows understanding of the mathematical concepts and procedures
- Satisfies all essential conditions of the Problem

3 Reasonably Complete Response

- Reasonably complete; may lack detail or clarity in work or explanations
- Shows understanding of most of the mathematical concepts and procedures
- Satisfies most of the essential conditions of the Problem

2 Partial Response

- Incomplete; work or explanations are unclear or lack detail
- Shows some understanding of the mathematical concepts and procedures
- Satisfies some of the essential conditions of the Problem

1 Inadequate Response

- Incomplete; work or written explanations are insufficient or not understandable
- Shows little understanding of the mathematical concepts and procedures
- Fails to address the essential conditions of the Problem

0 No Attempt

- Irrelevant response
- Does not address the conditions of the Problem

▼ Explore

Providing for Individual Needs

Have the students work in pairs to conduct their experiments. They can use their data to estimate the size of the "deer" population.

The basic proportion to be solved in making an estimate of the total number of beans has a few variations:

$$\frac{\text{marked beans in container}}{\text{total beans in container}} = \frac{\text{marked beans in sample}}{\text{total beans in sample}}$$

$$\frac{\text{total beans in container}}{\text{marked beans in container}} = \frac{\text{total beans in sample}}{\text{marked beans in sample}}$$

$$\frac{\text{marked beans in sample}}{\text{marked beans in container}} = \frac{\text{total beans in sample}}{\text{total beans in container}}$$

$$\frac{\text{marked beans in container}}{\text{marked beans in sample}} = \frac{\text{total beans in container}}{\text{total beans in sample}}$$

Suggested Questions

The benefit of having students work in groups is that they can discuss with one another the best ways to present their data.

- How do the different sample sizes change your estimates? (As the sample sizes get bigger, the estimates get closer and closer together.)

- Look at the line plots you made for Question D. Which line plots have the most variability? Which line plots have the least variability? (Students should see that the line plots cluster more around the mean/median for the greater sample sizes than for the lesser sample sizes. There is less variability in the larger sample sizes.)

- How do the line plots in Question D help you make a final estimate? (Students will be more likely to choose an average number (the mean or the median) from one of the line plots of the larger sample sizes for their final estimate. This shows that the summary statistics are getting more and more accurate as the sample sizes increase.)

Planning for the Summary

What evidence will you use in the summary to clarify and deepen understanding of the Focus Question?

What will you do if you do not have evidence?

▼ Summarize

Orchestrating the Discussion

As each team completes the Problem, ask them to prepare a summary of how they made a final estimate in Question C. Ask students how that estimate related to the estimate they made in Question D, part (2). Have the groups present these summaries and take questions from the class before you move on to the discussion questions below.

Suggested Questions

- Which of the line plots for Question D do you find most helpful in making an estimate? Why? (The line plot for the sample size of 150 beans; since this is the greatest sample size, the data are most likely the most accurate. Also, since all of the values cluster more around the measures of center, it is easy to choose the mean or the median of this line plot since they seem to be most representative of the greater population.)

- Did any group select a sample that gave an estimate that was very different from the final estimate you made in Question D, part (2)? Why do you think this estimate was so misleading? (Students may have made an error in solving the proportion, but it is more likely that the group chose and correctly used a small, misleading sample, which led to an inaccurate estimate.)

- Is it possible that a large sample can lead to an inaccurate estimate of the population? (On the line plot for the 150-bean samples in Question D, part (2), there may be a population estimate that lies far from the others. This is a good time to remind students that random samples, even large random samples, do vary from each other. They may not be representative of the underlying population. Most large random samples do, however, give accurate estimates of the population.)

• How else could you display your data if you were to give a report on your findings from Questions A and C? (Possible displays:

Capture–Tag–Recapture Sampling Data

Sample Size	Marked Beans	Unmarked Beans	Estimate of Total Number of Beans
25	8	17	313
50	20	30	250
75	29	46	259
100	42	58	238
125	36	89	347
150	58	92	259

Marked Beans in a Sample

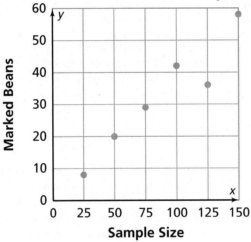

Estimated Population of Beans

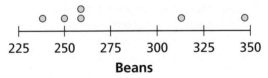

Estimated Population Beans

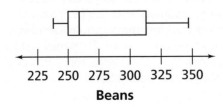

Finally, you can return to the Focus Question and discuss how this was answered in completing this Problem.

Reflecting on Student Learning

Use the following questions to assess student understanding at the end of the lesson.

- What evidence do I have that students understand the Focus Question?
  - Where did my students get stuck?
  - What strategies did they use?
  - What breakthroughs did my students have today?
- How will I use this to plan for tomorrow? For the next time I teach this lesson?
- Where will I have the opportunity to reinforce these ideas as I continue through this Unit? The next Unit?

ACE Assignment Guide

- **Applications:** 11–14
- **Extensions:** 29
- **Labsheet 3ACE: Exercise 11** (accessibility) is optional. It is an example of a way to provide students with additional support for an ACE Exercise.

Mathematical Reflections

Possible Answers to Mathematical Reflections

1. **a.** You can look at the measures of center (mean, median, and mode) and the measures of variability (range, IQR, and MAD) to compare samples from the same or different populations. If the measures of center and measures of variability are similar, you can conclude that the populations are similar in some way (they have a common attribute). If these statistics differ greatly, you may conclude that the samples come from populations with meaningful differences. The greater the difference, the more likely the difference is not just a result of natural variability from sample to sample.

   b. The summary measures of a sample are likely to be similar to the summary measures of the population from which it is drawn. This is more likely to be true, however, for large samples. For smaller samples, the summary statistics may be less similar to the population's summary statistics.

2. **a.** You can use box plots, medians, and IQRs to compare samples. Looking at the medians and summary statistics, you can compare the attributes of the samples. For example, in looking at the medians, box plots, and IQRs of arrowhead data in Problem 3.1, it is clear that Native Americans settled between 4000 B.C. and A.D. 500 made longer than arrowheads than Native Americans settled between A.D. 500 and A.D. 1600. This is because the box plots for the Native Americans settled between 4000 B.C. and A.D. 500 were located more to the right than the box plots for the Native Americans settled between A.D. 500 and A.D. 1600.

b. You can use means and MADs to compare two samples. When you compare means of two samples, you can see how the samples differ. For example, we used the means and MADs of samples to determine that male professional basketball players are generally taller than female professional basketball players. The mean of the male basketball player heights was quite a bit greater than the mean of the female basketball player heights. What's more is that the mean of the male basketball player heights was an unexpected value for the female basketball player distribution and vice versa (or close to unexpected). This means there is a meaningful difference between the heights of male professional basketball players and female professional basketball players.

c. As mentioned in part (b), you can use MADs to determine whether differences in samples are due to natural variability or due to meaningful differences in underlying populations. If a distribution's mean does not fall within 2 MADs of another distribution's mean, then the two distributions probably come from populations that have meaningful differences in the measured attribute.

3. a. You can simulate choosing data values at random by using probability concepts. Choosing data values in this way produces a representative, randomly selected sample. The simulation can involve using equally likely outcomes to determine which data values are part of the sample. Materials such as spinners or number cubes can help to generate these numbers.

b. You can use a capture–tag–recapture method to estimate the size of a population by initially tagging a sample of a population. Allow that sample to reintegrate, then take samples of different sizes at different points in time. For each sample, look at the number tagged out of the total number in a sample. Make an estimate based on that sample using proportions. Every time you take a new sample, you can refine your estimate of the population size.

4. Answers will vary based on the Problems the students choose. Make sure that students explain how the data were collected (either given in the Problem or collected as a class), which measures of center they chose to report (and why they reported those measures), and how they were able to draw conclusions to solve the Problem.

Possible Answers to Mathematical Practices Reflections

Students may have demonstrated all of the eight Common Core Standards for Mathematical Practice during this Investigation. During the class discussion, have students provide additional Practices that the Problem cited involved and identify the use of other Mathematical Practices in the Investigation.

One student observation is provided in the Student Edition. Here is another sample student response.

> In Problem 3.2, our group was trying to find the MAD of the heights of the sample of male professional basketball players. First we found the mean. Then, as we tried to find the MAD, we realized that it was taking forever! We decided that we should use a MAD calculator to help us find the MAD more quickly. We already know how to find the MAD, so we aren't missing out on any information. We're just helping ourselves to solve the Problem more quickly.
>
> **MP5: Use appropriate tools strategically.**

Investigation 3

Using Samples to Draw Conclusions

There are many different possible samples in any population. You can use a random sampling plan to help you choose your sample fairly. In general, large random samples are more representative than small random samples or samples chosen with other sampling methods.

3.1 Solving an Archeological Mystery
Comparing Samples Using Box Plots

Archeologists study past civilizations by excavating ancient settlements. They examine the artifacts of the people who lived there.

Common Core State Standards

7.SP.A.1 Understand that statistics can be used to gain information about a population by examining a sample of the population; generalizations about a population from a sample are valid only if the sample is representative of that population. Understand that random sampling tends to produce representative samples and support valid inferences.

7.SP.B.3 Informally assess the degree of visual overlap of two numerical data distributions with similar variabilities, measuring the difference between the centers by expressing it as a multiple of a measure of variability.

Also 7.RP.A.2, 7.NS.A.1, 7.NS.A.1b, 7.SP.A.2, 7.SP.B.4, 7.SP.C.5, and 7.SP.C.7b

56   Samples and Populations

Notes _____

_____

_____

On digs in southeastern Montana and north-central Wyoming, archeologists discovered the remains of two Native American settlements. They found a number of arrowheads at each site. The archeologists hoped to use the arrowheads to estimate the time period in which each site was inhabited.

The tables below give the lengths, widths, and neck widths of the arrowheads the archeologists found. The sets of data are samples from different populations of arrowheads from two different time periods.

Site I: 15 Arrowheads

Length (mm)	Width (mm)	Neck Width (mm)
24	19	8
27	19	10
29	19	11
29	22	12
31	16	12
31	32	16
37	23	11
38	22	12
38	26	14
40	25	16
45	22	11
45	28	15
55	22	13
62	26	14
63	29	18

SOURCE: *Plains Anthropologist*

Site II: 37 Arrowheads

Length (mm)	Width (mm)	Neck Width (mm)	Length (mm)	Width (mm)	Neck Width (mm)
13	10	6	24	13	8
15	11	7	24	13	8
16	12	8	24	14	10
16	13	7	24	15	9
17	15	9	24	15	8
18	12	10	25	13	7
19	12	8	25	13	7
19	13	9	25	15	10
20	12	7	25	24	7
20	12	9	26	14	10
21	11	7	26	14	11
22	13	9	26	15	11
22	13	9	27	14	8
22	13	8	28	11	6
22	14	10	28	13	9
23	14	9	32	12	8
23	15	9	42	16	11
24	11	8	43	14	9
24	12	7			

Investigation 3 **Using Samples to Draw Conclusions** 57

Notes _____

_____

_____

To help them with their work, the archeologists also used samples of arrowhead data from four other settlement sites. The data from those sites are on this page and on the next page.

The archeologists knew that the Big Goose Creek and Wortham Shelter sites were settled between A.D. 500 and A.D. 1600.

Big Goose Creek: 52 Arrowheads

Length (mm)	Width (mm)	Neck Width (mm)	Length (mm)	Width (mm)	Neck Width (mm)
16	13	9	26	12	12
16	14	10	26	14	9
17	13	8	26	16	10
17	13	10	27	13	9
18	12	7	27	13	9
18	12	8	27	14	9
18	13	7	27	14	9
18	15	11	27	17	13
19	11	8	28	10	5
20	11	6	28	13	7
20	12	8	28	13	8
21	11	7	28	15	9
21	12	7	29	15	8
21	12	9	30	11	7
22	12	9	30	13	8
22	13	8	30	14	8
22	13	10	30	14	8
23	13	8	30	14	9
23	13	9	30	15	11
23	14	9	31	12	8
24	14	9	33	13	7
24	14	11	33	15	9
25	13	7	34	15	9
25	13	8	35	14	10
25	14	8	39	18	12
26	11	8	40	14	8

SOURCE: *Plains Anthropologist*

Wortham Shelter: 45 Arrowheads

Length (mm)	Width (mm)	Neck Width (mm)
18	11	8
19	12	9
19	14	10
19	14	10
19	16	14
20	13	8
20	14	10
20	15	11
22	12	9
22	14	8
23	13	11
23	14	11
23	15	11
24	12	9
24	13	10
25	14	8
25	14	10
25	15	10
25	15	10
25	15	12
26	13	9
26	13	10
26	15	12
27	14	8
27	14	10
27	15	11
28	13	11
28	14	10
28	16	12
29	13	10
29	14	9
29	14	9
29	17	12
30	14	11
30	16	9
30	17	11
31	13	10
31	14	10
31	14	11
31	16	12
31	17	12
32	14	7
32	15	10
35	18	14
42	18	7

Notes _____

_____

_____

The archeologists knew that the Laddie Creek/Dead Indian Creek and Kobold/Buffalo Creek sites were settled between 4000 B.C. and A.D. 500.

- How could you use the data to estimate the length and width of a typical arrowhead from each time period?
- How could you use the data to determine the settlement periods for the unknown sites?

Laddie Creek/ Dead Indian Creek: 18 Arrowheads

Length (mm)	Width (mm)	Neck Width (mm)
25	18	13
27	20	13
27	20	14
29	14	11
29	20	13
30	23	13
31	18	11
32	16	10
32	19	10
35	20	15
37	17	13
38	17	14
39	18	15
40	18	11
41	15	11
42	22	12
44	18	13
52	21	16

Kobold/Buffalo Creek: 52 Arrowheads

Length (mm)	Width (mm)	Neck Width (mm)	Length (mm)	Width (mm)	Neck Width (mm)
25	18	15	45	22	13
30	17	12	46	17	13
30	19	15	46	20	14
31	16	13	46	23	14
31	17	12	47	19	13
32	20	13	47	20	12
32	22	17	47	22	13
32	23	18	49	20	14
35	19	11	50	21	13
35	22	14	50	23	15
37	18	12	50	23	16
37	21	11	51	18	10
38	18	9	52	17	12
38	24	15	52	22	15
39	21	14	52	24	16
40	19	15	54	24	13
40	20	12	56	19	12
40	20	13	56	21	15
40	21	12	56	25	13
41	21	13	57	21	15
42	22	14	61	19	12
42	22	15	64	21	13
44	20	11	66	20	15
44	20	12	67	21	13
44	25	14	71	24	13
45	20	13	78	26	12

Investigation 3 **Using Samples to Draw Conclusions** 59

Problem 3.1

The archeologists thought that Native Americans inhabiting the same area of the country during the same time period would have similar tools.

A **1.** For each known site and each unknown site, find the five-number summary of the arrowhead-length data. Then draw a box-and-whisker plot of each distribution.

2. Use your answers to part (1). Compare the lengths of the arrowheads found at the unknown sites with the lengths of the arrowheads found at the known sites.

a. During which time period (4000 B.C.–A.D. 500 or A.D. 500–A.D. 1600) do you think Site I was settled? Explain how your statistics and box plots support your answers.

b. During which time period do you think Site II was settled? Explain how your statistics and box plots support your answers.

B **1.** For each known site and each unknown site, find the five-number summary of the arrowhead-width data. Then draw a box plot of each distribution.

2. Do the box plots displaying data about arrowhead widths support your answers to Question A, part (2)? Explain.

C Suppose the archeologists had collected only a few arrowheads from each unknown site. Might they have reached a different conclusion? Explain.

A C E Homework starts on page 69.

Notes

3.2 Comparing Heights of Basketball Players

Using Means and MADs

Variability occurs naturally in all samples of a population. Distributions of two different samples will not be identical. When you compare two samples, you need to decide whether the samples differ more than what you would expect from natural variability.

The dot plots below show the heights of a random sample of 32 male professional basketball players and the heights of a random sample of 32 female professional basketball players.

Heights of Male Professional Basketball Players

Mean: 199.9063
MAD: 8.7871

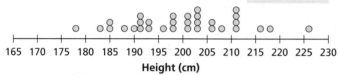

Height (cm)

Heights of Female Professional Basketball Players

Mean: 183.8125
MAD: 7.0625

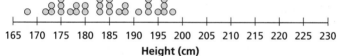

Height (cm)

- Do these samples give enough evidence to conclude that the population of male professional basketball players is taller than the population of female professional basketball players? Or is the difference you see in these samples just due to natural variation?

Notes _____

In Investigation 1, you looked at how the mean and MAD are related. You found that, in many distributions, most of the data are located within two MADs of the mean.

Problem 3.2

Use the dot plots of professional basketball players' heights on the previous page.

A Compare the means of the two sets of data. Compare the variabilities of the two sets of data.

B
1. On a copy of each dot plot, mark the locations of two MADs less than the mean and two MADs greater than the mean.

2. For each distribution, what percent of the data set is located within two MADs of the mean?

3. For each dot plot, mark the locations of three MADs less than the mean and three MADs greater than the mean. For each distribution, what percent of the data set is located within three MADs of the mean?

C
1. Mark the mean height of the men on the dot plot of the heights of the women.

   a. Use the MAD of the heights of the women as a unit of measure. Within how many MADs of the mean height of the women is the mean height of the men?

   b. Is the mean height of the men an unexpected height for a female professional basketball player? Explain.

2. Mark the mean height of the women on the dot plot of the heights of the men.

   a. Use the MAD of the heights of the men as a unit of measure. Within how many MADs of the mean height of the men is the mean height of the women?

   b. Is the mean height of the women an unexpected height for a male professional basketball player? Explain your reasoning.

3. Do these sample distributions provide enough evidence to draw conclusions about the heights of the populations from which the samples were drawn? Explain.

Notes _____

_____

_____

Problem **3.2** *continued*

D The dot plot below shows a distribution of heights for a sample of professional basketball players. Do you think this distribution shows a random sample of men or a random sample of women? Explain.

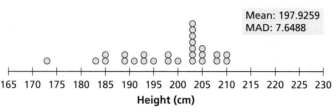

Heights of Mystery Players

Mean: 197.9259
MAD: 7.6488

Height (cm)

A C E Homework starts on page 69.

3.3 Five Chocolate Chips in Every Cookie
Using Sampling in a Simulation

Jeff and Hadiya work at the Custom Cookie Counter. Their advertising slogan is "Five giant chips in every cookie!"

One day, a customer complains that her cookie only has three chocolate chips. Jeff thinks she must have miscounted because he mixes 60 chips into the dough of each batch of a dozen cookies. Jeff and Hadiya examine a batch of cookies fresh from the oven. The picture at the right shows what they see.

• How might you correct Jeff's reasoning about how many chocolate chips to add to each batch of cookie dough?

• What advice would you give to Jeff and Hadiya to help them solve this quality-control problem?

Notes

STUDENT PAGE

Hadiya wants to figure out how many chocolate chips they should add to each batch of dough. She wants to be fairly confident that each cookie will have five chips. She simulates the situation by using random sampling. When Hadiya **simulates** the quality-control problem, she runs an experiment that models the relevant characteristics of the cookie-dough problem.

Hadiya says, "Think of a batch of dough as 12 cookies packed in a bowl. Each chip that we add to the dough lands in one cookie. There is an equally likely chance that a chip will land in any one of the 12 cookies. We can simulate the situation."

Hadiya's Simulation

- Select integers from 1 to 12 at random to assign chocolate chips to cookies. A "1" means a chip is included in Cookie 1. A "2" means a chip is included in Cookie 2, and so on.

- Keep a tally of where the chips land. Stop when each cookie includes at least five chips.

- The total number of tallied chips will be an estimate of the number of chips needed for each batch.

Jeff extends Hadiya's idea. He says, "Each time we simulate the situation, we might get a different number of chips. For some simulations, some cookies might be loaded with chips before each cookie gets five chips. We need to repeat the experiment enough times to find a typical result."

- What is the typical number of chips needed to have at least five chips in each cookie?

Notes _____

Problem 3.3

(A) 1. For each cookie, 1 to 12, what is the theoretical probability of a chip being assigned to that cookie?

2. Describe a method that you can use to give each chip a cookie number. Explain why your method makes it equally likely for each cookie to be assigned a chip.

3. Conduct the simulation Hadiya described. Record your results in a table such as the one below.

Cookie Simulation

Cookie Number	1	2	3	4	5	6	7	8	9	10	11	12
Number of Chips in the Cookie	▪	▪	▪	▪	▪	▪	▪	▪	▪	▪	▪	▪

(B) Find the total number of chips in your simulated batch of cookie dough.

(C) Ask each group in your class for the total number of chips in their simulated batches of cookie dough.

1. Make a *histogram* of the class data.

2. Describe your histogram. Explain how you chose the interval size. What does the histogram tell you about the results of the simulations?

3. Make a box-and-whisker plot of the class data.

4. Describe your box plot. What does the box plot tell you about the results of the simulations?

5. Compute the mean and the median of the class data. Compare the mean and the median. What do you notice?

(D) Jeff and Hadiya want to be sure that most of the cookies they make will have at least five chips. They do not want to waste money, however, by mixing in too many chips. How many chips do you predict they need to use in each batch? Use your answers to Question C to explain your reasoning.

continued on the next page >

STUDENT PAGE

Notes _____

Problem **3.3** *continued*

E **1.** As a class, discuss your answers to Question D. Choose a number to suggest to Jeff and Hadiya that the whole class agrees on.

2. Use the number of chips your class agreed on.

- As a class, conduct 30 simulations to distribute the recommended number of chips among 12 cookies.

- For each simulation, record whether each of the 12 cookies has at least five chips.

- Organize your information in a table such as the one below.

Trials for Recommended Number of Chips

Simulation Trial Number	Does Each Cookie Have at Least Five Chips?
1	■
2	■
3	■
4	■
⋮	■
30	■

3. What percent of the simulations resulted in at least five chips per cookie?

4. Make a final recommendation. How many chips should Jeff and Hadiya put in each batch? Use your simulation results to justify your choice.

5. Suggest a new advertising slogan for Jeff and Hadiya that might promote their cookies in a more accurate way.

A C E Homework starts on page 69.

Notes _____

_____

_____

3.4 Estimating a Deer Population
Using Samples to Estimate the Size of a Population

Scientists and environmentalists estimate populations of various animals in particular habitats.

- How can you estimate the deer population of a town, state, or region?

The **capture–tag–recapture method** is one way to estimate a deer population. Biologists capture a sample of deer in a specific area, tag the deer, and then release them. Later, they capture another sample of deer. They count the number of deer with tags and compare that number to the number of deer in the sample. Then, they use their comparison to estimate the number of deer in the area.

You can simulate the capture-tag-recapture method using beans. Think of each bean in a container as a deer. Your job is to estimate the total number of beans without counting them all.

How to Simulate the Capture–Tag–Recapture Method

Capture–Tag

- Remove 100 beans from the container. Mark them with a pen or marker.

- Put the beans back in the container. Gently shake the container to mix the marked and unmarked beans.

Recapture

- Without examining the beans, scoop out a sample from the container. Record the number of marked beans and the number of beans in the sample.

- Return the sample of beans to the container. Mix the beans together again.

- How does the sample of beans you recaptured help you determine how many beans are in the population?

When biologists use the capture-tag-recapture method, they do not collect samples of specific sizes. In this Problem, however, you will collect samples of specific sizes so that you can compare your answers with your classmates' answers.

Investigation 3 **Using Samples to Draw Conclusions** 67

Notes

Problem 3.4

Work with your group to simulate the capture–tag–recapture method.

A 1. Take a sample of 25 beans. Record the number of marked beans and the number of unmarked beans in a table such as the one below. Use the data to estimate the total number of beans in the container.

Capture–Tag–Recapture Sampling Data

Sample Size	Number of Marked Beans	Number of Unmarked Beans	Estimate of Total Number of Beans
25	▪	▪	▪
50	▪	▪	▪
75	▪	▪	▪
100	▪	▪	▪
125	▪	▪	▪
150	▪	▪	▪

   2. Follow the steps you used in part (1) with samples of 50 beans, 75 beans, 100 beans, 125 beans, and 150 beans. Record your data.

   3. Describe the strategy you used to estimate the total number of beans in the container.

B Explain why this experiment can be considered a simulation.

C Use the table from Question A. Make a final estimate for the number of total beans in the container. Explain your reasoning.

D Ask each group in your class for their estimates of total number of beans in the container for each sample size.

   1. For each sample size, draw a line plot of the data you collected from your class.

   2. Explain how the line plots you drew in part (1) might change your final estimate for the total number of beans in the container.

E Use what you have learned from this experiment. How do you think biologists count deer populations?

A C E Homework starts on page 69.

Notes _____

_____

_____

Applications

1. A zookeeper has tracked the weights of many chimpanzees over the years. The box plots below show the weights of two samples of chimpanzees. The top box plot shows a sample of 8-year-old chimpanzees. The bottom box plot shows a sample of 10-year-old chimpanzees.

8-Year-Old Chimpanzees

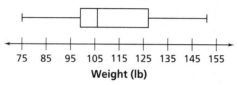

Weight (lb)

10-Year-Old Chimpanzees

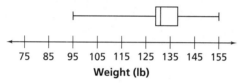

Weight (lb)

The zoo acquired some chimpanzees from a nearby zoo that was closing. They received a cage of 8-year-old chimpanzees and a cage of 10-year-old chimpanzees. The zoo forgot, however, to keep track of the cages. They weighed the chimpanzees in one cage and graphed the data.

Mystery Chimpanzees

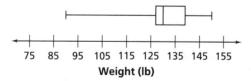

Weight (lb)

How old are the chimpanzees shown in the distribution above? Explain your reasoning.

STUDENT PAGE

Notes

2. a. Use the arrowhead tables from Problem 3.1. The tables include the neck widths of the arrowheads from two unknown sites and four known sites. For each of the six sites, calculate the five-number summaries of the neck-width data.

neck width

b. Make a box-and-whisker plot of the neck-width data for each site. You can use the same number line to plot all the box plots.

c. During which time periods do you think Sites I and II were settled? Use your answers to parts (a) and (b) to justify your response.

A sample of students measured their heights, arm spans, and foot lengths. Use the table below for Exercises 3–6.

Student Measurement Data

Gender	Height (cm)	Arm Span (cm)	Foot Length (cm)
F	160	158	25
M	111	113	15
F	160	160	23
F	152	155	23.5
F	146	144	24
F	157	156	24
M	136	135	21
F	143	142	23
M	147	145	20
M	133	133	20
F	153	151	25
M	148	149	23
M	125	123	20
F	150	149	20

3. a. Make a line plot displaying the foot lengths of the female students.

b. What is the mean of the data? The MAD?

c. On your line plot, mark the locations of one MAD and two MADs less than and greater than the mean.

Notes

_____

_____

_____

4. **a.** Make a line plot displaying the foot lengths of the male students.

   b. What is the mean of the data? The MAD?

   c. On your line plot, mark the locations of one MAD and two MADs less than and greater than the mean.

5. Use your answers to Exercises 3 and 4. Mark the mean male foot length on the line plot of female foot lengths. Is the mean male foot length an unexpected data value for the female line plot? Explain.

6. Use your answers to Exercises 3 and 4. Mark the mean female foot length on the line plot of male foot lengths. Is the mean female foot length an unexpected data value for the male line plot? Explain.

7. The line plots below display the name lengths of a sample of 30 U.S. students and a sample of 30 Chinese students.

   Keron and Ethan notice that U.S. names are longer than Chinese names for these samples. Keron thinks this is due to naturally occurring variability. Ethan thinks the differences are too great to be explained only by naturally occurring variability. Do you agree with Keron or with Ethan? Explain.

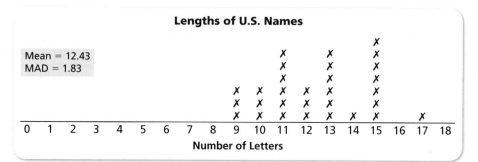

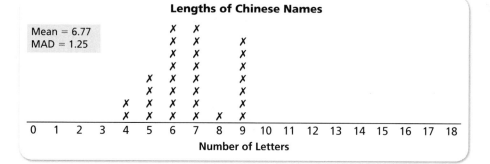

Notes _____

_____

_____

Keisha opens a bag containing 60 chocolate chip cookies. She selects a sample of 20 cookies and counts the chips in each cookie. For Exercises 8 and 9, use Keisha's data below.

Cookie Sample

Cookie Number	Number of Chips	Cookie Number	Number of Chips
1	6	11	8
2	8	12	7
3	8	13	9
4	11	14	9
5	7	15	8
6	6	16	6
7	6	17	8
8	7	18	10
9	11	19	10
10	7	20	8

8. Estimate the number of total chips in the bag. Explain your answer.

9. Copy and complete each statement with the most appropriate fraction: $\frac{1}{4}$, $\frac{1}{6}$, or $\frac{1}{2}$.

More than ▦ of the cookies have at least 8 chips.

More than ▦ of the cookies have at least 9 chips.

More than ▦ of the cookies have at least 10 chips.

10. a. A baker makes raisin muffins in batches of four dozen muffins. She pours a box of raisins into each batch. How could you use a sample of muffins to estimate the number of raisins in a box?

b. Suppose there are 1,000 raisins in each box. How many raisins would you expect to find in a typical muffin? Explain.

Notes

11. Yung-nan wants to estimate the number of beans in a large jar. She takes out 150 beans and marks each with a red dot. She returns the beans to the jar and mixes them with the unmarked beans. She then takes four samples from the jar. The table shows Yung-nan's data.

Bean Samples

Sample	Total Number of Beans	Number of Beans With Red Dots
1	25	3
2	150	23
3	75	15
4	250	25

a. For each sample, find the relative frequency of total beans that are marked with red dots.

b. Which sample has the greatest percent of marked beans? Use this sample to estimate the number of beans in the jar. Be sure to show your work.

c. Which sample has the least percent of marked beans? Use this sample to estimate the number of beans in the jar. Show your work.

d. Diya used the shaded bars below to make an estimate from Sample 3. Explain what the bars show and how they can be used to estimate the number of beans in the whole jar.

Sample 3

Number of beans in sample: 75

15, or 20% marked			

Whole Jar

Number of beans in jar: ?

150, or 20% marked			

e. Use your answers to parts (a)–(d). What is your best guess for the total number of beans in the jar? Explain your reasoning.

Notes

12. Salome is a biologist who studies the albatross, a type of bird. She lives on an island in the Pacific Ocean. Two summers ago, Salome's team trapped 20 albatrosses. They tagged and released them. This past summer, Salome's team trapped 50 albatrosses. They found that two of the albatrosses were tagged.

ALBATROSS

They have the longest wingspan of any bird (up to 11 feet).

They can live up to 50 years.

Their diet includes squid, krill, and fish, with some crustaceans.

They can travel long distances at high speeds (up to 80–85 mi/h).

19 of the 21 species of albatross are threatened with extinction.

a. Use Salome's findings. Estimate the number of albatrosses on the island. Explain how you made your estimate.

b. How confident are you that your estimate is accurate? Explain your answer.

c. Describe how Salome's team might use the capture–tag–recapture method to track how much the albatross population changes over time.

13. After independently testing many samples, an electric company determines that approximately 2 of every 1,000 light bulbs on the market are defective. Suppose Americans buy over one billion light bulbs each year. Estimate how many of these bulbs are defective.

14. Multiple Choice After testing many samples, a milk shipper determines that approximately 3 in every 100 milk cartons leak. The company ships 200,000 cartons of milk every week. About how many of these cartons leak?

A. 3   **B.** 600   **C.** 2,000   **D.** 6,000

Notes

Connections

Graphs tell stories. Suppose you are a news reporter. For Exercises 15 and 16, use the graphs to write a short news paragraph that tells the story portrayed.

15.

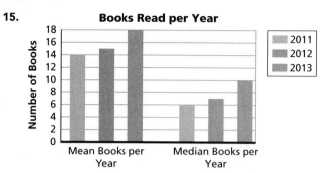

Books Read per Year

16.

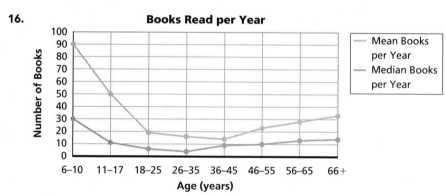

Books Read per Year

17. Multiple Choice The circle graph shows data for 1,585 students. About how many students are represented by the purple sector?

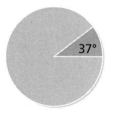

37°

F. 40   **G.** 160   **H.** 590   **J.** 58,650

STUDENT PAGE

Notes

18. Sometimes graphs can be misleading. The graphs below all display the same data about the percent of paper and paperboard recovered from 2001 to 2012.

a. Which graph do you think gives the clearest picture of the data pattern? Explain your reasoning.

b. Why are the other graphs misleading?

Percent of Recovered Paper and Paperboard (2001–2012)

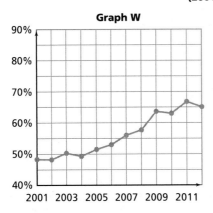

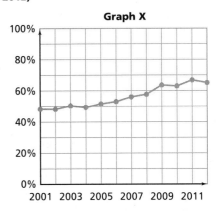

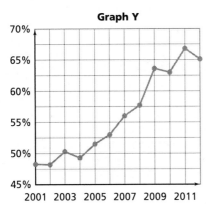

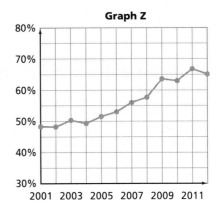

Notes _____

For Exercises 19–23, evaluate each survey described. Use the questions below to help you with your evaluation.

- What is the goal of the survey?
- What population is being studied?
- How is the sample chosen?
- How are the data analyzed and reported?
- Does the analysis support the conclusions?

19. A television manufacturer wants to design a remote control. Representatives for the company call 1,000 homes with televisions. They find that remote-control users sit an average of 3 meters from their televisions. Based on this finding, the company designs the remote control to work well at distances of 2.5 meters to 3.5 meters from a television.

20. A light bulb manufacturer wants to know the "defect rate" for its product. The manager takes 10 boxes of light bulbs from the assembly line and tests them. Each box contains 50 light bulbs. The manager finds that 5 bulbs are defective. He concludes that production quality is acceptable.

21. A nutritionist wants to know how many Calories in a typical U.S. teenager's diet are from fat. She asks Health teachers in Dallas, Texas to have their students record what they eat during one day. The nutritionist analyzes the records. The median intake is 500 Calories from fat per day, which is the recommended daily allowance. She concludes that Calories from fat are not a problem in the diets of teenagers.

22. A cookie maker claims that there are over 1,000 chocolate chips in a bag of its cookies. A consumer calls the company and asks how it knows this. A spokesperson says the company chooses a sample of bags of cookies. It soaks each bag in cold water to remove everything but the chips. Then the company weighs the chips that remain. In each case, the chips weigh more than a bag of 1,000 chocolate chips.

23. In the cafeteria line, Sam wrinkles his nose when he sees salami subs. The cook asks what he would prefer. Sam replies, "I like bologna better." The cook surveys the next ten students. Seven students say they prefer bologna over salami. The cook decides to serve bologna subs instead of salami subs in the future.

Notes

For Exercises 24–28, use the box plot below. Tell whether each statement is *true* or *false*. Explain.

Social Studies Test Scores

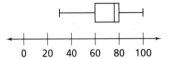

24. The class median is less than 80.

25. Half the class scored between 60 and 80.

26. At least one student earned a score of 100.

27. The class mean is probably less than the median.

28. If there are 30 students in the class, at least 10 scored above 80.

Extensions

29. Use a simulation to help you answer this question:

If you select five students at random from your class, what is the probability that at least two will have the same birth month?

a. Design a simulation to model this situation. Tell which month each simulation outcome represents.

b. Use your birth-month simulation to generate at least 25 samples of five people each. Use your results to estimate the probability that at least two people in a group of five will have the same birth month.

c. Explain how you could revise your simulation to explore this question:

What are the chances that at least two students in a class of 25 have the same birthday?

Notes _____

_____

_____

30. The percents of pushpin colors a company produces are on the bulletin board. A school secretary opens a large bag of pushpins. She puts the pins into boxes to distribute to teachers. She puts 50 pins in each box.

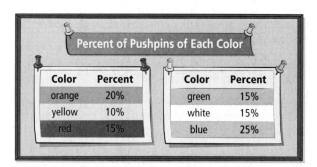

Percent of Pushpins of Each Color

Color	Percent
orange	20%
yellow	10%
red	15%

Color	Percent
green	15%
white	15%
blue	25%

a. How many pushpins of each color would you expect to be in a teacher's box?

b. How might the number of pushpins of each color vary across the boxes?

c. You can simulate filling the boxes by generating random integers from 1 to 20. Which numbers would you use to represent each color? How many numbers do you need to generate at random to simulate filling one box?

d. Carry out the simulation described in part (c) three times. Compare the distributions of colors in your simulated samples with the expected distribution from part (a).

e. Suppose the secretary selects a random sample of 1,000 pushpins from the bag. How closely would you expect the percents of each color in her sample to match the percents in the table?

Mathematical Reflections 3

In this Investigation, you developed strategies to draw conclusions about populations by analyzing samples. The following questions will help you summarize what you have learned.

Think about these questions. Discuss your ideas with other students and your teacher. Then write a summary of your findings in your notebook.

1. **a.** How can you use statistics to compare samples? How can you use samples to draw conclusions about the populations from which they are selected?

   b. In what ways might a data distribution for a sample be similar to or different from the data distribution for the entire population?

2. **a.** How can you use box plots, medians, and IQRs to compare samples? Give an example.

   b. How can you use means and MADs to compare samples? Give an example.

   c. How can you use statistics to decide whether differences between samples are expected due to natural variability or reflect measurable differences in underlying populations?

3. **a.** How can you use simulations to generate samples?

   b. How can you use data from a capture–tag–recapture simulation to estimate the actual size of a population?

4. The process of statistical investigation involves posing questions, collecting and analyzing data, and making interpretations to answer the original questions. Choose a Problem from this Investigation. Explain how you used the process of statistical investigation to solve the Problem.

Notes _____

_____

_____

Common Core Mathematical Practices

As you worked on the Problems in this Investigation, you used prior knowledge to make sense of them. You also applied Mathematical Practices to solve the Problems. Think back over your work, the ways you thought about the Problems, and how you used Mathematical Practices.

Shawna described her thoughts in the following way:

> In Problem 3.1, I compared arrowhead lengths. I used the mean, median, range, and MAD for each site.
>
> The mean arrowhead length for Site I (39.6 mm) is greater than the mean length for Site II (23.6 mm). The mean length for Site I is between the means for Laddie Creek/Dead Indian Creek (35 mm) and Kobold/Buffalo Creek (45.8 mm). These relationships are similar for the median values, too. Site I was probably settled between 4000 B.C. and A.D. 500.
>
> The data for Site II (mean of 23.6 mm, median of 24 mm) is similar to the Big Goose Creek (mean of 25.3 mm, median of 25.5 mm) and Wortham Shelter data (mean of 26.3 mm, median of 26 mm). Site II must have been settled between A.D. 500 and A.D. 1600.
>
> The minimum data values, maximum data values, and IQRs of all the sites also supported my ideas.
>
> ....
>
> **Common Core Standards for Mathematical Practice**
> **MP2** Reason abstractly and quantitatively.

 • What other Mathematical Practices can you identify in Shawna's reasoning?

• Describe a Mathematical Practice that you and your classmates used to solve a different Problem in this Investigation.

Notes

Looking Back

In this Unit, you learned about sampling data. You used samples to draw conclusions about the populations from which they were taken. You learned how to:

- Analyze and compare sets of data by using measures of center and measures of spread

- Select representative samples by using random sampling techniques

- Collect, organize, and display sample data

- Use your analyses of the samples to draw conclusions about populations

Use Your Understanding of Statistical Reasoning

1. Scientists often study the health of a habitat by gathering data about the number of animals that live there. Suppose you use the capture–tag–recapture method to find out how many butterflies live in a particular field.

   a. Suppose you capture and mark 20 butterflies and then release them. You return to the field and catch 10 butterflies. Only one butterfly is marked. Estimate the size of the population of butterflies in the field. Explain your reasoning.

   b. Suppose you return to the same field on a different day and catch 10 butterflies. Nine butterflies are marked. With this new information, estimate the size of the population of butterflies in the field. Explain.

   c. Suppose you return to the same field on a different day and capture and mark 80 additional butterflies. You then release them. You return to the field and catch 50 butterflies. Twenty-five are marked. Estimate the size of the population of butterflies in the field.

   d. For each part (a)-(c), how might you change your estimate to make sure that it is close to the actual number of butterflies in the field?

Notes

2. Glove makers are interested in the lengths and widths of their customers' hands. They look for patterns so they can make gloves that will fit most people. Each data value in the dot plots on the next page represents the mean of a sample of hand lengths.

- Two dot plots display data collected from 100 samples of males.

- Two dot plots display data collected from 100 samples of females.

- Two dot plots (one male and one female) show data from 100 samples of size 10.

- Two dot plots (one male and one female) show data from 100 samples of size 30.

- Assume that, on average, men's hands are longer than women's.

a. Which two distributions show data collected from males? Which two distributions show data collected from females? Explain your reasoning.

b. Look at the distributions of male data. Which distribution shows means from 100 samples of 10 males each? From 100 samples of 30 males each? Justify your reasoning.

c. Look at the distributions of female data. Which distribution shows means from 100 samples of 10 females each? From 100 samples of 30 females each? Justify your reasoning.

d. Compare the distribution of data collected from 100 samples of 30 males each with the distribution of data collected from 100 samples of 30 females each. How are the distributions alike? How are they different?

e. The MAD for the distribution of data collected from 100 samples of 30 males each is 0.072 centimeter. The MAD for the distribution of data collected from 100 samples of 30 females each is 0.077 centimeter.

How can you use this new information to support your answer to part (d)? What other comparisons can you now make?

Figure A

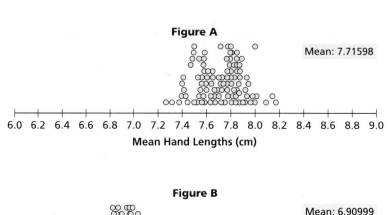

Mean: 7.71598

Mean Hand Lengths (cm)

Figure B

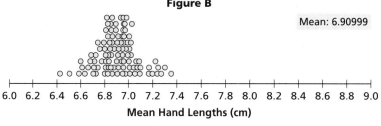

Mean: 6.90999

Mean Hand Lengths (cm)

Figure C

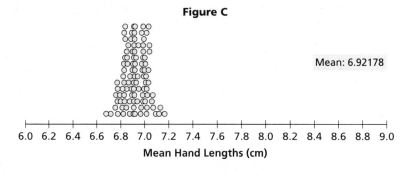

Mean: 6.92178

Mean Hand Lengths (cm)

Figure D

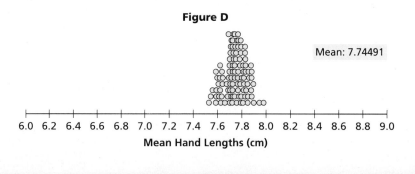

Mean: 7.74491

Mean Hand Lengths (cm)

Notes

3. Below are two box plots. One box plot is constructed from the data collected from 100 samples of 30 males each from Exercise 2. The other is constructed from the data collected from 100 samples of 30 females each from Exercise 2.

Figure E

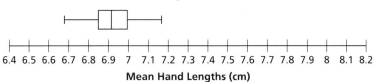

Mean Hand Lengths (cm)

Figure F

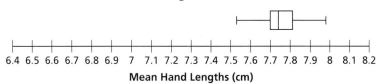

Mean Hand Lengths (cm)

   a. Which box plot shows data for males? For females? Explain.

   b. Identify the IQR from each box plot. Do these IQRs support your answers for Exercise 2, parts (d) and (e)? Explain.

   c. What other comparisons can you make using the box plots?

Explain Your Reasoning

When you choose samples, compare data sets, and use statistics to draw conclusions about populations, you should be able to justify your reasoning.

   4. When you report the mean, what related measure of spread can you report? What does this measure tell you about the data distribution?

   5. When you report the median, what related measure of spread can you report? What does this measure tell you about the data distribution?

   6. Describe three kinds of sampling methods that are not random sampling. Identify each method's strengths and weaknesses. Give an example of each kind of method.

   7. Give an example of a random sampling technique.

   8. When should you use sampled data to study a population?

Notes

English / Spanish Glossary

B

bar graph A graphical representation of a table of data in which the height or length of each bar indicates its frequency. The bars are separated from each other to highlight that the data are discrete or "counted" data. In a vertical bar graph, the horizontal axis shows the values or categories, and the vertical axis shows the frequency for each of the values or categories. In a horizontal bar graph, the vertical axis shows the values or categories, and the horizontal axis shows the frequencies.

gráfica de barras Representación gráfica de una tabla de datos en la que la altura o la longitud de cada barra indica su frecuencia. Las barras están separadas entre sí para subrayar que los datos son discretos o "contados". En una gráfica de barras vertical, el eje horizontal representa los valores o categorías y el eje vertical representa la frecuencia de cada uno de los valores o categorías. En una gráfica de barras horizontal, el eje vertical representa los valores o categorías y el eje horizontal representa las frecuencias.

Vertical Bar Graph

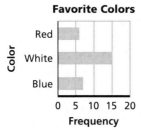

Horizontal Bar Graph

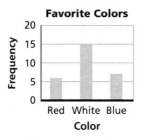

Gráfica de barras vertical

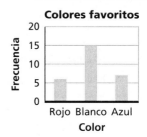

Gráfica de barras horizontal

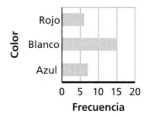

Notes _____

_____

_____

box-and-whisker plot, or box plot A display that shows the distribution of values in a data set separated into four equal-size groups. A box plot is constructed from a five-number summary of the data.

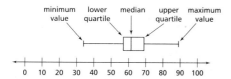

gráfica de caja y bigotes o diagrama de caja Una representación que muestra la distribución de los valores de un conjunto de datos separados en cuatro grupos de igual tamaño. Un diagrama de caja se construye a partir de un resumen de cinco números de los datos.

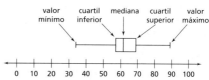

C

capture–tag–recapture method A sampling method used to estimate the size of a wildlife population. When using this method, scientists take a sample of animals, mark them in some way, then release them back into their habitat. Later, they capture another sample and count how many animals in that sample are marked. They use these data to estimate the population size.

método de captura-marcaje y recaptura Un método de muestreo que se usa para estimar el tamaño de una población de animales silvestres. Al usar este método, los científicos toman una muestra de los animales, los marcan de alguna manera y luego los vuelven a liberar en su hábitat. Más tarde, capturan otra muestra y cuentan cuántos animales de esa muestra están marcados. Usan estos datos para estimar el tamaño de la población.

categorical data Non-numerical data sets are categorical. For example, the responses to "What month were you born?" are categorical data. Frequency counts can be made of the values for a given category. The table below shows examples of categories and their possible values.

datos categóricos Los conjuntos de datos no numéricos son categóricos. Por ejemplo, las respuestas a "¿En qué mes naciste?" son datos categóricos. Los conteos de frecuencia se pueden hacer a partir de los valores de una categoría dada. La siguiente tabla muestra ejemplos de categorías y sus posibles valores.

Category	Possible Values
Month people are born	January, February, March
Favorite color to wear	magenta, blue, yellow
Kinds of pets people have	cats, dogs, fish, horses

Categoría	Valores posibles
Mes de nacimiento de las personas	enero, febrero, marzo
Color preferido para vestir	magenta, azul, amarillo
Tipos de mascotas que tienen las personas	gatos, perros, peces, caballos

census Data collected from every individual in a population.

censo Los datos recopilados de todos los individuos de una población.

Notes

convenience sampling Choosing a sample because it is convenient. For example, if you ask all the students on your bus how long it takes them to get to school and then claim that these data are representative of the entire school population, you are surveying a convenience sample.

muestreo de conveniencia Una muestra seleccionada porque es conveniente. Por ejemplo, si les preguntas a todos los estudiantes que van en el autobús cuánto tiempo tardan en llegar a la escuela y luego afirmas que esos datos son representativos de toda la población escolar, estás aplicando un muestreo de conveniencia.

D **describe** Academic Vocabulary
To explain or tell in detail. A written description can contain facts and other information needed to communicate your answer. A diagram or a graph may also be included.

related terms *express, explain, illustrate*

sample The band members want to conduct a survey. Describe a plan that uses systematic sampling.

> The band members can randomly select a starting time and then survey every sixth student who enters the school. This gives the band members a methodical way of collecting data.

describir Vocabulario académico
Explicar o decir con detalle. Una descripción escrita puede contener datos y otro tipo de información necesaria para comunicar tu respuesta. También puede incluir un diagrama o una gráfica.

términos relacionados *expresar, explicar, ilustrar*

ejemplo Los integrantes de la banda quieren hacer una encuesta. Describe un plan que use el muestreo sistemático.

> Los integrantes de la banda pueden seleccionar al azar un tiempo de inicio y luego aplicar la encuesta a cada sexto estudiante que entre a la escuela. Esto da a los integrantes de la banda una manera metódica de recopilar datos.

Notes

distribution The entire set of collected data values, organized to show their frequency of occurrence. A distribution can be described using summary statistics and/or by referring to its shape.

distribución Todo el conjunto de valores de datos recopilados, organizados para mostrar su frecuencia de incidencia. Una distribución se puede describir usando la estadística sumaria y/o haciendo referencia a su forma.

E

estimate Academic Vocabulary
To find an approximate answer that is relatively close to an exact amount.

related terms *approximate, guess*

sample A cup manufacturer knows that approximately 4 out of every 2,000 cups are defective. Estimate how many of 10,000 cups bought by a restaurant will be defective.

hacer una estimación Vocabulario académico
Hallar una respuesta aproximada que esté relativamente cerca de una cantidad exacta.

términos relacionados *aproximar, suponer*

ejemplo Un fabricante de tazas sabe que aproximadamente 4 de cada 2,000 tazas son defectuosas. Estima cuántas de 10,000 tazas compradas por un restaurante son defectuosas.

I can write 4 out of 2,000 as a percent.
$$\frac{4}{2,000} = 0.002 = 0.2\%$$
Then I can multiply 10,000 by 0.2% to estimate the number of defective cups bought by the restaurant chain.
$$0.002 \times 10,000 = 20$$
About 20 of the cups are defective.
I can also use a proportion.
$$\frac{4}{2,000} = \frac{x}{10,000}$$
$$2,000x = 40,000$$
$$x = 20$$

Puedo escribir 4 de 2,000 como un porcentaje. $$\frac{4}{2,000} = 0.002 = 0.2\%$$
Luego, puedo multiplicar 10,000 por 0.2% para estimar el número de tazas defectuosas compradas por el restaurante.
$$0.002 \times 10,000 = 20$$
Alrededor de 20 de las tazas están defectuosas.
También puedo usar una proporción.
$$\frac{4}{2,000} = \frac{x}{10,000}$$
$$2,000x = 40,000$$
$$x = 20$$

Notes

expect Academic Vocabulary
To use theoretical or experimental data to anticipate a certain outcome.

related terms *anticipate, predict*

sample A cook makes trail mix in 2-pound batches. She puts a bag of almonds into each batch. There are about 120 almonds in each bag. Explain how many almonds you would expect to find in $\frac{1}{2}$ pound of trail mix.

> If I divide 2 pounds of trail mix into half-pound parts, I will have 4 parts. Since the cook puts 120 almonds into each batch, divide 120 by 4 to determine the expected number of almonds in one-half pound. I can expect to find 30 almonds in one-half pound of trail mix because $120 \div 4 = 30$.

esperar Vocabulario académico
Usar datos teóricos o experimentales para anticipar un resultado determinado.

términos relacionados *anticipar, predecir*

ejemplo Una cocinera prepara una mezcla de nueces y frutas secas en recetas de 2 libras. Pone una bolsa de almendras en cada receta. Hay aproximadamente 120 almendras en cada bolsa. Explica cuántas almendras esperarías hallar en media libra de mezcla de nueces y frutas secas.

> Si divido 2 libras de mezcla de nueces y frutas secas en partes de media libra, tendré 4 partes. Dado que la cocinera pone 120 almendras en cada receta, divido 120 por 4 para determinar el número esperado de almendras en media libra. Puedo esperar hallar 30 almendras en media libra de mezcla de nueces y frutas secas, porque $120 \div 4 = 30$.

Notes

explain Academic Vocabulary
To give facts and details that make an idea easier to understand. Explaining can involve a written summary supported by a diagram, chart, table, or a combination of these.

related terms *analyze, clarify, describe, justify, tell*

sample Explain why the line graph is misleading.

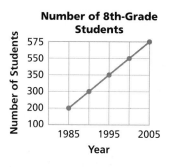

Number of 8th-Grade Students

The vertical axis of the graph does not start with zero and does not increase by the same amount for each interval. This causes the data to appear to increase at a constant rate, but it is increasing at different rates. Therefore, the graph is misleading.

explicar Vocabulario académico
Dar datos y detalles que hacen que una idea sea más fácil de comprender. Explicar puede incluir un resumen escrito apoyado por un diagrama, una gráfica, una tabla o una combinación de estos.

términos relacionados *analizar, aclarar, describir, justificar, decir*

ejemplo Explica por qué la gráfica lineal es engañosa.

Número de estudiantes del grado 8

El eje vertical de la gráfica no empieza en cero y no aumenta en la misma cantidad en cada intervalo. Esto hace que los datos parezcan aumentar en una tasa constante, pero están aumentando en diferentes tasas. Por tanto, la gráfica es engañosa.

F

five-number summary The minimum value, lower quartile, median, upper quartile, and maximum value for a data set. These five values give a summary of the shape of the distribution and are used to make box plots. The five-number summary is noted on the box plot below.

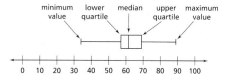

resumen de cinco números El valor mínimo, el cuartil inferior, la mediana, el cuartil superior y el valor máximo de un conjunto de datos. Estos cinco valores dan un resumen de la forma de una distribución y se usan para construir diagramas de caja. El resumen de cinco números se observa en el siguiente diagrama de caja.

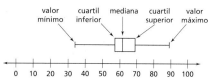

English/Spanish Glossary

END MATTER

STUDENT PAGE

Notes

frequency The number of times a given data value occurs in a data set.

frecuencia El número de veces que un valor de datos dado se produce en un conjunto de datos.

H **histogram** A display that shows the distribution of numeric data. The range of data values, divided into intervals, is displayed on the horizontal axis. The vertical axis shows the frequency in numbers or in percents. The height of the bar over each interval indicates the count or percent of data values in that interval.

histograma Una representación que muestra la distribución de datos numéricos. El rango de valores de datos, dividido en intervalos, se representa en el eje horizontal. El eje vertical muestra la frecuencia en números o en porcentajes. La altura de la barra sobre cada intervalo indica el conteo o porcentaje de valores de datos en ese intervalo.

The histogram below shows quality ratings for certain brands of peanut butter. The height of the bar over the interval from 20 to 30 is 4. This indicates that four brands of peanut butter have quality ratings greater than or equal to 20 and less than 30.

El siguiente histograma representa la calificación de la calidad de ciertas marcas de mantequilla de maní. La altura de la barra sobre el intervalo de 20 a 30 es 4. Esto indica que cuatro marcas de mantequilla de maní tienen una calificación mayor que o igual a 20 y menor que 30.

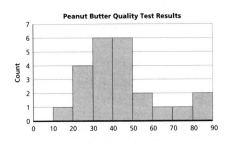

I **interquartile range (IQR)** The difference of the values of the upper quartile (Q3) and the lower quartile (Q1). In the box-and-whisker plot below, the upper quartile is 69, and the lower quartile is 58. The IQR is the difference 69–58, or 11.

rango entre cuartiles (REC) La diferencia de los valores del cuartil superior (C3) y el cuartil inferior (C1). En el siguiente diagrama de caja y bigotes, el cuartil superior es 69 y el cuartil inferior es 58. El REC es la diferencia de 69 a 58, u 11.

$$IQR = 69 - 58 = 11$$

$$REC = 69 - 58 = 11$$

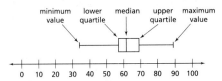

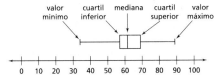

Samples and Populations

Notes

L **line plot** A way to organize data along a number line where the ✗s (or other symbols) above a number represent how often each value occurs in a data set. A line plot made with dots is sometimes referred to as a dot plot.

diagrama de puntos Una manera de organizar los datos a lo largo de una recta numérica donde las ✗ (u otros símbolos) colocadas encima de un número representan la frecuencia con que se menciona cada valor. Un diagrama de puntos hecho con puntos algunas veces se conoce como gráfica de puntos.

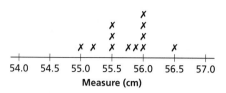

Measure (cm)

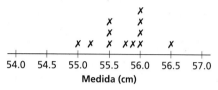

Medida (cm)

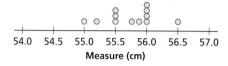

Measure (cm)

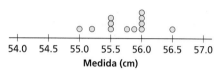

Medida (cm)

M **mean** The value found when all the data are combined and then redistributed evenly.

For example, the total number of siblings for the data in the line plot below is 56. If all 19 students had the same number of siblings, they would each have about 3 siblings.

Differences from the mean "balance out" so that the sum of differences below and above the mean equal 0. The mean of a set of data is the sum of the values divided by the number of values in the set.

media El valor que se halla cuando todos los datos se combinan y luego se redistribuyen de manera uniforme.

Por ejemplo, el número total de hermanos y hermanas en los datos del siguiente diagrama es 56. Si los 19 estudiantes tuvieran la misma cantidad de hermanos y hermanas, cada uno tendría aproximadamente 3 hermanos o hermanas.

Las diferencias de la media se "equilibran" de manera que la suma de las diferencias por encima y por debajo de la media sea igual a 0. La media de un conjunto de datos es la suma de los valores dividida por el número de valores en el conjunto.

Number of Siblings Students Have

Number of Siblings

Número de hermanos y hermanas que tienen los estudiantes

Número de hermanos y hermanas

mean absolute deviation (MAD) The average distance of all of the data values in a data set from the mean of the distribution.

desviación absoluta media (DAM) La distancia media de todos los valores de datos en un conjunto de datos a partir de la media de la distribución.

median The number that marks the midpoint of an ordered set of data. At least half of the values lie at or above the median, and at least half lie at or below the median.

For the sibling data (0, 0, 0, 1, 1, 2, 2, 2, 2, 3, 3, 3, 4, 4, 5, 5, 5, 6, 8), the median of the distribution of siblings is 3 because the tenth (middle) value in the ordered set of 19 values is 3. When a distribution contains an even number of data values, the median is computed by finding the average of the two middle data values in an ordered list of the data values.

For example, the median of 1, 3, 7, 8, 25, and 30 is 7.5 because the data values 7 and 8 are third and fourth in the list of six data values.

mediana El número que marca el punto medio de un conjunto ordenado de datos. Por lo menos la mitad de los datos se encuentran en o encima de la mediana y por lo menos la mitad se encuentran en o debajo de la mediana.

Para los datos de los hermanos y hermanas (0, 0, 0, 1, 1, 2, 2, 2, 2, 3, 3, 3, 4, 4, 5, 5, 5, 6, 8), la mediana de la distribución de hermanos y hermanas es 3 porque el décimo valor (el del medio) en el conjunto ordenado de 19 valores es 3. Cuando una distribución contiene un número par de valores de datos, la mediana se calcula hallando el promedio de los dos valores de datos del medio en una lista ordenada de los valores de datos.

Por ejemplo, la mediana de 1, 3, 7, 8, 25 y 30 es 7.5, porque los valores de datos 7 y 8 son tercero y cuarto en la lista de seis valores de datos.

mode The value that appears most frequently in a set of data. In the data set 2, 2, 2, 2, 3, 3, 7, 7, 8, 9, 10, 11, the mode is 2.

moda El valor que aparece con mayor frecuencia en un conjunto de datos. En el conjunto de datos 2, 2, 2, 2, 3, 3, 7, 7, 8, 9, 10, 11, la moda es 2.

N

numerical data Values that are numbers such as counts, measurements, and ratings. Here are some examples.

- Number of children in families

- Pulse rates (number of heart beats per minute)

- Heights

- Amounts of time people spend reading in one day

- Ratings such as: on a scale of 1 to 5 with 1 as "low interest," how would you rate your interest in participating in the school's field day?

datos numéricos Valores que son números como conteos, mediciones y calificaciones. Los siguientes son algunos ejemplos.

- Número de hijos e hijas en las familias

- Pulsaciones por minuto (número de latidos del corazón por minuto)

- Alturas

- Cantidades de tiempo que las personas pasan leyendo en un día

- Calificaciones como: en una escala de 1 a 5, en la que 1 representa "poco interés", ¿cómo calificarías tu interés por participar en el día de maniobras de tu escuela?

Notes

outlier A value that lies far from the "center" of a distribution and is not like other values. *Outlier* is a relative term, but it indicates a data point that is much higher or much lower than the values that could be normally expected for the distribution.

To identify an outlier in a distribution represented by a box plot, measure the distance between Q3 and any suspected outliers at the top of the range of data values; if this distance is more than $1.5 \times \text{IQR}$, then the data value is an outlier. Likewise, if the distance between any data value at the low end of the range of values and Q1 is more than $1.5 \times \text{IQR}$, then the data value is an outlier.

valor extremo Un valor que se encuentra lejos del "centro" de una distribución y no es como los demás valores. El *valor extremo* es un término relativo, pero indica un dato que es mucho más alto o mucho más bajo que los valores que se podrían esperar normalmente para la distribución.

Para identificar un valor extremo en una distribución representada por un diagrama de caja, se mide la distancia entre C3 y cualquier valor que se sospeche es extremo en la parte superior del rango de los valores de datos; si esta distancia es mayor que $1.5 \times \text{REC}$, entonces el valor de datos es un valor extremo. Del mismo modo, si la distancia entre cualquier valor de datos en la parte inferior del rango de valores y C1 es mayor que $1.5 \times \text{REC}$, entonces el valor de datos es un valor extremo.

population The entire collection of people or objects you are studying.

población El grupo completo de las personas o los objetos que se están estudiando.

quartile One of three points that divide a data set into four equal groups. The second quartile, Q2, is the median of the data set. The first quartile, Q1, is the median of the lower half of the data set. The third quartile, Q3, is the median of the upper half of the data set.

cuartil Uno de los tres puntos que dividen un conjunto de datos en cuatro grupos iguales. El segundo cuartil, C2, es la mediana del conjunto de datos. El primer cuartil, C1, es la mediana de la mitad inferior del conjunto de datos. El tercer cuartil, C3, es la mediana de la mitad superior del conjunto de datos.

random sampling Choosing a sample in a way that gives every member of a population an equally likely chance of being selected.

muestreo aleatorio Elegir una muestra de manera que todo miembro de una población tenga la misma probabilidad de ser seleccionado.

range The difference of the maximum value and the minimum value in a distribution. If you know the range of the data is 12 grams of sugar per serving, you know that the difference between the minimum and maximum values is 12 grams. For example, in the distribution 2, 2, 2, 2, 3, 3, 7, 7, 8, 9, 10, 11, the range of the data set is 9, because $11 - 2 = 9$.

rango La diferencia del valor máximo y el valor mínimo en una distribución. Si se sabe que el rango de los datos es 12 gramos de azúcar por porción, entonces se sabe que la diferencia entre el valor mínimo y el máximo es 12 gramos. Por ejemplo, en la distribución 2, 2, 2, 2, 3, 3, 7, 7, 8, 9, 10, 11, el rango del conjunto de datos es 9, porque $11 - 2 = 9$.

Notes

relative frequency The ratio of the number of desired results to the total number of trials. Written as a percent, relative frequencies help you compare samples of different sizes.

frecuencia relativa La razón del número de resultados deseados al número total de pruebas. Escritas como porcentajes, las frecuencias relativas ayudan a comparar muestras de diferentes tamaños.

representative sample A sample whose characteristics accurately reflect those of the larger population from which the sample was selected.

muestra representativa Una muestra cuyas características reflejan con exactitud las características de la población más grande de la que se seleccionó la muestra.

S **sample** A group of people or objects selected from a population.

muestra Un grupo de personas u objetos seleccionados de una población.

sampling distribution The distribution of the means (or medians) from a set of same-size samples, each selected randomly from the same population.

distribución muestral Distribución de las medias (o medianas) de un conjunto de muestras del mismo tamaño, seleccionadas al azar de la misma población.

sampling plan A detailed strategy for selecting a sample from a population, including what data will be collected, in what manner, and by whom.

plan de muestreo Una estrategia detallada para seleccionar la muestra de una población, incluyendo los datos que se recopilarán, de qué manera y por quién.

simulate To run an experiment modeling the relevant characteristics of a real-world situation for use in studying the behavior of the real-world situation.

simular Llevar a cabo un experimento representando las características relevantes de una situación de la vida diaria para usarlas en el estudio del comportamiento de esa situación.

systematic sampling Choosing a sample in a methodical way. For example, if you survey every tenth person on an alphabetical list of names, you are surveying a systematic sample.

muestreo sistemático Una muestra seleccionada de una manera metódica. Por ejemplo, si se encuesta a cada décima persona de una lista de nombres en orden alfabético, se estaría aplicando el muestreo sistemático.

V **voluntary-response (or self-selected) sampling** A sample that selects itself. For example, if you put an ad in the school paper asking for volunteers to take a survey, the students who respond will be a voluntary-response sample.

muestra de respuesta voluntaria (o autoseleccionada) Una muestra que se selecciona a sí misma. Por ejemplo, si se pone un anuncio en el periódico escolar pidiendo voluntarios para participar en una encuesta, los estudiantes que respondan serán una muestra de respuesta voluntaria.

Notes _____

_____

_____

Index

Notes _____

Notes _____

_____

_____

Index

END MATTER

STUDENT PAGE

Notes

Acknowledgments

Cover Design
Three Communication Design, Chicago

Text

American Forest and Paper Association
076 Data from the **"Paper & Paperboard Recovery"** from WWW.PAPERRECYCLES.ORG

George C. Knight
057 From **"Site 1 and Site 2 Arrowhead Sizes"** by George C. Knight and James D. Keyser from PLAINS ANTHROPOLOGIST VOLUME 28, NUMBER 101, 1983. Reprinted by permission of the author.

058 From **"A Mathematical Technique for Dating Projectile Points Common to the Northwestern Plains (Big Goose Creek Arrowheads)"** by George C. Knight and James D. Keyser from PLAINS ANTHROPOLOGIST VOLUME 28, NUMBER 101, 1983. Reprinted by permission of the author.

058 From **"A Mathematical Technique for Dating Projectile Points Common to the Northwestern Plains (Wortham Shelter Arrowheads)"** by George C. Knight and James D. Keyser from PLAINS ANTHROPOLOGIST VOLUME 28, NUMBER 101, 1983. Reprinted by permission of the author.

059 From **"A Mathematical Technique for Dating Projectile Points Common to the Northwestern Plains (Kobold/Buffalo Creek Arrowheads)"** by George C. Knight and James D. Keyser from PLAINS ANTHROPOLOGIST VOLUME 28, NUMBER 101, 1983. Reprinted by permission of the author.

059 From **"A Mathematical Technique for Dating Projectile Points Common to the Northwestern Plains (Laddie Creek/Dead Indian Creek Arrowheads)"** by George C. Knight and James D. Keyser from PLAINS ANTHROPOLOGIST VOLUME 28, NUMBER 101, 1983. Reprinted by permission of the author.

Duane Marden
016 "Roller Coaster Census Report" by Duane Marden from WWW.RCDB.COM/CENSUS.HTM

National Geographic Stock
026 "Survey 2000: Census Information" from WWW.NATIONALGEOGRAPHIC.COM. Used by permission of NGS/National Geographic Stock.

Pew Research Center
034 Data on teen text messaging and teen cell phone ownership from the Pew Research Center from WWW.PEWRESEARCH.ORG

Photographs
Photo locators denoted as follows: Top (T), Center (C), Bottom (B), Left (L), Right (R), Background (Bkgd)

002 (TR) AndreAnita/Shutterstock , (BR) David R. Frazier Photolibrary, Inc./Alamy; **003** Fritz Polking/The Image Works; **070** Hemera Technologies/Alamy; **074** AndreAnita/Shutterstock; **016** (BL) David R. Frazier Photolibrary, Inc./Alamy, (BR) David Kleyn/Alamy; **034** (BL) iStockphoto/Thinkstock, (BCL) Milosluz/Fotolia, (BCR) Marco Desscouleurs/Fotolia, (CR) SP-PIC/Fotolia; **056** Alberto Paredes/Alamy; **057** Hemera Technologies/Alamy.

Notes _____

_____

_____

1.1 Comparing Performances: Using Center and Spread

> **Focus Question** Given a set of results, how might you use measures of center and variability (spread) to judge overall performance?

Launch

Use the Investigation introduction to set up Problem 1.1. Discuss what is involved in conducting a statistical investigation: posing a question, collecting data, analyzing the data, and interpreting the results. In talking about the analysis phase, have students discuss why deciding what is typical for a data set or describing how a data set varies can help them compare distributions.

In Problem 1.1, students use measures of center and spread to compare distributions. Students find that they need to use measures of spread, in conjunction with measures of center, to judge performance.

Suggested Questions

- *What might you consider when comparing these sample test scores?*

- *How do you find a mean? A median? The MAD? What do these statistics tell you?*

> **Materials**
>
> There are no additional materials for this Problem.

Explore

If some students are confused by Question A, other teams can help them recall the two measures of center: mean and median.

Suggested Question

- *How is it possible that both Jun and Mia have the same mean and median math scores when their test scores are different?*

For Question B, two measures of variability—range and mean absolute deviation (MAD)—are highlighted.

You may need to review the mean absolute deviation (MAD) as a statistic. The MAD is determined using the mean of a distribution. It is used to describe how much, on average, the math test scores (in this example) differ from the mean score.

Questions C and D ask whether having more information (a larger sample) provides better evidence for making a decision, and which measure of spread best reflects the samples.

- *Does having more data change the measures you found in Questions A and B?*

- *Does having more data change the decision you made in Question C?*

Summarize

It may surprise students that the test scores have the same measures of center. In this situation, a lower measure of spread indicates a more consistent test performance. Have students discuss how they found the range and what it means for one range to be 40 points and the other 10 points in terms of evaluating performance.

Suggested Questions

- *What do you think the word "sample" means?*
- *Does the sample include all of Jun's or Mia's math test scores?*
- *Does it make sense to make general statements about the two performances?*

Students may conclude that Mia performs more consistently, since she does not have low values, nor as great a range in scores, as Jun does.

Assignment Guide for Problem 1.1

Applications: 1–2 | Connections: 17–18

Answers to Problem 1.1

A. **1.** Mean = 80; median = 80; The two measures are identical.

2. Mean = 80; median = 80; The two measures are identical.

3. All measures of center are identical, so who performed better cannot be distinguished.

B. **1.** Range = 40; MAD = 13.33

2. Range = 10; MAD = 3.33

3. Comparing the measures of spread, Mia's results are less variable than Jun's results. Mia's performance is more successful than Jun's if success is judged on how consistently each student performs.

C. There is probably not enough data since 3 scores each do not constitute a large data set.

D. **1.** Jun: mean = 80, median = 80; Mia: mean = 83.33, median = 80; Mia's mean score is higher than Jun's, but their median scores are the same.

2. A range of 40 points makes Jun's scores appear inconsistent compared to Mia's smaller range of 25 points. However, the MADs are closer (6.67 for Jun and 6.1 for Mia) and make the scores seem not so different.

3. Answers may depend on which measures students use to justify.

- One student is a stronger math student than the other: Mia could be considered a stronger student. Her mean (83.3) is higher than Jun's (80), but the difference is small. They are both B students.

- One student is more consistent than the other: The MADs are somewhat similar, so the students are equally consistent using this measure.

- The two students perform equally well on math tests: The big range (40) and low minimum value (60) make it appear that Jun does not do as well as Mia. The other measures are fairly consistent, however. It is reasonable to conclude that both students perform equally well.

- You can make better comparisons using the larger data set: Most students will agree with this one. With only three pieces of data, Jun looked very inconsistent. With six pieces of data, the apparent inconsistency is seen to be the result of one poor test score. With the larger data set, Jun is more consistent than previously thought.

At a Glance

Problem 1.2   Pacing 1 Day

1.2 Which Team Is Most Successful?
Using the MAD to Compare Samples

> *Focus Question*   What strategies might you use to evaluate numerical outcomes and judge success?

Launch

Students should be familiar with the concepts of center and spread from *Data About Us*. In particular, the mean absolute deviation (MAD) is explored as a way to evaluate variability in data distributions. Not only do students find the MAD, they now evaluate "how many" MADs each data value is away from the mean.

Pose the fundraising context faced by the Hiking Club. Have students examine the table of data.

Suggested Questions

- *In this Problem, you have a larger number of samples with more data values. It makes sense to represent the data on a graph. What kind of graph might you choose?*
- *How do you make a line plot?*
- *What might you see on a line plot that helps you make comparisons?*

Have students brainstorm strategies they might use in order to decide how to answer the question posed. Resist actually carrying out strategies during this stage—the intent is to get ideas out. Some strategies students are likely to suggest: find which of the six groups collected the most money, find the mean or the median, find a way to measure the contributions of individual members in terms of how "equal" they are, etc.

Have students work in pairs on Problem 1.2. Labsheet 1.2 contains a table version of the team data in the SE.

Materials

Labsheet
- 1.2: Fundraising Money Collected

Accessibility Labsheet
- 1ACE: Exercises 3–7

Teaching Aid
- 1.2: Line Plots of Fundraiser Data

- Data and Graphs Tool

Explore

Question A involves students making line plots for each set of data; this allows them to look at the distributions differently.

In Question B, students interpret other students' thinking. In each of the three parts, different approaches are proposed. Each one is designed to highlight key strategies that can be used.

Students might be puzzled as they work through parts (1)–(3). In part (1), they discover that all teams raised the same amounts of money, but one team has five people and the rest have six people each. In part (2), all teams except Team 5 have the same mean; Team 5 has a higher mean, yet it also has fewer team members.

Suggested Questions

- *How can Team 5 have a higher mean when all teams raised the same amount?*
- *Do the means help you compare the teams?*
- *What does the MAD represent in each case?*
- *How do the MADs help you compare teams?*

Question C asks students to use any other strategies not yet tried to see how the results will help them answer the question.

Question D engages students in examining locations of data values in relation to MADs. Remind students that they are finding the number of data values within one MAD (or two MADs). Data values that fall on a MAD marker should not be counted as within, since they are not less than one MAD (or two MADs) from the mean. Students may want to use a calculator at this point.

Summarize

You may want to use Teaching Aid 1.2, which displays the line plots of the team data. Using the same scale for each graph makes it easier to compare the distributions. Teams 1, 2, and 6 seem to have less variability than the other three teams.

Have students discuss the strategies posed in Question B. For identifying the most successful team, Jonah's strategy of using the MADs is probably the one that can help students focus on performance among group members.

For Question C, have students discuss any other strategies not considered in Question B. Students may focus on locating medians. This statistic is different for each group. Students might want to consider which statistic—the median or MAD—best characterizes groups working "fairly" together to raise money.

Question D engages students in thinking about how the data values relate both to the mean and to the MADs of a distribution.

Suggested Questions

- *It looks like it is quite unusual for data to be more than 2 MADs from the mean. Does this give us a way to measure whose contributions may be considered unusual? Was any contribution unusually high? Low?*
- *Are all the data values within 3 MADs of the mean? If not, do you think a data value more than 3 MADs from the mean is unusual, when compared to other data values?*

ⒶⒸⒺ
Assignment Guide for Problem 1.2

Applications: 3–7 | Connections: 19–20

Answers to Problem 1.2

A. (See Figures 1 through 6, next page.)

Student answers will vary. Possible answers: Team 3 has the biggest range ($90). Team 1

has the smallest range ($20). Team 4 has the smallest minimum value ($0), whereas, Team 3 has the greatest maximum value ($100).

B. 1. If the teams raised different amounts of money, identifying the team that raised the most money would be one way to answer the question. In this case, the total amount raised by each team is the same. This method will not determine the most successful team.

Figure 1

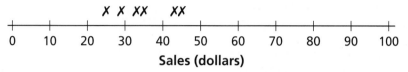

Team 1 Fundraising

Sales (dollars)

Figure 2

Team 2 Fundraising

Sales (dollars)

Figure 3

Team 3 Fundraising

Sales (dollars)

Figure 4

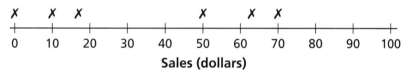

Team 4 Fundraising

Sales (dollars)

Figure 5

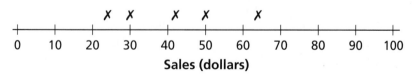

Team 5 Fundraising

Sales (dollars)

Figure 6

Team 6 Fundraising

Sales (dollars)

2. Since the totals are the same, the means of all teams (except Team 5) will be the same (total money raised ÷ number of team members). Team 5 has five team members, not six, so that team's mean will be higher. If a team's success is measured by the average amount raised, this strategy helps determine the most successful team.

3. Team 1 MAD = $6; Team 2 MAD = $10; Team 3 MAD = $25; Team 4 MAD = $26; Team 5 MAD = $12; Team 6 MAD = $5.

   Since Team 6 has the lowest MAD, you can see that members of Team 6 are more consistent in their performance. Team 6 individual fundraising differs, on average, only $5 from the mean. Teams 2–5 have greater variability among the amounts raised. Team 1 follows closely with a low variability ($6 from the mean).

   If a team's success is measured in terms of variability (or low variability), this strategy helps determine the most successful team.

C. Students may have other strategies. They might suggest that the median be found. Medians: Team 1 (34), Team 2 (30), Team 3 (20), Team 4 (33.5), Team 5 (42), Team 6 (35). The medians are different. Team 5 has the greatest median, yet it also has the fewest members. Other strategies may vary.

D. This question is designed to help students realize that, generally, most of the data in a distribution are located less than two MADs from the mean. Students can think about the distance of one MAD or two MADs by making sketches to mark both on a graph.

   1. Team 1 has two data values closer than one MAD (about 33.3%).

   2. Team 1 has six data values closer than two MADs (100%).

   3. Team 1 has zero data values more than twice the team's MAD (0%).

   4. Team 1 markers:

      One MAD: 35 + 6 = 41 and 35 − 6 = 29; two data values are closer (about 33.3%).

      Two MADs: 35 + 12 = 47 and 35 − 12 = 23; six data values are closer (100%).

      More than two MADs: zero data values (0%).

Team 2 markers:

One MAD: 35 + 10 = 45 and 35 − 10 = 25; one data value is closer (about 16.7%).

Two MADs: 35 + 20 = 55 and 35 − 20 = 15; six data values are closer (100%).

More than two MADs: zero data values (0%).

Team 3 markers:

One MAD: 35 + 25 = 60 and 35 − 25 = 10; four data values are closer (about 66.7%).

Two MADs: 35 + 50 = 85 and 35 − 50 = 0; five data values are closer (83%).

More than two MADs: one data value (17%).

Team 4 markers:

One MAD: 35 + 26 = 71 and 35 − 26 = 9; five data values are closer (about 83.3%).

Two MADs: 35 + 52 = 87 and 35 − 52 = zero; six data values are closer (100%).

More than two MADs: zero data values (0%).

Team 5 markers:

One MAD: 42 + 12 = 54 and 42 − 12 = 30; two data values are closer (40%).

Two MADs: 42 + 24 = 66 and 42 − 24 = 18; five data values are closer (100%).

More than two MADs: zero data values (0%).

Team 6 markers:

One MAD: 35 + 5 = 40 and 35 − 5 = 30; four data values are closer (about 66.7%).

Two MADs: 35 + 10 = 45 and 35 − 10 = 25; four data values are closer (66.7%).

More than two MADs: two data values (33.3%).

5. For most teams, 100% of the data values are located within two MADs of the mean of the distribution. Only Team 3 and Team 6 have data values located greater than two MADs from their means. These data values may be considered to be unusual in their distributions.

At a Glance — Problem 1.3   Pacing 1 Day

1.3 Pick Your Preference: Distinguishing Categorical Data From Numerical Data

Focus Question How might you compare results to see if each sample responded to a survey in a similar way? How can using percentages help you make comparisons?

Launch

In this Problem, students compare different-sized data sets and use bar graphs to display these data. In *Data About Us*, students used counts or frequencies. Now, to make data sets "comparable," students see that the data sets need to be the "same size." This can be done by reporting percentages, not counts. In statistics, this is called *relative frequency*. By using percents, students report responses "out of one hundred" to compare three sets of data.

Give students Labsheet 1.3, which contains the two tables of Roller Coaster Seating Preferences and Other Roller Coaster Preferences. The tables are like the ones found in the Student Edition, but with an added column for "Your Class Votes." Introduce the students to the surveys on roller-coaster preferences. Collect and tally the total responses from the class to each question. Add class data in the appropriate column.

Suggested Questions

- *Is it OK to say that more people online than 7th grade students want to sit up front?*

- *Do more 7th grade students like to sit up front than the people in our class?*

- *How can we make comparisons when sample sizes are different?*

- *How do we calculate the percent of each group that prefer to sit up front?*

- *Suppose you go online, respond to a survey, and then see a set of graphs dynamically updated to show the latest results of the survey once you have taken it. What kinds of graphs would be easiest to use?*

- *How would you set up the graphs?*

- *We have results of the survey from three different sample groups. How might we compare these results to see whether each group responded to the survey in a similar way?*

Key Vocabulary
- relative frequency

Materials

Labsheet
- 1.3: Roller Coaster Survey Responses

Teaching Aid
- 1.3: Bar Graphs for Roller Coaster Survey Responses

Explore

Teachers have completed this activity in one of two ways. One option is to work through the making of the graphs as a class. This means that the activity takes a short amount of time. It also takes away the opportunity for students to decide whether percents or counts are the better way to represent these data.

Another way is to organize students in teams of three. Students may prepare their solutions on chart paper so that they can present and post their solutions. The class discusses the variety of solutions.

As you visit groups, focus on using the same frequency scales for different graphs and on displaying frequencies using percents vs. counts. [**Note:** Bar graphs of the internet survey and 7th-grade responses are on Teaching Aid 1.3.]

Suggested Questions

- *For Question A, how might you compare the collected responses with the other two sets of data?*
- *How would you determine percents for each data set? For example, you know that 97 out of 165 respondents to the Internet survey voted for sitting at the front of a roller coaster. What percent of the votes is this?*
- *How does reporting relative frequencies help you compare the three sets of data?*

Question C is important. Since these are categorical data, only one measure of center may be used — the mode. Students may have trouble realizing that the median or mean will not work. Often, they will try to report the mean frequency or median frequency. Help them to see that the actual data are the responses to the survey; they are not numerical data.

- *For Question D, did you find any differences between groups?*
- *Did these differences surprise you, or do you have explanations for them?*
- *If you wanted to make a general statement about how people respond to the first survey question, what might you say based on our data?*
- *For Question E, how do you use statistics to help the manager predict how many people want to sit at the front of the roller coaster?*

Students may want to use the percents from the larger sample. If they want to use their own data, you can approach the idea that maybe one class of 7th-grade students is not similar in tastes to the varied age levels that the manager is thinking about. If they want to combine data sets, ask why—perhaps they intuitively think that a larger set is a more reliable predictor.

Summarize

Teaching Aid 1.3 displays the relative frequency bar graphs from the online survey and the group of 7th-grade students. With the students, look at the two different bar graphs for the first survey question (the one about seating preferences). For comparison, include a bar graph of your own class data from the survey. Specifically, consider why relative frequencies as opposed to actual frequencies are needed to make the data sets appear as if they each are the same size. (Each data set is redefined as "out of 100.") It is as if each survey had been given to exactly 100 people in that survey group.

Suggested Questions

- *What percent of the votes from the online-survey respondents like to ride up front in a roller coaster? How does this percent compare with that of the 7th graders?*
- *How do the other seat locations compare for the two groups?*

You can have a similar conversation about the second survey question (about roller coaster characteristics).

Assignment Guide for Problem 1.3

Applications: 8 | Connections: 21
Extensions: 27–33

Answers to Problem 1.3

A. Answers will vary depending on class data collected.

B.

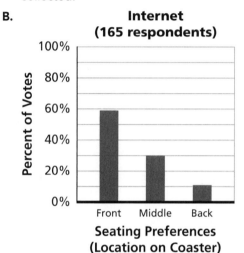

Internet
(165 respondents)

*Seating Preferences
(Location on Coaster)*

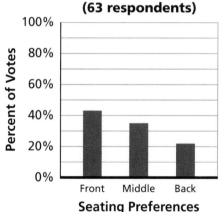

7th Graders
(63 respondents)

*Seating Preferences
(Location on Coaster)*

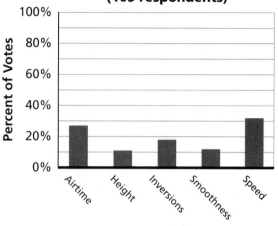

Internet
(165 respondents)

Coaster Characteristics

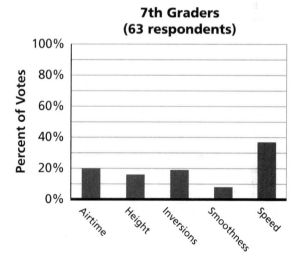

**7th Graders
(63 respondents)**

Coaster Characteristics

Students will also provide bar graphs of their own class data.

Bar graphs showing percent frequencies of the categories of responses are probably the better way to represent these data. Using percent frequencies treats each category of the responses as a part–whole situation expressed as a percent. Using counts for frequencies makes comparisons difficult.

C. The mode can be used to describe these results because it is a measure of center for categorical (nominal) data.

D. 1. The comparison statements may include class data, so answers will vary. Possible statements include: For Question 1, both groups had "front" as their first choice and "back" as their last choice. The online respondents had a stronger preference for the front (about 60%) than did the original sample of three 7th-grade classes. For Question 2, both samples indicated a preference for "airtime" and "speed" when riding a roller coaster. Again, the online respondents had stronger preferences for each of these choices when compared to the 7th-grade classes. You might think that the votes from the Web site sample reflect avid coaster riders; they can choose to respond and it's likely that responses to the online survey attract those who like to ride coasters.

2. Student answers will vary. Possible statements include: Most people surveyed like to ride at the front of the coaster, although the 7th graders like to ride in the middle almost as much as the front. Most people also like "speed" when they ride roller coasters. Summaries are helpful in order to make general conclusions about the data, although these are just samples.

E. About 200 people would prefer to sit in front. Reasoning will vary: Students can apply the thinking developed in *Comparing and Scaling*. Students might decide to look at the relative frequency reported to answer this question for each of the three surveys. For example, for Votes from the Web site, 59% preferred to sit up front. For Votes for 7th Graders, 43% had this preference. You can also look at the percent related to your class vote. Some students may want to combine the data – total number of responses to sit up front to total number of responses possible and use this percent. Then they would take this percent of 400 to find an answer to this question.

1.4 Are Steel-Frame Coasters Faster Than Wood-Frame Coasters? Using the IQR to Compare Statistics

> *Focus Question* How might you decide whether steel-frame coasters or wood-frame coasters are faster?

Launch

Discuss Labsheets 1.4A and 1.4B.

Suggested Questions

- *Is there any information that surprises you? Why or why not?*
- *What other information might we collect about roller coasters?*
- *How might you go about collecting this information?*

Explore

Ask students what might be considered a fast speed for a roller coaster *before* analyzing the data. Encourage students to think about whether they use speed as a criterion when choosing to ride a roller coaster.

Suggested Questions

- *Do you need the same scale for each graph? Why or why not?*
- *Look at the shapes of the two distributions. What do you notice?*
- *What statistics might you use to compare the two distributions?*

Students can identify that the means are not the same, but the difference between the two is not important in this context. The same is true for the difference between the medians.

- *The measures of center differ by about 2 to 3 miles per hour. Do you think you would notice that difference if you were riding a coaster?*

Summarize

Have each group prepare and share a report explaining which type of coaster is faster. Students should realize that comparisons of samples have to take both centers and spread into account.

Suggested Questions

- *For Question D, do you agree with Charlie's overall conclusion?*
- *Do you agree with Rosa's overall conclusion that steel-frame coasters are faster in general, but not all steel-frame coasters are faster?*

Key Vocabulary

- census
- population

Materials

Labsheets
- 1.4A: Sample of 30 Steel-Frame Roller Coasters
- 1.4B: Sample of 30 Wood-Frame Roller Coasters

Accessibility Labsheet
- 1.4C: Dot Plots of Top-Speed Data

Assessment
- Check Up

- Data and Graphs Tool

Answers to Problem 1.4

A. Answers will vary for all parts (1)–(3), since students are asked opinions/predictions. Possible answers:

  1. 60 mi/h and higher seems fast for a roller coaster since that speed is like driving on a highway.

  2. Yes. Knowing the top speeds of the roller coasters, I would choose the coaster with the faster speed.

  3. Some wood-frame roller coasters are faster than steel-frame roller coasters, but not all. For example, Wood-Frame Coaster 30 has a top speed of 66 mi/h, but Steel-Frame Coasters 21–30 all have speeds of 66 mi/h or above.

B. **1.** For steel-frame coasters: minimum value = 22; maximum value = 90; range = 68 mi/h; mean ~ 55.03 mi/h

    For wood-frame coasters: minimum value = 25 mi/h; maximum value = 66 mi/h; range = 41 mi/h; mean ~ 52.6 mi/h

    The speeds of steel-frame roller coasters appear to be faster than the speeds of wood-frame coasters because the mean of the wood-frame data is greater than the mean of the steel-frame data.

  2. The IQR for steel-frame coasters is 28 mi/h; the median is 54.5 mi/h; the IQR for wood-frame coasters is 10 mi/h; the median = 53 mi/h. The IQR for steel-frame coasters is more than twice the IQR for wood-frame coasters. The median of the steel-frame coasters is greater than the median of the wood-frame coasters, but the middle 50% of speeds of steel-frame coasters are more variable than those of wood-frame coasters.

  3. At least 25% of the steel-frame coasters have speeds that are faster than those of wood-frame coasters. (See Figures 1 and 2.)

C. Answers will vary. In summary, the measures of center for steel- and wood-frame coasters are somewhat similar. Speeds of steel-frame coasters vary greatly. Measures of spread (specifically the IQR), show that at least 25% of the steel-frame coasters have speeds that are faster than those of wood-frame coasters.

D. Answers will vary. It is possible to agree with Charlie while still criticizing his lack of attention to measures of spread. Charlie looked only at measures of center to conclude that there was no real difference in the speeds of steel-frame and wood-frame roller coasters. He is correct to point out that outliers affect the mean, and so the measures of center for the steel-frame roller coasters and wood-frame roller coasters are actually rather similar. He does not, however, pay any attention to measures of spread. Looking at measures of spread (as Rosa did) highlights the variability in the steel-frame-coaster speeds.

Figure 1   **Steel-Frame Roller Coaster Top Speeds** ⊥ Median

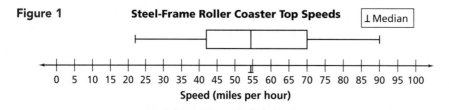

Speed (miles per hour)

Figure 2   **Wood-Frame Roller Coaster Top Speeds** ⊥ Median

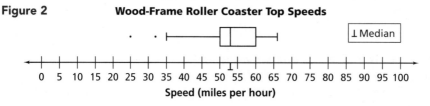

Speed (miles per hour)

Problem 2.1 Pacing 1 *Day*

2.1 Asking About Honesty: Using a Sample to Make Predictions

> *Focus Question* What is a population? What is a sample? What is a sampling plan?

Launch

Explain that we can often use data about a sample to draw conclusions about an entire population.

Introduce the survey about honesty, Teaching Aid 2.1. Ask students to read the survey and to consider how it describes honest behavior.

Suggested Questions

- *If you wanted to use this survey to study the honesty of the students in our school, how would you go about collecting the data?*

- *In order to draw conclusions about the students in our school, is it necessary to ask everyone in the school to complete the survey?*

- *If you wanted to gather information from a sample of students in our school, how would you decide whom to ask? In other words, what would your sampling plan be?*

> *Key Vocabulary*
> - sample
> - sampling plan
>
> *Materials*
>
> **Teaching Aid**
> - 2.1: Honesty Survey

Explore

Students may need help constructing a graph in Question C. Since the data are categorical, students should use a bar graph reporting percent frequencies. Placing bars for "honest" and "dishonest" answers next to each other allows for comparisons across questions.

Look for different strategies in Question D. Students have opportunities to apply concepts they learned in *Decimal Ops* and *Comparing and Scaling*.

Suggested Questions

- *How might you scale up the results of the survey to try to predict something about the whole population of U.S.?*

- *Why would percentages help?*

Summarize

Questions B, C, and D are rather straightforward mathematically and offer a brief review of percents. Discuss students' solution strategies. If more than one answer is presented, resolve any questions about working with percents.

Suggested Questions

- *Why are percentages useful in Question C?*

Have students share their responses to Question E, which asks why the results of this survey may not apply to all Americans.

Students will have a variety of ideas about revising the sampling plan in response to Question E, part (2). Ask them to identify the problems they are trying to remedy by using a plan other than the one developed by the magazine.

- *Is that sampling plan more likely to give results that represent the entire population [i.e., the sample has characteristics that accurately reflect those of the larger population from which they were chosen]?*

Applications: 1–4 | Connections: 18–19
Extensions: 39

Answers to Problem 2.1

A. The population is the population of the United States; the sample is the readers of this particular magazine who log on and respond to the Internet survey. The sampling plan is to ask people to answer the survey.

B. 1. a: 3,960 ÷ 5,280 = 75%, **b:** 792 ÷ 5,280 = 15%, **c:** 528 ÷ 5,280 = 10%.

  2. 4,752 ÷ 5,280 = 90% of respondents would tell the cashier about the error.

  3. 4,224 ÷ 5,280 = 80% of respondents said they would not cheat on an exam.

  4. 5,280 − 1,584 = 3,696; 3,696 ÷ 5,280 = 70% of respondents said they would not download music from the Internet.

C. 1. (See Figures 1 and 2.)

  2. People are honest 70%–90% of the time. It appears that the more personal the interaction, the more likely the person is to act honestly.

D. 1. About 80% of 314 million, or about 251.2 million people, would not cheat on an exam.

  2. About 70% of 314 million, or about 219.8 million people, would not download music from the Internet.

E. 1. Possible answer: Only people who read this magazine and have the time and interest to respond will answer this survey. This group of people might be very different from an average group of U.S. citizens, and some people may have answered the survey more than once.

  2. Answers will vary. Possible suggestions may include using a sample other than readers of the magazine or using a method of survey other than the Internet.

Figure 1

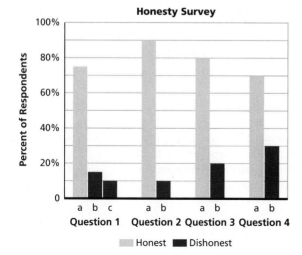

Figure 2

Relative Frequencies From Honesty Survey

Question Number	Honest Response	Dishonest Response
1	75%	25%
2	90%	10%
3	80%	20%
4	70%	30%

Samples and Populations **At a Glance**

At a Glance   Problem 2.2   Pacing 1 *Day*

2.2   Selecting a Sample: Different Kinds of Samples

> *Focus Question*   How could you select a sample of your school population to survey?

Launch

Introduce the topic by reading, or having students read, the two questions in the hypothetical research project.

Suggested Questions

- *How might you word these as survey questions for students?*
- *Do you think your questions are clear? What would happen if you asked students in your school each question?*
- *What sampling plan might you design to conduct this research?*
- *Suppose there are more students in one grade than another and you want to represent both grades. How will you address this in your sampling plan?*
- *What are some ways you might represent and analyze your data?*
- *When you are finished with the research project, what might you be able to say about how students in the school spend their time?*

Explore

If students have trouble understanding a particular sampling method, ask them to focus on the name of the strategy. Each is descriptive of the important feature of that method.

Suggested Questions

- *Will group X's plan result in a sample that is representative of the whole school? Explain.*
- *For Group 1, is it possible that students have some common characteristic that is more usual for bus riders than for students in the whole school?*
- *For Group 2, is it possible that this method systematically skips some groups of students?*
- *For Group 3, is it possible that having surveys from only students who want to respond distorts the results?*
- *For Group 4, is it possible that each student in the school has an equally likely chance of being included in the sample? Would this make the sample representative?*

Summarize

Post four sheets of paper at the front of the classroom. Divide each sheet into halves titled "Advantages" and "Disadvantages." Record students' ideas.

Key Vocabulary

- convenience sampling
- random sampling
- representative sample
- systematic sampling
- voluntary-response sampling

Materials

Accessibility Labsheet
- 2ACE: Exercises 20–22

- Data and Graphs Tool

- Expression Calculator Tool

After the class has reviewed the sampling plans, ask students to share their ideas about which plan would give the most representative sample. Ask students to explain their ideas and to critique the ideas of the other students.

ACE

Assignment Guide for Problem 2.2

Applications: 5–9 | Connections: 20–24
Extensions: 40

Answers to Problem 2.2

A. Possible advantages and disadvantages:

Group 1's plan is easy to implement, but the students on a particular bus probably all live in the same neighborhood and, as a result, won't necessarily be typical of all students.

Group 2's plan seems to offer a better prospect of surveying a variety of students from the school, but it is possible that the students who buy cafeteria lunches are not typical of all students. For example, it may be that students who wear braces don't buy cafeteria food as much as students who don't wear braces.

Group 3's plan is similar to the magazine's survey about honesty, with the disadvantage being that the sample will include only students that want to take the time to volunteer for the survey.

Group 4's plan would make each student equally likely to be chosen, but it may be more difficult to implement because each selected student would need to be tracked down.

B. Group 4's plan would probably give the most representative sample since each student has an equally likely chance of being chosen.

C. 1. Convenience sampling is choosing a sample based on the availability of respondents, people who are easy to locate and ask. Possible plans: Survey the students in a particular math class or homeroom or who belong to the same club or team.

2. Systematic sampling is choosing a sample by using a methodological technique. Possible plans: Choose every fifth name from an alphabetical list of students in each grade level, the first off each school bus one morning, or the student at the head of each row of seats in an auditorium assembly.

3. Voluntary-response sampling is asking people to choose to participate. Possible plan: Hand out surveys to all students, and ask them to return completed forms to a box in the school office.

4. Random sampling is giving every member of a population an equally likely chance of being selected. Possible plan: Choose student names or numbers by writing them all on slips of paper, mixing them in a bowl, and selecting slips of paper without looking.

D. 1. Groups 1, 2, and 3 are likely to result in samples that may not be representative. Group 1 is surveying only students who ride on their buses; they won't survey any students who don't take those buses. Group 2 will only survey students who eat school lunches. Group 3 is surveying only students who are motivated enough to respond.

2. i. It actually produces a *stratified* sample, which is not quite the same as a random sample.

ii. It does represent the student body, assuming the teachers choose the students randomly.

iii. Answers will vary. Students might raise the additional problem of unintended bias if the teachers asks the questions. To avoid this, the selection process could be as given, but the actual questions could be asked by a peer or students could be surveyed anonymously.

2.3 Choosing Random Samples: Comparing Samples Using Center and Spread

Focus Question How could you use statistics of a random sample of data to make predictions about an entire population?

Launch

Discuss the desirability of sampling plans that produce random samples.

Explore

Every student in each group of 3 should select a random sample of 30 students from the table of 100 7th-grade students found in the Student Edition. Because each sample will be different, students will explore variability related to sample data.

Have groups draw line plots of the distributions on Labsheet 2.3B. Students may use a MAD calculator.

Discuss Questions A and B before having students work on Question C.

Have groups draw box plots of the distributions on Labsheet 2.3C.

Summarize

Summarize after students complete Questions A and B. As the class views sets of line plots made by various groups of students, ask students to evaluate the plots.

Suggested Questions

- *Are there any apparent differences in the variability among the three samples drawn by each group of students?*
- *Now that you have seen the line plots produced by other students how would you answer the question asked in Question B, part (4)?*
- *What can you conclude about the movie-watching behavior of the population based on the patterns you have seen in the samples selected by the various groups?*

Choose data from a single sample and use just the one line plot.

- *What might you be able to say about the population if we had only one sample?*
- *What can you conclude about the movie-watching behavior of the population?*

A similar summary can take place after students explore Question C (refer to Explore). Distribute Labsheet 2.3C to each group.

- *What can you conclude about the hours of sleep of the population of 100 students based on the patterns in the samples selected by your group?*
- *Why might it be difficult to gather accurate data on topics like these?*

Materials

Labsheets
- 2.3A: Responses to Grade 7 Movie and Sleep Survey
- 2.3B: Blank Number Lines for Movies Watched Line Plots
- 2.3C: Blank Number Lines for Hours Slept Box Plots
- 10-Section Spinner

Teaching Aids
- 2.3: Graphs for Grade 7 Survey (Whole Population)

- 10-sided solids
- paper clips or bobby pins
- Probability Tool
- Data and Graphs Tool

Display Teaching Aid 2.3. Then ask:

- *How well did we predict the mean number of movies from a single sample? The median number of hours of sleep?*
- *Would some samples give better predictions than others?*
- *Does a line plot or box plot of your sample help you make a better prediction?*
- *Would any of our samples have given a very poor prediction?*

Note: Make the point that a random sample resulting in a poor prediction is not anyone's fault. This happens occasionally.

Applications: 10–14 | Connections: 25–31

Answers to Problem 2.3

A. **1.** Answers are the list of 30 student numbers selected as a sample.

   2. Answers will vary depending on sample selected. Students will record the number of movies watched and the number of hours slept for each student in the sample.

B. **1.** Dot plots of the distribution of data (movies watched) from the sample will vary.

   2. a. Answers will vary depending on the sample. However, as a point of reference, the mean of the 100-student database is 4.22 movies watched.

   b. The distribution may show some variability due to outliers, but the data may clump between 0 and 4 and cluster around 3 or 4. It is likely to be more balanced around the mean, but may still have some gaps.

   3. Possible answer: The range in number of movies may be different because there are outliers, but the data will probably clump between 0 and 4. The range for the population of 100 students is 17 movies (0 to 17 movies). The MAD indicates the spread of the data; a small MAD indicates less variability. The MAD for the movie data of the population is about 3.29 movies.

4. Answers will vary. Students can compare means, MADs, spread and shape.

5. Possible conclusion: The patterns in the samples collected by the class may show that the number of movies watched per week by the 100 students varies from about 0 to 17 (the range of the data), and clusters between 0–5 movies.

C. **1.** Box plots of the distribution of data (hours slept) from the sample will vary.

   2. Answers will vary depending on the sample. However, as a point of reference, the median of the 100-student database is 8 hours of sleep. Clustering in the data will probably occur around 7 or 8 hours of sleep. The IQR (interquartile range) can be used to talk about the variability of the data.

   3. Samples with a smaller IQR (or shorter box) have less variability in their data. The range for the population of 100 students is 9.8 hours (2 to 11.8 hours of sleep). The IQR for the sleep data of the population is 1.35 hours.

   4. Possible answer: The distributions have similar medians; the IQRs (and the boxes in the box plots) have similar spread.

   5. Possible conclusion: Although there may be some variation ranging from 5 to 11 hours, the population of 100 students typically sleeps around 8 hours, where the data cluster.

At a Glance   Problem 2.4   Pacing *2 Days*

2.4 Growing Samples: What Size Sample to Use?

> *Focus Question* Can you make good statistical estimates with less work by selecting smaller samples? How does sample size relate to the accuracy of statistical estimates?

Launch

Suggested Questions

- *In Problem 2.3, you analyzed samples of 30. Do you think you would get similar results from smaller sample sizes?*

For Question B, part (2), record the statistics on the board.

Using the class data, students will make a line plot of the distribution of the means for each of the size samples (5, 10, and 30 students).

Have students work in their groups to complete Questions D and E. Save Questions F and G until after the Problem Summarize.

Explore

Have students choose methods for generating random samples. Designate places for groups to record the movie data and the hours-slept data. For each sample size, let the class know when all groups have recorded their results so that they can draw line plots.

Students may need help understanding that the data in the line plots are not data about single students; each data value is a mean.

Suggested Questions

- *What does each point in your line plot represent? How is this the same as or different from the line plot you made in Problem 2.3?*
- *When you found the mean in Problem 2.3, what did it tell you?*
- *What does the mean of the data in this Problem tell you?*
- *Compare the line plot you made for your single sample of 30 in Problem 2.3 and the line plot of means from samples of 30 in Problem 2.4, Question C. What do you notice?*
- *What do you observe about the distribution of the means? How do the distributions of means for each sample size compare?*

Summarize

Display class line plots of the distributions of each set of data for the sample sizes.

Suggested Questions

- *What do you observe about the overall distributions?*
- *How do the three distributions for each sample size compare?*

Key Vocabulary
- sampling distribution

Materials

Labsheets
- 2.3A: Movie and Sleep Survey
- 2.4A: Movies Watched Last Week (Means)
- 2.4B: Movies Watched Last Week (Medians)
- 2.4C: Hours of Sleep Last Night (Means)
- 2.4D: Hours of Sleep Last Night (Medians)
- 2.4E: Group Organizer
- 2.4F: Class Organizer

Teaching Aid
- 2.3: Graphs for Grade 7 Survey (Whole Population)

Assessment
- Partner Quiz

- 10-sided solids
- paper clips or bobby pins
- Probability Tool
- Data and Graphs Tool

For Question G, bring the class back to the initial collection of data and statistics.

* *What do you notice about the MADs and IQRs?*

Assignment Guide for Problem 2.4

Applications: 15–17 | Connections: 32–38
Extensions: 41

Answers to Problem 2.4

A. Answers will vary (depends on samples).

B. **1.** Answers will vary (depends on samples).

2. Answers will vary (depends on samples).

C. **1.** Line plots will vary. The means for the samples of size 30 should cluster about the population mean of about 4. The means for samples of size 5 should show considerable variation. The means for samples of size 10 should show less variation than the means of samples of size 5, but more than the means for samples of size 30.

2. The mean number of movies for the 100 students is about 4.22. The larger the sample size, the better the estimate.

D. **1.** Medians for the samples of size 30 should cluster about the population median of 3. The medians for samples of size 5 may show variation and may not cluster closely around the population median of 3. For samples of size 10, the medians may show some variation, but not as much as the medians of samples of size 5. Medians may show less variation than means, even for small samples, since medians are less influenced by extreme data values than means.

2. The median number of movies for the 100 students is 3. The larger the sample size, the better the estimate.

E. Line plots for the means and the medians will vary. The medians for the samples of size 30 should cluster about the population median of 8. The medians for samples of size 5 may show variation, perhaps with a clustering around 7 to 9. The medians for samples of size 10 may also show some variation, less than the medians for samples of size 5, but more than the medians for samples of size 30.

The means for the sample size of 30 should cluster about the population mean of 7.7 hours. The means for samples of size 5 should show considerable variation, perhaps with a tendency to cluster between 7 and 9. The means for samples of size 10 should show less variation than the means of the samples of size 5, but more than the means for samples of size 30.

F. Possible answer: With a sample size of 50 students, the mean or the median number of movies watched or the hours slept, the line plots would show less variation than the line plots of samples of size 30. For the movie data: The line plots of the means will probably show a more pronounced clustering around the population mean of about 4. The line plots of the median will show a pronounced clustering around the population median of 3. For the hours slept, the line plots of the mean will show a more pronounced clustering around the mean of the population of about 7.7 hours. The line plots of the median will show a more pronounced clustering around the median of the population of 8 hours.

G. Answers will vary. Students should notice that variability drops as sample size increases. The characteristics of the sample become closer to those of the population as a whole.

3.1 Solving an Archeological Mystery: Comparing Samples Using Box Plots

Focus Question How might you analyze samples from known and unknown populations to determine whether the unknown population has one or more attributes in common with the known population?

Launch

In Problem 3.1, students extend the understanding they built in Investigation 2. Students have explored using data collected with random sampling to make inferences about a population. Investigation 3 extends this by asking students to draw conclusions by comparing more than one population.

Suggested Questions

- *There are six tables showing data in this Problem. In each table, there is a lot of data listed. How might you make these large sets of data easier to compare?*

- *What statistics might be helpful in comparing these data? What displays might be helpful?*

Discuss the archeological digs described in Problem 3.1. Give students time to familiarize themselves with the tables.

As a class, discuss how your students might approach this Problem.

- *What does this Problem ask you to figure out?*

- *What do you know that can help you with this Problem?*

- *How can you estimate the time period during which each of the two unknown sites was settled?*

- *Do you have enough data to make good comparisons?*

Materials

Labsheets
- 3.1A: Arrowhead Data
- 3.1B: Blank Tables for Arrowhead Summary Statistics
- 3.1C: Arrowhead Summary Statistics
- 3.1D: Box Plots for Arrowhead Data
- Graph Paper

- calculators
- Data and Graphs Tool

Explore

The Problem is stated in an open-ended way. Students can develop their own strategies for determining when each unknown site was settled. For each site, students are asked to both calculate summary statistics as well as construct box plots to represent the data and make comparisons. They can rely either on the box plots or the statistics to draw conclusions about Sites I and II.

If students are using graphing calculators, they may want to calculate statistics with the calculator and then construct the box plot on paper to summarize their findings. If they are using statistical software, it may be possible to display all six box plots on one scale. Such a display can then be printed and analyzed.

Suggested Questions

- *How do you construct box plots to display the data?*
- *How can you use summary statistics to determine when the unknown sites were settled? The box plots?*
- *Are the summary statistics for either of the unknown-site samples identical to the statistics for a known-site sample? If they are not identical, how can you decide what time period the unknown-site samples are from?*

Summarize

Ask students to discuss their conclusions and justify their answers. The box plots students have drawn will yield two distinct groups of data, one with generally higher medians than the other. These data provide a way to identify the time periods during which the new sites may have been settled.

Ask questions to help students think about how to apply what they have learned.

Suggested Questions

- *Are you able to make comparisons among samples of different sizes?*
- *For the known sites, which populations can you group together? What similarities do you see between these sites?*
- *What inferences can you make about the two unknown sites by comparing their data? What inferences can you make about the two unknown sites by comparing their data to the data from the known sites?*

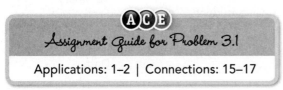

Applications: 1–2 | Connections: 15–17

Answers to Problem 3.1

A. 1. (See Figures 1 and 2, next page.)

   Note: Students may or may not show outliers on their box plots.

   2. a. Site I was most likely settled between 4000 B.C. and 500 A.D. The box plots for the Site I data are more similar to the box plots for the Laddie Creek/Dead Indian Creek and Kobold/Buffalo Creek data. Site I has a similar variability and similar mean to the sites settled between 4000 B.C. and 500 A.D. Also, when compared to the Site II, Big Goose Creek, and Wortham Shelter box plots, the Site I box plot is very different.

   Looking at the statistics, the medians of the sites from the 4000 B.C. to A.D. 500.

period vary from 33.5 to 45 and the means vary from 35 to 45.9. These statistics are a bit more spread out but, again, when the statistics are compared with the statistics of the three other sites, it is clear that Site I is similar to the Kobold/Buffalo Creek and Laddie Creek/Dead Indian Creek sites.

b. Site II was most likely settled between A.D. 500 and A.D. 1600. The box plot for Site II is similar to the plots for Big Goose Creek and Wortham Shelter.

Looking at the statistics, the medians vary from 24 to 26 and the means vary from 23.6 to 26.3. The ranges of data are also similar (between 24 and 30), whereas the ranges for the other three sites are between 27 and 53. The data for the two known sites are a bit more spread out, but Site II has two outliers which extend the box plot.

Samples and Populations At a Glance

B. **1.** (See Figures 3 and 4, next page.)

2. The statistics and box plots for arrowhead width do support the conclusions drawn in Question A.

Site I data are similar to the data from the Kobold/Buffalo Creek and Laddie Creek/Dead Indian Creek settlements. The widths are greater and the data are more spread out.

Site II data are similar to the data from the Big Goose Creek and Wortham Shelter settlements. The widths are shorter and the data are less spread out.

C. The sample sizes for Laddie Creek (18 arrowheads) and Site I (15 arrowheads) data are somewhat small. However, the data in this Problem imply that it is possible to make predictions based on sample sizes that

Figure 1

Arrowhead Lengths (in millimeters)

Statistics	Kobold/ Buffalo Creek	Laddie Creek/Dead Indian Creek	Site I	Site II	Big Goose Creek	Wortham Shelter
Minimum	25	25	24	13	16	18
Q1	38	29	29	20	21	23
Median	45	33.5	38	24	26	26
Q3	52	40	45	25.5	29.5	30
Maximum	78	52	63	43	40	42
Range	53	27	39	30	24	24
Mean (nearest tenth)	45.9	35	39.6	23.6	25.4	26.3
MAD (nearest tenth)	8.7	5.9	9.7	2.6	4.5	3.9

Figure 2

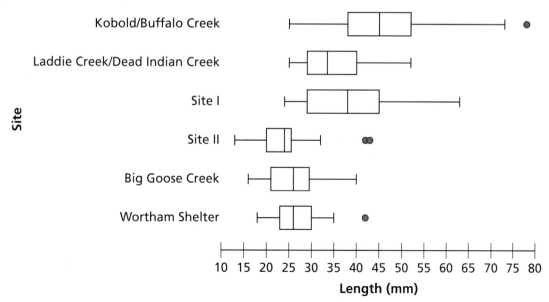

Arrowheads

Site

Length (mm)

AT A GLANCE 3

are somewhat smaller than we might like to have. The samples from the known sites and the unknown sites are of relatively reasonable size. They can be used to draw conclusions about the characteristics of the populations.

If archeologists had collected only a few arrowheads from each new site, however, the data they collected might not have been representative. For example, if the shortest arrowheads from Site I and the longest arrowheads from Site II had been chosen, the two data sets might have been classified in the same time period.

This Question solidifies concepts explored in Investigation 2. In that Investigation, students learned that there is less variability in medians and means for samples of 30 than for samples of 5 or 10.

Figure 3

Arrowhead Widths (in millimeters)

Statistics	Kobold/ Buffalo Creek	Laddie Creek/Dead Indian Creek	Site I	Site II	Big Goose Creek	Wortham Shelter
Minimum	16	14	16	10	10	11
Q1	19	17	19	12	12	13
Median	21	18	22	13	13	14
Q3	22	20	26	14	14	15
Maximum	26	23	32	24	18	18
Range	10	9	16	14	8	7
Mean (nearest tenth)	20.7	18.6	23.3	13.4	13.3	14.4
MAD (nearest tenth)	1.8	1.8	3.5	1.5	1.2	1.2

Figure 4

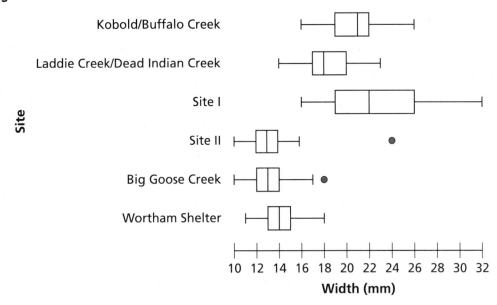

Samples and Populations   **At a Glance**

3.2 Comparing Heights of Basketball Players: Using Means and MADs

Focus Question How can you determine whether differences in sample data are large enough to be meaningful, or just due to naturally occurring variability from one sample to another?

Launch

In Investigation 1, students learned that most of the data values in a distribution are usually located within two MADs from the mean of that distribution. Data values greater than two MADs from the mean (or less than two MADs from the mean) are generally few in number. They are, therefore, seen as unexpected values for the overall distribution.

Suggested Questions

- *How might you determine which values are unexpected for a distribution of data?*

- *In this Problem, you will be comparing two distributions of data that have similar variabilities. How can you tell whether two distributions of data have similar variabilities?*

Discuss heights of basketball players as a class. The data values are given in centimeters. Make sure your students can visualize the magnitude of these heights.

- *Look at the two dot plots. What information does each dot plot give?*

- *How much taller do you think these basketball players are than the students in our class?*

Students need to develop a sense of how tall these players are, especially since they may not be familiar with measurements taken with the metric system. Ask students about the conversion rate from centimeters to inches (2.5 cm ≈ 1 inch).

- *Who is taller, the male basketball players or the female basketball players? How do you know?*

- *These two distributions have similar variabilities. Because of this, we can compare the means of the distributions rather accurately. The difference between the means is about 16 centimeters (or about 6 inches). Do you think this difference in means is just due to the fact that heights vary from sample to sample? Or do you think that you can say that male basketball players are generally taller than female basketball players? In other words, if you were given two other samples from the male basketball player and the female basketball player populations, might you find there is no difference in heights?*

Materials

Labsheet
- 3.2: Heights of Basketball Players

Accessibility Labsheets
- 3ACE: Exercises 3–6
- 3ACE: Exercise 7
- calculators
- Data and Graphs Tool

AT A GLANCE 3

• *In this Problem, you need to find a way to show whether the sample means differ this much because of naturally occurring variability from one sample to another, or whether they differ this much because the population of male professional basketball players is measurably taller than the population of female professional basketball players.*

Explore

After students finish Question C, you may want to do a mini-summary.

Suggested Questions

• *Where does the mean height of the male players fall on the dot plot of the heights of the female players?*

• *What does this tell you about the mean male player height in comparison to the female player heights?*

• *Where does the mean height of the female players fall on the dot plot of the heights of the male players?*

• *What does this tell you about the mean female player height in comparison to the male player heights?*

Students will likely think that the distribution shown in Question D is of male professional basketball player heights. Encourage them justify their answer by explaining how they compared the distribution in Question D to each of the distributions discussed in the introduction.

Summarize

During the Summarize, spend time making sure that students justify the reasoning behind their comparisons. First have the students provide answers to Problem 3.2. Then have them explain generally how they can discuss differences in sample data by addressing the Focus Question.

Suggested Questions

• *For Question D, how did you determine whether the sample data was taken from a male professional basketball player population or a female professional basketball player population?*

• *Do you think that the differences between the male basketball player sample heights and the female basketball player sample heights prove that there are meaningful height differences in those populations? Or, do the differences in the samples simply show naturally occurring variability?*

A C E

Assignment Guide for Problem 3.2

Applications: 3–7 | Connections: 24–28

Answers to Problem 3.2

A. The MADs of the two distributions are similar. They are only about 2 units away from one another. So, the variabilities are similar. On the other hand, the means are quite different. The means differ by about 16 centimeters, which is a noticeable difference in height.

B. **1.** (See Figures 1 and 2, next page.)

2. Female professional basketball player distribution: 93.75% (30 of the 32 data values) are within two MADs of the mean.

Male professional basketball player distribution: 90.625% (29 of the 32 data values) are within two MADs of the mean.

3. (See Figures 3 and 4.)

100% of the data values fall within three MADs of the mean for each distribution.

Figure 1

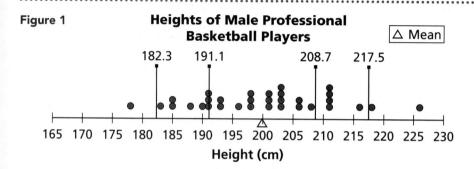

Heights of Male Professional Basketball Players

Figure 2

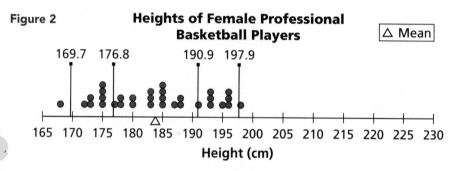

Heights of Female Professional Basketball Players

Figure 3

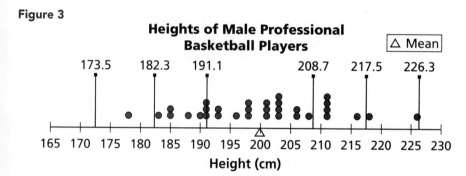

Heights of Male Professional Basketball Players

Figure 4

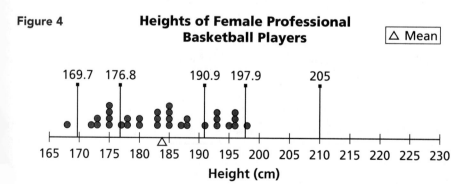

Heights of Female Professional Basketball Players

AT A GLANCE 3

C. 1. (See Figure 5.)

    a. The mean of the male professional basketball player distribution, 199.9063, is greater than two MADs from the mean of the female professional basketball players.

    b. The mean of the male professional basketball player distribution, then, is considered to be an unexpected height for female professional basketball players.

  2. (See Figure 6.)

    a. The mean of the female professional basketball player distribution, 183.8125, is close to two MADs less than the mean of the male professional basketball players, but it does fall within two MADs of the mean.

    b. This is within the expected range of male professional basketball player heights, but at the very low end.

  3. The samples are large, random samples, so they are likely to be representative of the population. If you have evidence that the mean of the sample of male heights is an unexpected value for the sample of female heights, you can extend that conclusion to the populations, as well. The mean (or typical) height of the male population of basketball players is noticeably different from the mean height of the female population of basketball players.

D. This distribution has a mean of 197.9259 and a MAD of 7.6488. Because of the mean, this distribution is more likely a sample of male professional basketball players than a sample of female professional basketball players.

If you mark the mean of 197.9259 on the female professional basketball players' distribution of heights, it is just slightly within the 2 MADs mark, so it probably not a distribution of female professional basketball players. If you mark the mean of 197.9259 on the distribution of male professional basketball player heights, it is located very close to the mean of the male professional basketball player distribution, and it is clearly less than one MAD from the mean. It is likely that this data value would occur in the male professional basketball player distribution.

Figure 5

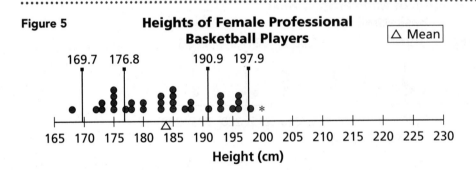

Heights of Female Professional Basketball Players

Figure 6

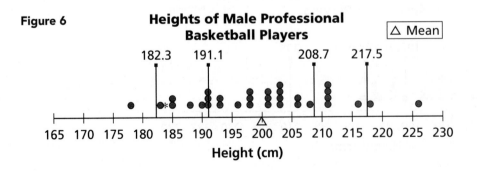

Heights of Male Professional Basketball Players

  Samples and Populations   **At a Glance**

Problem 3.3 Pacing $1\frac{1}{2}$ Days

3.3 Five Chocolate Chips in Every Cookie: Using Sampling in a Simulation

> **Focus Question** How can you simulate a real-world problem? How can you analyze the data that you collect from that simulation to draw conclusions?

Launch

Problem 3.3 includes applications of probability in its structure, building upon Investigation 2 and *What Do You Expect*. In this Problem, students consider the number of total chocolate chips that should be mixed in the dough for a batch of 12 cookies so that each cookie gets at least 5 chips.

You may want to review the process of constructing a histogram before students work on their own. They are required to construct one for Question C.

As a class, discuss the illustration of a sample batch of cookies in the Student Edition, which shows that the chocolate chips often will not be evenly distributed among 12 cookies.

Suggested Questions

- *There are 60 total chips in this batch of cookies. Why does Jeff think that 60 chips should be added to the dough?*
- *Does each cookie have five chips?*
- *What does this Problem ask you to figure out?*

Before discussing Hadiya's Simulation in the Student Edition, ask students to think about ways that they might explore this Problem. Students may or may not suggest that they need to simulate this situation.

- *Why is it important that you share your results with your classmates? Why is it important that you use your classmates' results to come up with a solution to the problem?*

Make sure the students understand the overall plan for how to simulate distributing chocolate chips among 12 cookies in a batch.

Explore

Students need to track the process of their simulations and data analysis as they complete the Problem. The data collection and analysis shifts throughout the Problem.

In Question A, students work on collecting individual data as they assign cookie numbers to each "chip" that they place in the batch of dough.

Suggested Questions

- *How might you generate integers from 1 to 12 at random?*
- *On average, how many chips are there per cookie? What do you think of Jeff's earlier reasoning based on your results?*

Key Vocabulary
- simulate

Materials

Labsheets
- 3.3: Cookie Simulation Tables
- 3ACE: Exercises 8 and 9
- 12-Section Spinners
- Graph Paper

- spinners
- number cubes
- coins
- calculators
- Probability Tool
- Coordinate Grapher Tool

- *What does the box plot tell you about batches of cookies mixed with the median number of chips? What does the histogram tell you about batches of cookies mixed with the maximum number of chips?*

At any stage of the Problem (during Question A or E), students who are finished early can conduct an additional simulation. Having more sets of results by completing the simulations several times can only be beneficial. It is essential that students have enough samples to support their conclusions with confidence.

Summarize

Throughout the Problem, students should be sharing their data and responses so that all students can benefit from multiple samples of data. Ensure that students share their answers for Questions D and E in the Summarize.

Suggested Questions

- *How did you decide on the number of chips to put in a batch?*
- *Did you use the simulation that results in the greatest number of chips, or did you choose a lesser number? Is adding this many chips to a batch of a dozen cookies practical? Why?*
- *Were you surprised by the results of the simulations?*
- *What is the average number of chips per cookie that would result from your recommendation?*
- *In each simulation, the cookie with the fewest chips contained 5 chips. How many chips did the cookie(s) with the most chips contain? Is this many chips in a cookie realistic?*
- *What kinds of displays can you construct with these data? Which displays are most useful for addressing the Problem? Explain.*

Assignment Guide for Problem 3.3

Applications: 8–10 | Connections: 18–23
Extensions: 30

Answers to Problem 3.3

A. 1. $\frac{1}{12}$, $0.08\overline{3}$, or $8.\overline{3}\%$

  2. Answers will vary. All methods should rely on there being an equal probability that any number 1–12 will be generated for each trial. Possible methods: cards labeled with numbers 1–12 (which would need to be re-shuffled after each trial); a combination of a number cube and a coin toss; a spinner with 12 sections.

  3. Simulation results will vary.

B. The total number of chips will vary. Ensure that your students have tallied up the total number of chips in all the cookies when they provide this answer to the class.

C. Figures 1 and 2 show the results from a class in which 20 simulations were conducted; both a histogram and a box plot are shown.

  1. (See Figure 1, next page.)

  2. Answers will vary based on the data collected. Students should comment on the range and overall spread, whether or not the histogram is symmetric, any measures of center or variability, and the shape of the distribution (where the data cluster or gap). Students should also describe why they chose their interval size and what patterns are visible because of that interval size. Last, students should describe conclusions they can draw based on the histogram. For example, using the histogram above, a student might say that using 160 chips would ensure that each cookie will always have 5 chips. This gives an average, however, of 13 chips per cookie. This number is too many average chips per cookie.

3. (See Figure 2.)

4. Answers will vary based on the data collected. Students should comment on where 50% of the data are located (the box of box plot). They can comment on the range and overall spread, the presence or absence of outliers, and the median and IQR. Students can comment on the shape of the distribution, noting where the data appear to cluster based on the four quartiles of the box plot. They can describe whether the box plot is symmetric or skewed. Last, students should describe conclusions they can draw based on the box plot. For example, using the box plot above, a student might say that using 160 chips would ensure that each cookie will always have 5 chips. This gives an average, however, of 13 chips per cookie. This number is too many average chips per cookie. They might state that using the number of chips identified at Q3 (in the example above, about 118) would give enough chips per cookie for about 75% of the batches.

Figure 1

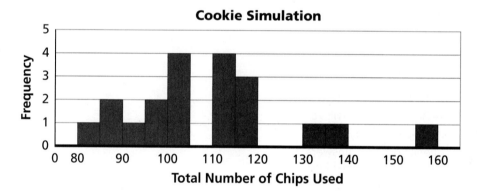

Figure 2

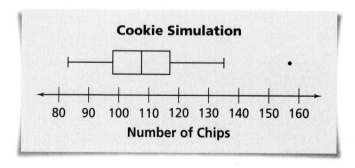

5. Answers will vary based on the data collected. All students should arrive at the same mean and median, as they are computing class data. Students can comment on how different the mean and median are, and draw conclusions based on whether the median and mean are similar or different.

D. In their answers, students might decide to add at least as many chips as required in the worst-case batch (which is the greatest number of chips found in the simulation). If they do this, you may want to point out that the question states that Jeff and Hadiya do not want to waste money. Students may, on the other hand, suggest a number that works most of the time. Students will need to define what that means. With any recommended number, students must explain their reasoning. This explanation is the critical portion of the answer. A good answer might be to choose Quartile 3 as a recommendation.

E. **1.** The recommended number of chips will vary from class to class.

2. The results of the 30 simulations will vary.

3. Students can calculate this answer by dividing the frequency of "yes" answers by 30, then converting this decimal into a percent.

4. Recommendations will vary. Again, the justification of the recommendation is the most important part of this answer.

5. Slogans will vary. Student answers might use specifics statistics from their simulation. A possible slogan may be, "We are reasonably certain that _____% of the time, every cookie in a batch will have at least five chips!"

3.4 Estimating a Deer Population: Using Samples to Estimate Size of a Population

Focus Question   How can you estimate the size of a large population?

Launch

Suggested Questions

Ask students what they know about estimating the size of populations that can't be easily counted.

Review the steps of the bean experiment. You may want to model the experiment with a small container of beans:

- Take a sample of beans and mark them. Remember how many you marked.

- Return the marked beans to the container. Ask students what they should do now.

- Mix the marked and unmarked beans together. Ask your students how they might use the marked beans to estimate the total number of beans in the container.

- Take a new sample and count the marked and unmarked beans. Ask students how they can use the gathered information.

Students now know the number of marked beans in the population, the number of marked beans in the sample, and the sample size.

- *How can you use ratios to estimate the number of beans in the whole population?*

Key Vocabulary

- capture–tag–recapture

Materials

Labsheets
- Labsheet 3.4: Capture–Tag–Recapture Table
- Graph Paper

Accessibility Labsheet
- 3ACE: Exercise 11

Assessments
- Self-Assessment
- Notebook Checklist
- Unit Test
- containers of beans
- markers or pens
- calculators
- Probability Tool

Explore

The basic proportion to use has a few variations:

$$\frac{\text{marked beans in container}}{\text{total beans in container}} = \frac{\text{marked beans in sample}}{\text{total beans in sample}} \qquad \frac{\text{total beans in container}}{\text{marked beans in container}} = \frac{\text{total beans in sample}}{\text{marked beans in sample}}$$

$$\frac{\text{marked beans in sample}}{\text{marked beans in container}} = \frac{\text{total beans in sample}}{\text{total beans in container}} \qquad \frac{\text{marked beans in container}}{\text{marked beans in sample}} = \frac{\text{total beans in container}}{\text{total beans in sample}}$$

Suggested Questions

- *How do the different sample sizes change your estimates?*

- *Look at the line plots you made for Question D. Which line plots have the most variability? The least? How do these plots help you make a final estimate?*

Summarize

Suggested Questions

- *Which of the line plots you drew do you find most helpful in making an estimate? Why?*

- *How else could you display this data?*

Applications: 11–14 | Extensions: 29

Answers to Problem 3.4

A. 1. and 2. Answers will vary depending on how many beans are in the container. Be sure that students fill out the entire table shown in the Student Edition and provide a sufficient explanation as to how they made their estimates.

Capture–Tag–Recapture Sampling Data

Sample Size	Marked Beans	Unmarked Beans	Estimate of Total Number of Beans
25	8	17	313
50	20	30	250
75	29	46	259
100	42	58	238
125	36	89	347
150	58	92	259

3. The basic proportion to be solved in making an estimate of the total number of beans is below. There are four variations of the same proportion. Students can scale up for each trial to estimate the total number of beans in the container.

$$\frac{\text{marked beans in container}}{\text{total beans in container}} = \frac{\text{marked beans in sample}}{\text{total beans in sample}}$$

$$\frac{\text{total beans in container}}{\text{marked beans in container}} = \frac{\text{total beans in sample}}{\text{marked beans in sample}}$$

$$\frac{\text{marked beans in sample}}{\text{marked beans in container}} = \frac{\text{total beans in sample}}{\text{total beans in container}}$$

$$\frac{\text{marked beans in container}}{\text{marked beans in sample}} = \frac{\text{total beans in container}}{\text{total beans in sample}}$$

B. Possible answer: This experiment can be considered a simulation because it models a real-world process. People who study populations use the capture–tag–recapture method to estimate population sizes. This is similar to the capture–tag–recapture method, except it samples objects instead of living things.

C. Answers will vary. Students' explanations should match the data in their tables and give good support to their estimates. For the sample table provided for Question A, the mean of the estimates is about 278 and the median is about 259. Either of these would be sufficient estimates for the sample table.

D. 1. Answers will vary based on the data collected. Each group should draw the same line plots since the data is class-wide.

2. Answers will vary. Students should mention that the line plots displaying greater sample sizes will most likely contain more accurate data. Students might choose the mean or median of the class data collected for a sample size of 150 as their final estimate.

E. Biologists might count deer populations using the capture–tag–recapture method. They would catch a sample of deer, mark them with tags of some sort, and release them. Later, the biologists would catch another sample of deer and compute the ratio of tagged deer in the new sample to the total number of deer sampled. From this ratio, they would find an equivalent ratio using the total number of tagged deer and the expected number of deer in the population.

At a Glance

Pacing ☐ Day

Mathematical Goals ....

_____

_____

_____

_____

Launch ....

_____

_____

_____

_____

_____

Materials

Explore ....

_____

_____

_____

_____

_____

Materials

Summarize ....

_____

_____

_____

_____

_____

Materials

Notes

Applications

1. **a.** Mean = 8.5; Median = 8.5. The mean and median are identical.

    b. Mean = 8.5; Median = 8.5. The mean and median are identical.

    c. Both sets of measures of center are identical; students can only say that Jarrod's and Pascal's performances appear to be the same.

2. **a.** Range = 3.6; MAD = 1.0.

    b. Range = 1.8; MAD = 0.6.

    c. Jarrod's scores vary more than Pascal's scores. Jarrod's range is twice Pascal's; whereas his MAD is $1\frac{2}{3}$ times Pascal's MAD. Jarrod's performance is less consistent than Pascal's, so we can say that Pascal performs better overall.

3. Each team collected a sum of $270. You cannot answer which team performed better since the totals are all the same.

4. **a.** mean = $45 (Teams 1, 2, and 3); mean = $54 (Team 4); median = $44 (Teams 1, 2, and 4); median = $40 (Team 3)

    b. All but one team has the same mean. Team 4 only has 5 people instead of 6, so its mean will be different since each team raises the same total amount of money. Based on the similar means, you cannot answer which team performed better. All but one team has the same median, so you cannot use the median to answer which team performed better. Some students may note that the mean in Team 4 is highest, so it was the most successful.

5. **a.** Range = $20 (Teams 1 and 2), $85 (Team 3), $45 (Team 4). Two teams have the same range. Team 3 has a large range due to the extreme values (high and low). MAD = 6 (Team 1), 8 (Team 2), 20 (Team 3), 18 (Team 4). The MADs indicate that Teams 3 & 4 have the greatest variability (lack of consistency) amongst team members.

    b. The different ranges do not answer the question of which team performed

better. Team 1 has the smallest MAD, so it performed more successfully due to the consistency of its members.

6. **a.** Team 1: 2 (33%)
    Team 2: 2 (33%)
    Team 3: 3 (50%)
    Team 4: 2 (40%)

    b. Team 1: 6 (100%)
    Team 2: 6 (100%)
    Team 3: 5 (83%)
    Team 4: 5 (100%)

    c. Team 1: 0 (0%)
    Team 2: 0 (0%)
    Team 3: 1 (17%)
    Team 4: 0 (0%)
    (See Figure 1, next page.)

7. Team 3 had one person whose money collected is greater than twice the MAD. This is not typical.

8. **a.** Students may draw a triple bar graph or three individual bar graphs. Students will need to use relative frequencies.

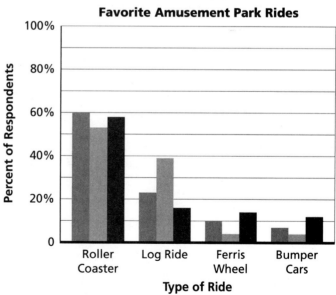

Favorite Amusement Park Rides

■ West Jr. High   ■ East Jr. High   ■ Internet

    b. Possible answers: Students from East Jr. High do not prefer the Ferris Wheel as often as West Jr. High or the Internet Survey. Students from East Jr. High prefer the Log Ride more commonly than the people from the Internet Survey. The West Jr. High students prefer the Roller Coaster more often than any other group.

9. For every one wood-frame roller coaster, there are about 18 steel-frame roller coasters.

10. North America has about 5.5 times as many roller coasters as South America.

11. Asia has about 2 times as many roller coasters as North America.

12. North America has 70% of all the wood-frame roller coasters in the world.

13. Possible answers: North America has about 3.5 times as many wood-frame coasters as Europe. Asia has 47% of all the steel-frame roller coasters in the world.

14. **a.** steel-frame: 15 coasters or 50%; wood-frame: 17 coasters or about 57%

    b. steel-frame: 26 coasters or about 87%; wood-frame: 27 coasters or 90%

    c. steel-frame: 4 coasters or about 13%; wood-frame: 3 coasters or 10%

15. **a.** Answers will vary. Possible statements: Roller coasters built in 1960 or later were taller and had greater maximum drops. You can see this by (1) comparing the means and medians and (2) by the general shift to the right in the distributions after 1959. It looks like the distributions of maximum heights and maximum drops are similar in shape and location. This probably means that there is a relationship here. The speeds of coasters built before 1960 are not as variable as those of coasters built after 1959; it looks like roller coasters were able to go faster (greater than 60 mph) after 1959.

    b. Answers will vary. Sample size is addressed in Investigation 2, but it certainly is appropriate for students to note that the sample size of coasters build before 1950 is small. One question might be whether there are others that could be included. If students want to pursue this, they can visit the website that has the census table about kinds of coasters for more data.

16. B

Figure 1

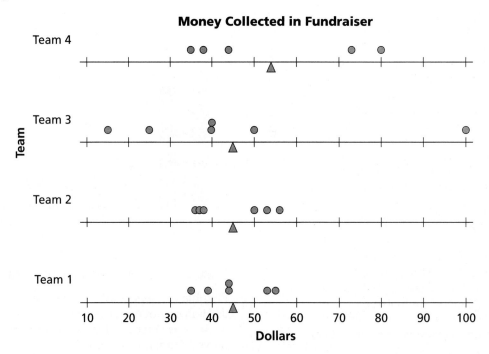

Money Collected in Fundraiser

Samples and Populations   ACE Answers

Connections

17. J

18. C

19. J

20. C; [(3 × 90) + 86] ÷ 4 = 89

21. a. Table 1: 9.1% (735 ÷ 8,114; students can also check by adding percents and subtracting total from 100%. This result will be 9.1%)
Table 2: 12.2% (968 ÷ 7,934; students can also check by adding percents and subtracting total from 100%. This result will be 12.2%)
Table 3, Boys: 41.1% (100% − 58.9%)
Table 3, Ages 5–12: 57.9% (100% − 42.1%)

b. (See Figure 2.)

c. Most children have lived in 1–3 apartments or houses (about 60%). The data peak at two apartments or houses (the mode) and then seem to taper off.

d. Use data from Table 1: 6% + 6.5% + 6.3% + 4.1% + 2.8% + 2.2% = 27.9% (you could also add all the counts and then divide the sum by 8,114).

e. Use data from Table 2: 20.7% have lived only in one home (taken directly from the question).

f. About $\frac{2}{5}$ of the boys have lived in the same city or town all their lives; 41.1% is close to 40%.

22. a. Wood-Frame Roller Coasters by Continent

b. Steel-Frame Roller Coasters by Continent

Sample explanation: There are no wood-frame roller coasters in Africa, so the graph in part (a) must show wood-frame coasters.

23. The shape appears to be clumped in two clusters, one from 0 g to 4 g and the other from 12 g to 15 g. The sugar per serving (g) has a range of 20 g (20 − 0).

24. Based on the shape, one can estimate that the mean and median are in the area of 10–12 grams of sugar; the halfway mark for the data is in this interval, and the mean and median are probably somewhat similar.

25. About one half of the cereals have serving sizes of 1 cup; only a few have larger serving sizes, and the rest have serving sizes of three-fourths cup, two-thirds cup, or one-half cup.

26. The mean is less than 1 cup and median is 1 cup serving size; the median has to be in this group at 1 cup, but there are more values below 1 that are a greater distance below 1 cup than the values above 1 cup, so the mean is less than 1 cup.

Figure 2

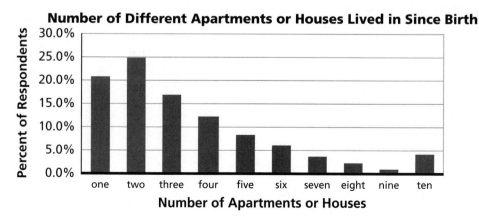

Number of Different Apartments or Houses Lived in Since Birth

Extensions

27. A mean of 143.3 bpm corresponds to exercise heart rates, and a mean of 89.4 bpm corresponds to resting heart rates. This is because 143.3 is close to the median of the exercise heart rate data (143), and all values for resting heart rates are less than 143.3 bpm. Also, 89.4 bpm is close to the median for the resting heart rate data (86 bpm).

28. A MAD of 8.9 bpm corresponds to the resting heart rate data, and a MAD of 27.3 bpm corresponds to the exercise heart rate data. The exercise heart rate data has greater variability (as shown by the greater range and IQR seen in the box plots), so its MAD must be greater.

29. The exercise heart rates distribution has the larger MAD. You compare MADs of the resting and exercise heart rates in order to report which distribution appears to have the greatest spread.

30. A resting heart rate distribution would have an IQR of 15.5 bpm. An exercise heart rate distribution would have an IQR of 59.5 bpm. This is because the sample distributions shown indicate that the variability in exercise heart rates is greater than the variability in resting heart rates.

31. Exercise heart rates' distribution has the larger IQR. You compare the IQRs of the resting and exercise heart rates in order to report which distribution appears to have the greatest spread.

32. Answers will vary. For example: Almost all the resting pulse rates are less than 75% of the exercise pulse rates. OR The spread of the exercise pulse rates is more than there times the spread of the resting pulse rates.

33. a.

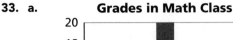

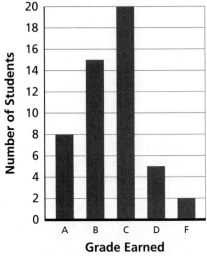

b. Relative frequencies: A (16%), B (30%), C (40%), D (10%), F (4%)

c.

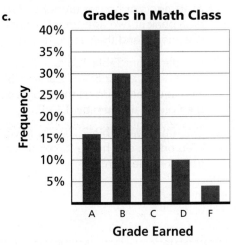

d. The shapes as shown in each bar graph are the same.

e. You would report relative frequencies if you wanted to make a prediction about a group that may have a different number of students. The percent can be used to calculate the actual counts.

Applications

1. The population being studied is the teenagers who read the magazine. The sampling method is to ask readers to voluntarily write in to the magazine. The sample is the volunteers.

2. The population being studied is middle-school students. The eighth-grade students keep records of the time they spend on the phone each day for a week. The sample is the eighth-grade class conducting the plan.

3. The population being studied is middle-school students. Forty cards are chosen from a box containing cards with the names of all the students in the school. The sample is the forty students chosen.

4. The population being studied is students who attend the particular school. The sampling method is to choose 26 students, one with a name beginning with A, one with B, etc. The sample is the 26 students chosen.

5. Systematic selection; Systematic selection from class lists would probably give a representative sample, provided the lists include the names of all students in the school.

6. Random selection; Based on the assumption that 350 students attend the assembly, selection by choosing red and white beans could produce a representative sample because every student has an equal chance of being in the sample.

7. Convenience sampling; Selection by surveying all members of particular classes would probably not give a representative sample because all students do not have an equally likely chance of being surveyed. It may be that students in these classes are assigned more homework on average and thus spend more time doing homework.

8. Voluntary response; This voluntary-response method would not give a representative sample because it depends on people's willingness to complete and return the surveys. Not everyone will complete a survey, and those who do might not place it in the box at the end of the day. Those who complete surveys may have some special reason for responding.

9. Voluntary response; Possible explanation: the results of this survey may not describe the opinions of all the show's listeners because only those listeners that have the time and want to call in with their opinion will be included. Some may try to call in and may not get through, while others may not listen to the radio program at the time that the opinion question is asked because they are at work.

10. The company could randomly select a certain number of video-game systems as they come off the production line. Or, the company could systematically select every nth video game as it comes off the production line. The company might increase the frequency of testing when a tested item shows flaws.

11. The company could randomly test a certain sample of compact discs for each recording artist. The number would depend on the difficulty, and thus the cost, of testing. It also depends on the number of defects found in previous samples.

12. The company may want to use a systematic sampling method or randomly select a certain percent of fireworks to test. However, since fireworks that have been tested cannot then be sold, keeping testing numbers to a minimum while still assuring safety is important.

13. Since tested bottles probably cannot be sold, it makes sense to use a sampling strategy that involves inspecting only a small sample of all bottles produced. A systematic sample might make sense because the machinery could be programmed to select every nth bottle and move it aside for testing.

14. **a.** This strategy may produce some biased samples because the students are most likely listed in some sort of order (such as alphabetically). You want to guarantee that every student has an equal chance of being included in a sample.

b. Again, this strategy does not give every student a chance of being included in the sample, and the students might be listed in some order—perhaps with odd-numbered students differing from even-numbered students in some way.

15. **a.** Answers will vary. Possible sampling method: find a random sample of 50 students by taking a numbered student list and using slips of paper to choose the sample. For example, if there are 700 students in the school, place the numbers 0, 1, 2, ..., 9 in a bucket. Pick one slip from the bucket for the hundreds digit, replace and pick another for the tens and replace that and pick another for the ones digit. If a number is picked that is greater than 700, disregard and repeat the process.

b. Take the percent of students that said yes in the sample and multiply it by 700, the population of the school.

16. about 8 hours

17. Possible answer: 30 students is better because if you choose too small a sample, for example 5 students, you could end up picking 2 students with outlier data values. These outliers affect the data more since you only have 5 in your sample. With more students in your sample, you are more likely to get a representative sample.

Connections

18. 5.1 (use the range to help make this decision)

19. **a.** One jar makes approximately 15 sandwiches; so 100 jars would make 1,500 sandwiches.

b. From age 5 to 18 is 14 years; $100 \div 14$ is approximately 7 jars per year for each student.

c. 15 sandwiches per jar $\times$ 7 jars per year = 105 sandwiches per year. Given 52 weeks in a year, a child eats about 2 peanut butter sandwiches a week ($105 \div 52$).

20. **Time Spent on Homework (minutes)**

Grade	Mean	Median	MAD
6	25.8	20	18.56
7	36.129	35	14.53

21. **a.** Grade 6: The mean is greater than the median because there are some unusually high values. Because of the spread, the MAD is also large.

Grade 7: The distribution looks more typical; the mean and median are similar, and the MAD is not as great as that of Grade 6.

b. If you compare means, the mean time for Grade 7 is about 11 minutes greater than that for Grade 6; the MAD for Grade 7 is a little more than $\frac{2}{3}$ of the MAD for Grade 6; if you compare the medians, the median time for Grade 7 is 15 minutes greater than that for Grade 6.

22. These data may not be representative of all school nights because students may typically have more homework on some nights than on others. Also, depending on the sampling plan, the sample may not be representative.

23. **a.** The mean is 23; the range is $25 - 20 = 5$.

b. Answers will vary. Possible answers: Add 44, 45, and 45, which gives a new mean of 29.5 and a range of 25 ($45 - 20 = 25$). Or add 0, 0, and 10,000, which gives a new mean of 1,016.1 and a range of 10,000 ($10,000 - 0 = 10,000$).

c. Answers will vary. Possible answer: Add 5, 9, and 8, which gives a new mean of 18.3 and a range of 20 (5 to 25). Or add 22, 22, and 22, which gives a new mean of 22.7 and a range of 20 to 25.

d. Answers will vary. Generally speaking, students may find that the ranges change. Adding values above the mean will shift the mean higher; adding values below the mean will shift the mean lower.

24. C

25. a. $\frac{8}{25} = \frac{112}{350}$ (32%); 112 students.

b. $\frac{7}{28} = \frac{87.5}{350}$ (25%); 88 students.

c. Sample 1 predicts the greater fraction of students.

d. Answers will vary. It is quite possible to get different results from different samples, even when using a random sample.

26. $\frac{1}{18}$; Since Annie is one person in a class of 18 she has a $\frac{1}{18}$ chance of being chosen on any day. So there is a $\frac{1}{18}$ chance she will be picked on Monday.

27. $\frac{1}{18}$; Since Annie is one person in a class of 18 she has a $\frac{1}{18}$ chance of being chosen on any day. So there is a $\frac{1}{18}$ chance she will be picked on Tuesday.

28. $\frac{1}{324}$; To understand what the chance is of being chosen on both days students might make a chart that is 18-by-18, with each row representing the chance for any one student to be chosen on Monday, and each column representing the chance for any one student to be chosen on Tuesday (like tossing a numbered solid twice, only this time an 18-sided solid). Choosing Annie on both days would be represented by a single square in this grid. The area model indicates a $\frac{1}{324}$ chance that Annie will be chosen BOTH days.

29. $\frac{12}{18}$ or about 67% (12 of the 18 students are girls).

30. $\frac{11}{17}$ or about 65% (once Annie is chosen, 11 girls remain).

31. Since $\frac{2}{3}$ of the class are girls, you would expect $\frac{2}{3}$ of the chosen students to be girls, that is, 4 out of 6. But this is a very small sample, so it would not be surprising if there were only 2 girls chosen.

32. a. $\frac{400}{800} = \frac{1}{2}; \frac{399}{799}; \frac{398}{798}$

b. 12.5%;
$\frac{400}{800} \times \frac{399}{799} \times \frac{398}{798} = \frac{63,520,800}{510,081,600} \approx 12.5$

33. a. $\frac{1}{2}$; P(6th-grade girl) $= \frac{150}{300}$ or $\frac{1}{2}$

b. $\frac{1}{8}$; P(3 girls) $= \frac{150}{300} \times \frac{150}{300} \times \frac{100}{200} = \frac{1}{8}$ or $\frac{1}{2} \times \frac{1}{2} \times \frac{1}{2} = \frac{1}{8}$

34. 150 students would prefer healthful snacks $\frac{1}{2} \times 300 = 150$.

35. 500 students;
$150 + 150 + 100 + 100 = 500$ students.

36. $\frac{200}{800} = \frac{1}{4}$

37. Install 1 healthful snack machine; $\frac{500}{800}$ of all students surveyed chose a healthful snack machine so this would be an option that would probably satisfy most students.

38. a. $\frac{600}{800}$ or 75% probability

b. You cannot answer this question; you don't know the breakdown of male/female for the 600 who chose healthful snacks. You can't tell this from the Principal's poll. It may be that a preference for healthful snacks is dependent on gender. (In fact Alyssa's sample seems to indicate this.)

c. You cannot answer this question; you don't know the breakdown of male/female for the 600 who chose healthful snacks.

d. Install 1 healthful snack machine; $\frac{6}{8}$ of all students surveyed chose a healthful snack machine so this would be an option that would probably satisfy most students. It seems that the Principal has a large majority supporting the decision. The Principal may want to check that proportion in favor is the same for both genders by checking a sample of males and females separately.

Extensions

39. Possible answer: Pre-election polls can be inaccurate as a result of a poor sampling method. When sensitive issues are being contested in an election, polled voters may not accurately report their views, especially if those views are unpopular or are believed to be unacceptable for voicing in public. (**Note:** Pollsters now often ask people whether or not they are likely to actually vote. Also, it is known that polls in recent years about voting issues that involve race and gender have led to inaccuracies.)

40. Possible answer: A political party may poll people from areas in which the majority of people are of their same party or hold views similar to those held by the candidates. They might frame questions in a way that encourages responses favorable to their candidate with the intent being to create a public impression that their candidate is "on a roll" in the hopes that others will be persuaded to join that side.

41. a. $1{,}000 \div 207{,}000{,}000 \approx 0.000005\%$

b. Possible answer: The sample is probably taken from a cross section of people rather than just from people in one geographical location, occupation, political party, age group, gender, or the like.

Applications

1. The chimpanzees are 10-year-old chimpanzees. The box plot of the mystery chimpanzees looks more like the box plot for the 10-year-old chimpanzees than the 8-year-old chimpanzees. The mystery chimpanzees' summary statistics more closely resemble the 10-year-old chimpanzees' as well.

2. a. (See Figure 1.)

b. (See Figure 2.)

c. The statistics for Site I seem closest to those for Kobold/Buffalo Creek, with minimums of 8 or 9, medians of 12 or 13, and the same maximum of 18. The statistics for Site II seem closest to those for Big Goose Creek, with minimums of 6 or 5, medians of 8 or 8.5, and maximums of 11 or 13. This would indicate that Site I was likely settled between 4000 B.C. and A.D. 500 and Site II was likely settled between A.D. 500 and A.D. 1600.

Figure 1

Arrowhead Neck Widths (in millimeters)

Statistics	Kobold/ Buffalo Creek	Laddie Creek/Dead Indian Creek	Site I	Site II	Big Goose Creek	Wortham Shelter
Minimum	9	10	8	6	5	7
Q1	12	11	11	7	8	9
Median	13	13	12	8	8.5	10
Q3	15	14	15	9	9	11
Maximum	18	16	18	11	13	14
Range	9	6	10	5	8	7
Mean (nearest tenth)	13.3	12.7	12.9	8.5	8.7	10.1
MAD (nearest tenth)	1.3	1.4	2.1	1.1	1.2	1.2

Figure 2

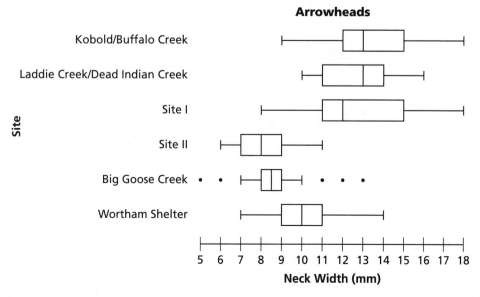

ACE ANSWERS 3

3. a. (See Figure 3.)

   b. The mean is about 23.44; the MAD is about 1.08.

   c. (See Figure 4.)

4. a. (See Figure 5.)

   b. The mean is about 19.83; the MAD is about 1.61.

   c. (See Figure 6.)

Figure 3

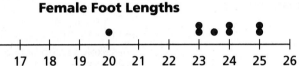

Female Foot Lengths

Figure 4

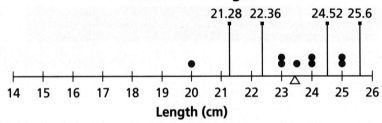

Female Foot Lengths

Figure 5

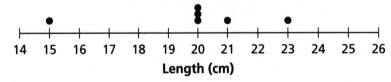

Male Foot Lengths

Figure 6

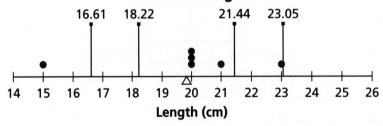

Male Foot Lengths

    Samples and Populations   **ACE Answers**

5. Yes; the mean male foot length is greater than two MADs away from the mean of the female foot length. (See Figure 7.)

6. Yes; the mean female foot length is greater than two MADs away from the mean of the male foot length. (See Figure 8.)

7. Students can use the same steps as they used for Problem 3.2.

- Locate the markers for one and two MADs from the means for each distribution.

- Mark the mean for U.S. name lengths on the distribution of Chinese name lengths; note its location in relation to the mean for the Chinese name lengths and the benchmark of two MADs. The

mean US name length is greater than two MADs away from the Chinese name length mean.

- Mark the mean for Chinese name lengths on the distribution of U.S. name lengths; note its location in relation to the mean for the U.S. name lengths and the benchmark of two MADs. The mean Chinese name length is greater than two MADs away from the US name length mean.

(See Figure 9; see Figure 10, next page.)

The differences between samples are more than we would expect from naturally occurring variability.

Figure 7

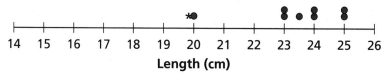

Figure 8

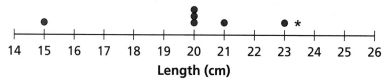

Figure 9

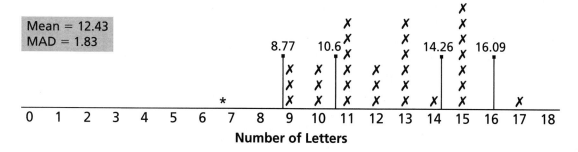

8. The mean for this sample is 8 chips per cookie. So, a good estimate of the number of chips in the bag is 8 × 60 = 480 chips. Another way to do this is to add all the chips in the sample of 20 (157), then multiply 157 by 3, since 20 × 3 = 60 cookies. This gives you an estimate of 471 chips in the bag.

9. $\frac{1}{2}; \frac{1}{4}; \frac{1}{6}$

10. a. You could randomly choose some number of muffins (for example, five). Find the average number of raisins per muffin. Then, multiply the average by 48 (which is equal to four dozen) to estimate the number of raisins in a box.

   b. 1,000 ÷ 48 ≈ 21 raisins

11. a. Sample 1: 12%; Sample 2: 15.$\overline{3}$%; Sample 3: 20%; Sample 4: 10%

   b. Sample 3; 20% of this sample is marked. If this represents the entire jar, then 20% of the entire jar is marked. You know that 150 beans are marked. You can use a proportion: $\frac{20}{100} = \frac{150}{b}$. b (the total number of beans in the jar) must be 750.

   c. Sample 4; If 10% of the beans are marked and this sample represents the entire jar, then 10% of the entire jar is marked. You can use a proportion: $\frac{10}{100} = \frac{150}{b}$. The total number of beans in the jar must be 1,500.

d. The first shaded bar is the number of beans in the sample. The total sample is 75; the number of marked beans is 15. Since 20% of the beans are marked, 20% of the percent bar is shaded.

Diya uses proportional reasoning in the second percent bar. She knows that, 20% of the beans are marked (from her sample data), so she shades in 20% of the bar. She knows that 150 total beans are marked, so that number is represented by the 20% shading as well. She is looking to see how much the entire bar represents.

e. Students might average all the predictions for the total:

$\frac{1}{4}$ × (1,250 + 750 + 978 + 1,500) = 1,120.

Or they might average all the percentages marked:

$\frac{1}{4}$(12 + 20 + 15.3 + 10) = 14.3%, which means that 150 represents 14.3% of the total. The total is 1,049.

Students might not want to count each sample as equally valid. They might note that the number marked across all samples as 66 out of 500 sampled (as if it were one large sample) and get a total of 1,136.

Figure 10

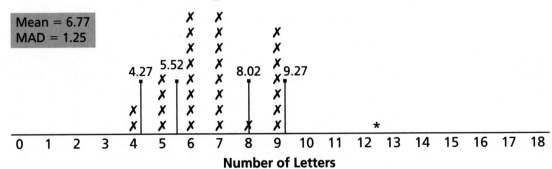

Lengths of Chinese Names

Mean = 6.77
MAD = 1.25

Number of Letters

12. a. 20 albatrosses originally marked : x number of albatrosses in population = 2 albatrosses marked : 50 albatrosses in sample

Solving for x, there must be 500 albatrosses in the population.

b. If Salome's team's sample is representative, you can be confident that your estimate is realistic. If there is some reason, however, why the sample would not be representative, then this estimate could be unrealistic.

c. Salome's team can continue sampling the albatrosses and estimating the population every couple of months or years. They can compare their estimates over time to see how the population might be growing or declining.

13. $\frac{2}{1,000} = \frac{x}{1,000,000,000}$; $x = 2,000,000$

Note: You may want to discuss the vocabulary in this Exercise with your students before they work on answering it. They might not be aware of market/quality control vocabulary.

14. D

Connections

15. Reading is on the rise! New data comparing the mean and median number of books read per year in 2011, 2012, and 2013 show there has been an increase in reading. The mean number of books read per year in 2013 is 18 as compared to a much smaller 14 in 2011. What is interesting is that the median number of books read in 2013 is 10. So, 50% of those surveyed read 10 or less books. Since the mean is much larger, it suggests that the remaining 50% are doing a great deal more reading.

16. Young children of ages 6 to 10 are the leaders in reading according to this graph! This graph compares median and mean books read per year, as did the previous graph. This graph, however, shows the data as grouped by age ranges. There is a major drop in the number of books read per year from 6- to 10-year-olds to 11- to 17-year-olds. This may be due to the lengths of the books. After a minimum number of books read between 26 and 45, book reading steadily inclines again as adults age.

17. G

18. Note: You may want to discuss the vocabulary of this Exercise with your students. Recovered paper is paper collected for recycling. Recycled paper is actually re-processed paper that was not damaged before the recycling process.

a. Graph X gives the most honest picture because it shows the full 100% scale on the vertical axis. The other graphs are truncated.

b. Graphs W and Y exaggerate the growth of recycling because the vertical axes are labeled from 40% and 45%. Graph Z exaggerates the growth because the vertical axis starts at 30% and is extended to only 80% rather than 100%.

19. The goal of the study was to determine the distance from a television set at which a typical person might use a remote control. It appears that the population being studied was owners of television sets; the sampling procedure is unclear. The report indicates only an average viewer distance, but it seems important to consider variability as well. The remote seems to have been designed for a fairly small operational range.

A box plot or stem plot of the data would help in determining the range over which the remote control should be functional. The single data piece, average distance, doesn't seem to give much confidence in the conclusion.

20. The population being studied was light bulbs produced by a particular manufacturer. The purpose of the study was to discover the defect rate of the product. The sampling procedure is not clearly random, and testing was done on a single morning. Variability in production quality over time would not be guaranteed by this brief study. In fact, industrial production processes are generally monitored regularly. A defect rate of 1% might seem acceptable, though some companies aim for lower rates. For a product whose dependability is critical, 1% would seem a fairly high defect rate.

21. The nutritionist's study set out to find the typical number of calories derived from fat in the diet of U.S. teenagers, yet the population being studied consists solely of teenagers in Dallas. Their diets may differ significantly from those of teenagers in other parts of the country. Students in health classes might be more than typically conscious of their diets. Many students may have had the same school lunch the day of the survey, which might give results far from those that would be obtained from a random survey. Also, only the median was considered; some students may be considerably over the daily allowance.

22. The aim of the study was to test whether or not there are 1,000 chips in a bag of cookies. The company may have randomly selected the bags to be tested; however, it is not clear that the company consistently tests bags of cookies. The chips in one bag may weigh more than 1,000 chocolate chips but may not actually amount to that number. It is possible that the soaking process adds weight to the remaining chips.

23. The purpose of the school cafeteria survey was to determine whether the population of students in a school preferred salami or bologna sandwiches. The convenience sample chosen runs the risk of not producing data that are representative of the whole school population. Therefore, the data do not strongly support the conclusion that students prefer bologna.

24. True; vertical line inside the box is at the median.

25. True; the box runs from 25th percentile to 75th percentile. The box is within the 60 and 80 tick marks.

26. True; the right end whisker reaches 100.

27. True; the data spreads farther to the left than the right, pulling the mean down below the median.

28. False: the data show only one-quarter (about 7.5 in a class of 30) of the class above 80.

Extensions

29. **a.** Generate random integers from 1 to 12, with the numbers assigned to the months January through December. Use a calculator, a 12-sided number cube, or a spinner divided into 12 equal sections to generate the numbers. Generate sets of five random numbers to simulate groups of five students; two of the five numbers matching in a set indicates two students with the same birth month.

   b. Results will vary. The theoretical probability—based on the assumption that each birth month is equally likely—that at least two individuals in a group of five will have the same birth month is about 0.6.

   Note: One way to reason about this is to notice that the probability of at least two people having the same birth month is 1 minus the probability that all five people have different birth months, a calculation involving combinations and permutations. One approach is as follows: probability (no matches) =

   $$1 - \left[\left(\frac{11}{12}\right)\left(\frac{10}{12}\right)\left(\frac{9}{12}\right)\left(\frac{8}{12}\right) \right] = 0.618$$

   This explanation is, of course, beyond the scope of this course.

   c. Generate random integers from 1 to 365, and inspect samples of 25 random numbers looking for samples in which at least 2 numbers match.

30. a. white: 7 or 8; yellow: 5; red: 7 or 8; orange: 10; green: 7 or 8; blue: 12 or 13

   b. Some variation is expected. One teacher may have more of one color than estimated, while another teacher may have less of that color.

   c. You could let white be represented by 1, 2, and 3 (3 numbers is 15% of 20 numbers); yellow by 4 and 5 (2 numbers is 10% of 20 numbers); red by 6, 7, and 8; orange by 9, 10, 11, and 12 (4 numbers is 20% of 20 numbers); green by 13, 14, and 15; and blue by 16, 17, 18, 19, and 20 (5 numbers is 25% of 20 numbers). Fifty random numbers would be needed to simulate filling one box.

   d. Results will vary.

   Note: You might have students pool their results. The distributions for each color should cluster around the numbers given in part (a).

   e. The percent of each color should come quite close to the percents in the table because this is a relatively large sample.